ESSAYS BY EDWIN MORGAN

ESSAYS
by Edwin Morgan

A CARCANET NEW PRESS PUBLICATION

First published 1974
by Carcanet New Press Ltd.
266 Councillor Lane
Cheadle Hulme, Cheadle
Cheshire SK8 5PN

820.9
M847

Printed in Great Britain
by W & J Mackay Limited, Chatham

CONTENTS

PREFACE   vii

PART ONE
   A Glimpse of Petavius   3
   The Poet and the Particle   16
   Into the Constellation: Some Thoughts on the Origin
      and Nature of Concrete Poetry   20
   The Walls of Gormenghast: An Introduction to the
      Novels of Mervyn Peake   35
   Three Views of Brooklyn Bridge   43
   Introduction to *Wi the Haill Voice: 25 Poems by Vladimir
      Mayakovsky Translated into Scots*   58
   Zbigniew Herbert   67
   Heraclitus in Gorky Street: The Theme of Metamor-
      phosis in the Poetry of Andrei Voznesensky   71

PART TWO
   Dunbar and the Language of Poetry   81
   Dryden's Drudging   100
   A Prelude to *The Prelude*   118
   Wordsworth in 1970   130
   The Poetry of Robert Louis Stevenson   135

PART THREE
   Registering the Reality of Scotland   153
   The Resources of Scotland   158
   The Beatnik in the Kailyaird   166
   Scottish Poetry in the 1960s   177
   Edwin Muir   186
   MacDiarmid Embattled   194
   Poetry and Knowledge in MacDiarmid's Later Work   203
   MacDiarmid at Seventy-five   214
   The Raging and the Grace: Some Notes on the Poetry of
      Iain Crichton Smith   222
   James Bridie   232
   The Novels of Robin Jenkins   242

PART FOUR

The Bicentenary   249
A Hantle of Howlers   255
The Compleat Writer's Guide, USA–USSR   277

Preface

THIS book contains a selection of essays and critical articles written between 1952 and 1973. A few minor corrections have been made, but I thought it was best not to attempt any substantial alteration or rewriting, even when some statement had been overtaken by events or when some emphasis that seemed right at the time might read oddly now. Most of the essays were written under the immediate pressure of personal interest or enthusiasm, or of some congenial request or commission, and inevitably over the years they become like archeological layers, now re-exposed and betraying habits of style and thought that may very well sit uneasily together. CHANGE RULES is the supreme graffito. Gathering up the shards – 'performances, assortments, résumés' – can hope perhaps to scatter values through a reticulation that surprises thought rather than traps it.

E.M.

Part One

A Glimpse of Petavius

Nous sommes dans un temps comparable à celui de la Renaissance,
mais aujourd'hui Ronsard et du Bellay feraient de la Pléiade une équipe
de chercheurs scientifiques et non plus de poètes: les deux vocations ne
sont-elles pas d'ailleurs en train de se rejoindre ?

Louis Pauwels

IN 1847, Edward FitzGerald wrote in a letter to Edward Cowell:

> Yet, as I often think, it is not the poetical imagination, but bare Science
> that every day more and more unrolls a greater Epic than the Iliad . . .
> I never take up a book of Geology or Astronomy but this strikes me
> . . . So that, as Lyell says, the Geologist looking at Niagara forgets
> even the roar of its waters in the contemplation of the awful processes
> of time that it suggests. It is not only that this vision of Time must
> wither the Poet's hope of immortality; but it is in itself more wonderful
> than all the conceptions of Dante and Milton.

These remarks of FitzGerald's are acute and prophetic. Anyone in
the nineteenth century could have seen that the sciences were becoming more and more important, and that that was involving an
intense search for *truth*; but FitzGerald was one of the few who saw
how this was going to affect the *imagination*, and his fear (very different from Keats's fears about the rainbow in 'Lamia') was that truth
would become stranger and more impressive than fiction, that science
would absorb and yet feed and flatter people's capacity for wonder,
and that poetry as an imaginative art might be fighting a losing battle
because it could no longer hold the world's attention. Kubla Khan's
river Alph that ran through caverns measureless to man was no
match for the Niagara Falls; and the very phrase 'measureless to man'
which no doubt seemed so impressive to the romantic-minded would
now tell against the poem – because men were more eager to measure
caverns, and the true measurements might be far more breathtaking
than the rhetorical gesture of 'measureless'. FitzGerald himself

offered no solution to this problem, and did not consider the possibility of a poet making use of this kind of truth.

A little later, in 1859, we find another aspect of the pressure of truth upon imagination. In a letter to Tennyson from John Ruskin, discussing his *Idylls of the King* which had recently been published, Ruskin criticized an escapist trend in Tennyson's poetry. He said:

> . . . it seems to me that so great power ought not to be spent on visions of things past but on the living present . . . And merely in the facts of modern life, not drawing-room formal life, but the far-away and quite unknown growth of souls in and through any form of misery and servitude – there is an infinity of what men should be told, and what none but a poet can tell. I cannot but think that the intense, masterful, and unerring transcript of an actuality . . . would make all men feel more or less what poetry was, as they felt what Life and Fate were in their instant workings. This seems to me the true task of the modern poet.

Although this quotation is not concerned with science, it is equally concerned with truth to fact, and with the impact of the contemporary situation on the poet, and Ruskin gives indeed a kind of answer to FitzGerald's dilemma. If science reveals the full wonder of the Niagara Falls, the poet should be willing to make use of the fillip to imagination which extended knowledge can give, and stop inventing marvellous cascades, like Peter the Great, in his own mind. Ruskin, wanting here to rescue poetry from romance, hammers home these phrases: *living present, facts of modern life, unerring transcript of an actuality.* The poet has a *social* task, and the modern poet's social task is to be as true and close to actual modern experience as he can. This links up with FitzGerald in an interesting way: for if science enters everyday experience, as X-rays enter the hospital ward or the comptometer enters the office or the television set enters the living-room, then it will be the poet's job to bring these things into his poetry, and he will have (ideally) three tasks to fulfil – to seize their imaginative possibilities, to understand them as far as he can (so that he won't merely use science as a new springboard into the romantic), and to see how they fit into people's lives.

My third quotation draws these various worries and diagnostics together. Walt Whitman, in the preface to his *November Boughs* of 1888, wrote:

> I see in an article on Wordsworth, in one of the current English magazines, the lines 'A few weeks ago an eminent French critic said that,

owing to the special tendency to science and to its all-devouring force, poetry would cease to be read in fifty years.' But I anticipate the very contrary. Only a firmer, vastly broader, new area begins to exist – nay, is already form'd – to which the poetic genius must emigrate. Whatever may have been the case in years gone by, the true use for the imaginative faculty of modern times is to give ultimate vivification to facts, to science, and to common lives . . . Without that ultimate vivification – which the poet or other artist alone can give – reality would seem incomplete, and science, democracy, and life itself, finally in vain.

Whitman puts the main point very clearly. The poet, the man of imagination, is to be a mediator between the complex technological modern world and the ordinary person who lives in that world but doesn't understand it or see his place in it as having any significance. Dry facts are to be made vivid; science has to be humanized; and the slogging monotonous workaday life of the mass of the people is in some way to be illuminated, both to themselves and to others. And these things, he says, the poet can do, or can help to do. 'The words of the true poems give you more than poems.'

If Whitman could come back today, and we were to show him the most admired and the most influential of our 'modern' poetry, the works of Yeats and Pound and Eliot, would he not object to a lack of interest in his facts, science, or common lives?

It would not be hard to rake up an answer to Whitman. We could remind him that as against the view of the poet having a duty to society there is the view of the poet being true to his own experiences and beliefs, and it has so happened that these leading poets have in general strongly disliked or disapproved of the main trends of their time towards technological complexity, material progress, and mass culture: Whitman's mood of prophetic optimism has been impossible for them, and the whole material transformation of the universe is to them the crackling of thorns under a pot. But my main task is to examine the situation from Whitman's point of view rather than from the more familiar point of view of Yeats, Eliot, and Pound, because I think this is much needed as a corrective, expecially when we are asked to look on a man like Eliot as 'speaking for his generation' or 'expressing the anguish of a period', as we often are.

Whitman's complaint would be that not only the critic, but the poet too, has forgotten how to be 'a man speaking to men'. If it is true that the poet is a seer, it is also true that he is a teacher and an entertainer. If it is true that in one sense he must know *more* than the people he is addressing (in that he has some insight, some vision, some exhortation to contribute to human society), it is also true that he must know *what* people know – and this is perhaps at the present moment more worthy of emphasis. Many modern poets have not started from a knowledge of what the ordinary person's knowledge and interests are, and so they have communicated only to exceptional or to well-educated people. And this situation is usually accepted. It is argued that communication must be very restricted and partial, because poetry cannot compromise its own standards to meet even halfway a popular taste that has been coarsened by the more violent stimulants of the cinema or the variety theatre or the football ground. Certainly the days are long past when the Old English or Celtic bard was called for at the end of supper and asked to recite his lays to an audience that was no doubt boisterous but nevertheless would listen, could be captured, was not prejudicially contemptuous of poetry. What hopes are there now, it may well be asked, of reaching a live audience?

In the 1920s the Russian poet Mayakovsky travelled all over the USSR, reading his poems to big audiences in public halls, and people flocked excitedly to listen to him. He had a very strong personality, and a powerful dramatic style of reading, and what he read was undoubtedly poetry, sometimes very great poetry. Yet even he felt the strain and difficulties of keeping up this position. His comments on it are particularly valuable, since he was equally and intensely concerned to be true to himself as a poet, and to produce a truthful and useful poetry which would both entertain and educate the people. Herbert Marshall in his book on Mayakovsky (Pilot Press, 1945) quotes a verbatim report of what he said at the last of his public readings, shortly before his death in 1930. Before he began to read his poems he said:

It's easy enough to write poetry that does not irritate anybody: March, march again you working men . . . The Red Flag waves higher like the flame of a fire – etc. It will be liked very much and forgotten the next day . . . It is very difficult to work in the way I want to work, trying to establish real contact between the working auditorium and big poetry, poetry genuinely created and without ever lowering its standard and its meaning . . . Poets often write so that you can't understand them. It happens often even to our quite famous poets. Very often a poet writes in such a way that it's quite unintelligible, or if it is intelligible it's just nonsense. Poetry must be made so that without getting rid of the seriousness of your idea, you make your verses necessary to the masses, so that when one has read it about five times you say, well, it was hard to understand, but having grasped it, it enriched our brain, our imagination, and it has sharpened our will in the fight for socialism.

If Mayakovsky found these difficulties in Soviet Russia, where communication is an essential part of poetic doctrine, where Yevtushenko and Voznesensky are carrying on the same tradition of public readings today, and where minor poets will sell in editions of 10,000 copies, it is hardly surprising that in the west we should find the crisis more acute: a crisis neatly and tacitly commented on when T. S. Eliot left poetry for his series of drawing-room verse plays, thereby reaching a much wider public but at the same time producing less satisfactory works of art. The brilliant success of the poetry-readings of Dylan Thomas in America had so many special attendant circumstances that it could hardly then be seen optimistically as a typical portent; though we may note in passing that Dylan Thomas claimed to write not for 'the proud man apart' but for the simple lovers with 'their arms round the griefs of the ages' and their ignorance of his craft or art. It may also be significant that he was gradually turning away from 'book poetry' to the poetry of radio, cinema, and opera. He felt an audience was there to be reached – *had* to be reached – and he was making various experimental gestures towards it at the time of his death. Since then, the poetry of the spoken rather than the written word has made many advances in both America and Britain, and the readings and recordings of Ginsberg and Kerouac, Pete Brown and Christopher Logue, have once more brought a reasonably general public sharply up against the poetry that is completely contemporary with it.

Has Whitman anything to contribute to this situation? If the 'common life' today is inescapably and increasingly within a world of 'fact and science' – however dimly grasped, however indifferently regarded – can the poet effect any illumination of this life and this world not so much in *his* as in *its* terms? Can he raise *its* voice, *its* language, *its* facts into a viable poetry (as the cinema and television can do visually), or, to put it another way, can he study the secrets of how to *release* its own inhering (but how indomitably opposed and rejected!) poetry? Can he escape from the sterile antipathy towards any real confrontation of art and science which once marked Yeats and Lawrence, and still marks F. R. Leavis? It is an undertaking most heads will shake over; still, let us look at some of the evidence.

To go back to the beginning of the century, there is the Scottish poet John Davidson, a man whose works would repay more examination than they have yet had. Davidson, whom Yeats described as having 'enough passion to make a great poet', and who nearly disintegrated the Rhymers' Club by introducing four of his less couth compatriots (one of them 'read out a poem upon the Life-boat, evidently intended for a recitation'), tried to embody a scientific materialism in a lyrico-rhetorical style of verse that was meant to be able to take the life-boat as well as the lily in its stride. He tried hard to vivify terms from astronomy and chemistry by bringing them into human contexts. He wrote a poetry of the city, of modern city life, endeavouring to carry the actual names of things into poetry as Whitman had done – trains and motors, drain-pipes and printing-presses, Christian Science and Democracy, wireless and queues and cigarettes. He tried to present relation and analogy in contemporary terms. A poem on the Crystal Palace begins like this:

> Contraption, – that's the bizarre, proper slang,
> Eclectic word, for this portentous toy,
> The flying-machine, that gyrates stiffly, arms
> A-kimbo, so to say, and baskets slung
> From every elbow, skating in the air.

The Palace itself receives this description.

> So sublime! Like some
> Immense crustacean's gannoid skeleton,
> Unearthed, and cleansed, and polished! Were it so
> Our paleontological respect
> Would shield it from derision; but when a shed,
> Intended for a palace, looks as like
> The fossil of a giant myriapod! . . .

This almost Wellsian imaginative realism was something new in the poetry of 1909, but Davidson's use of scientific terms was not followed up, and Pound and Eliot were soon to turn poetry in a different direction (though Eliot admired the realism of 'Thirty Bob a Week'). It was Davidson's concern for truthfulness and contemporaneity that allowed him to employ 'unpoetic' words taken from non-committal or abstract contexts, but he still found it difficult to imbue such words with even the minimum emotional impact he felt they must have. This is shown in the following verses from a poem called 'Snow' in which he tries to 'humanize' the snowflake's situation, while at the same time giving a scientific account of the process; the attempt is interesting, but it doesn't quite come off.

> Once I saw upon an object-glass,
>   Martyred underneath a microscope,
> One elaborate snow-flake slowly pass,
>   Dying hard, beyond the reach of hope.
>
> Still from shape to shape the crystal changed,
>   Writhing in its agony; and still,
> Less and less elaborate, arranged
>   Potently the angle of its will.
>
> Tortured to a simple final form,
>   Angles six and six divergent beams,
> Lo, in death it touched the perfect norm
>   Verifying all its crystal dreams!

– Here, one feels that 'martyred' is too strong, too rhetorical, for 'microscope'; but also one can see why he used it, and what he was trying to do.

But the poets who have perhaps done most to meet Whitman's desiderata, and who have therefore taken the greatest risks aesthetically (and also reputationally, since they have been working against the twentieth-century orthodoxy), are Hugh MacDiarmid and William Carlos Williams. MacDiarmid, in the face of more opposition and indifference than encouragement, has stirred himself to keep the worlds of art and science in contact, partly because he believes history is at a point where this ought to be one's concern, and also probably because of a Scottish fondness for fact as against symbol. He has more than once quoted with approval Whitman's remarks about the 'true use for the imaginative faculty of modern times', and he sees poetry as what he calls

> A protest, invaluable to science itself,
> Against the exclusion of value
> From the essence of matter of fact.

This interesting attitude, perverse or quixotic as it may seem in relation to the intractable and highly specialized 'facts' of modern science, does strike to the heart of the subject. *Against the exclusion of value* is the two-edged weapon the contemporary poet must take up: attacking with it *both* the last-ditch village-maypole humanists who growl about cultureless technocracies *and* the Astronomers Royal who step off aircraft and pronounce that 'interplanetary travel is bilge'.

The difficulty of producing such a poetry is admitted, and the main problem is how the faculty of imagination is to gain entry to a world of fact. There are two possible approaches: through a science-fiction poetry paralleling the development of science-fiction in prose, and through a poetry which selects, juxtaposes, and broods on interesting features of the scientific (factual or theoretical) scene and tries to relate these to human experience. MacDiarmid attempted the former method in his translation of Harry Martinson's *Aniara* (1963). This long poem had a big enough conception behind it – the reactions of the passengers during the drifting to destruction of a giant space-ship – but is so unconvincing and indeed puerile in its details that the latent imaginative possibilities are aborted, and the poem (at any rate in MacDiarmid's version of it) is an almost complete failure. Although, being an adaptation of another man's work, it is not a fair test, *Aniara* does nevertheless suggest when one compares it with the rest of MacDiarmid's 'scientific' poetry that for him at least it is more important to start from fact and arouse the imagination than to start from imaginative scientific fantasy and throw in a few concessions to fact. His best poetry in the genre is a poetry which makes us aware, often through highly original analogies, of the interest or relevance of some fact which is not a part of the ordinary reader's general knowledge. He wants to set such facts within our knowledge, to the enriching of our experience of course, but also to make us more receptive of his belief that there is a 'point where science and art can meet', a satisfactory fusion of 'scientific data and aesthetic realization'. 'Stony Limits', for instance, the elegy on Charles Doughty, uses geology and astronomy to do three things: (i) to link the poet and his subject through the quest for knowledge which preoccupies them both, (ii) to present intimations of new or strange worlds – the forms of crystallography, the prehistoric upheavals of the earth, the craters of the moon, and (iii) to claim the relevance of such parallels as that between crystal growth and poetic creation.

> . . . How should we have anything to give you
>   In death who had nothing in life,
> Attempting in our sand-riddles to sieve you
> Who were with nothing but the sheer elements rife?

Anchor of truth, facile as granite you lie,
A plug suspended in England's false dreams.
Your worth will be seen by and by,
Like God's purpose in what men deem *their* schemes,
Nothing ephemeral can seek what lies in this ground
Since nothing can be sought but the found.

The poem that would praise you must be
Like the glass of some rock, sleek brown, crowded
With dark incipient crystal growths, we see;
Or a glimpse of Petavius may have endowed it
With the tubular and dumb-bell-shaped inclusions surrounded
        By the broad reaction rims it needs.
I have seen it in dreams and know how it abounded
–Ah! would I could find in me like seeds! –
As the north-easterly garden in the lunation grows,
A spectacle not one man in ten millions knows . . .

What matters is the imaginative response, first of the poet and then
of his readers, and it is clear that this can come from contemplation
of fact – can come better from that, indeed, than from the clumsily
inventive pseudo-fact of *Aniara*'s 'goldonda', 'phototurb', 'gopta',
and 'dormijun'.

If, in MacDiarmid's development, 'facts and science' have tended
to overshadow 'common lives', the work of William Carlos Williams
helps to restore this particular balance. Williams, like MacDiarmid,
saw his work as having a relation to Whitman, and being an American he felt something more: that he was to produce a continuation
and fulfilment of Whitman's ideals, both as regards form and as
regards content. Being himself a man of technical training, a busy
medical practitioner whose poetry and other writings filled the
interstices of a life where willy-nilly 'facts and science' met 'common
lives' at every step, Williams was able to develop a humane, earthbound, wonderfully honest poetry: a poetry of which 'earthbound'
cannot be used pejoratively. In a letter to Kenneth Burke in 1947 he
spoke of his desire 'to find some basis for avoiding the tyranny of
the symbolic without sacrificing fullness of imagery', and went on:

> My whole intent, in my life, has been, as with you, to find a basis (in
> poetry, in my case) for the actual. It isn't a difficult problem to solve
> theoretically. All one has to do it to discover new laws of the metric
> and use them. That's objective enough and little different from the
> practical deductions of an Edison. The difficulty lies in the practice.

Williams's poetry does in fact have a good deal of success in both of these directions: in producing a spontaneous, speech-directed prosodic phrasing, and in escaping the 'tyranny' of symbolism without falling into drabness or niggardliness of effect. Recent developments in American poetry suggest that the importance of his achievement has been seen, and although he saw himself as ploughing a fairly lonely furrow his doggedness was justified. 'It is as sure that good work lives (if any be written) as that scientific discoveries into the depths of physics and chemistry will not be lost. But one must be at the advancing edge of the art: that's the American tradition.' (Letter to T. C. Wilson, 12 July 1933.)

Both in his long poem *Paterson* with its loving, utterly committed portrayal of a city and its life and his life in it in actual place and time – 'Say it, no ideas but in things' – and in his shorter and more lyrical poems Williams shows this 'advancing edge' of art as a sharp, stinging, splintery immediacy, sensuous, cinematic, and human. Detail is essential to it; appearances are essential to it; prosaic material is forced to shine and cry by the subtle speech-movements of the verse. Williams is not the first poet to be called an observer, but he bears little resemblance to the rather sinister bloodless God's-private-eye portrait of Browning's 'How It Strikes a Contemporary'. Here are the closing sections of his 'January Morning':

> x
> The young doctor is dancing with happiness
> in the sparkling wind, alone
> at the prow of the ferry! He notices
> the curdy barnacles and broken ice crusts
> left at the ship's base by the low tide
> and thinks of summer and green
> shell-crusted ledges among
> the emerald eel-grass!

> xi
> Who knows the Palisades as I do
> knows the river breaks east from them
> above the city – but they continue south
> – under the sky – to bear a crest of
> little peering houses that brighten
> with dawn behind the moody
> water-loving giants of Manhattan.

XII
Long yellow rushes bending
above the white snow patches:
purple and gold ribbon
of the distant wood:
                    what an angle
you make with each other as
you lie there in contemplation.

XIII
Work hard all your young days
and they'll find you too, some morning
staring up under
your chiffonier at its warped
bass-wood bottom and your soul –
out!
– among the little sparrows
behind the shutter.

XIV
– and the flapping flags are at
half mast for the dead admiral.

XV
All this –
                    was for you, old woman.
I wanted to write a poem
that you would understand.
For what good is it to me
if you can't understand it?
                    But you got to try hard
But –
        Well, you know how
the young girls run giggling
on Park Avenue after dark
when they ought to be home in bed?
Well,
that's the way it is with me somehow.

'We cannot long resist,' wrote James Kirkup, 'the sight of actual things.' But is this a weakness? Poets, who have been so careful to distinguish shades of feeling and subtleties of mood, have been slow to distinguish shades of difference in the material, technical, and intellectual world in which they live. Kathleen Raine remarked in the

Introduction to her *Collected Poems* (1956): 'It was David Gascoyne who said to me that nature remains always in the Year One ... The ever-recurring forms of nature mirror eternal reality; the never-recurring productions of human history reflect only fallen man.' These phrases are loaded dice, harmful assumptions masquerading as grandeurs; they indicate a point of view which most of all this essay desires to disturb. If the poet travels by transcontinental jet instead of by pony and trap, let him not pretend that no change has 'really' occurred: that he is still 'just travelling'. If artificial satellites are launched from the earth, let the poet not pretend that 'reality' remains unaffected by these geophysical pranks. What involves man involves reality; what involves many men is the great neglected material of our poetry.

Most people might agree that it is important to assert human values in an age of science and technology as complex as ours; but this is not quite the point. It is here that our Lawrences and Leavises take the wrong turning. To go on 'asserting human values' in terms that are isolated from the world of rockets and computers and television sets, as if they did not exist within the same frame of reality at all, will in the end make these values less and less convincing, because it is man himself who sends up and travels in rockets and who makes and watches television sets. When Yuri Gagarin was circling the earth in his spaceship Vostok he was not only exposed to a new physical and mental experience which can be only partially simulated under laboratory conditions; he also received an aesthetic experience which no man had had before, and his reaction to the 'delicate and lovely' and 'hard-to-describe' blue aureole surrounding the globe – his exclamations during the flight and his later remarks to reporters – deserve to be noted both by non-scientists who say there is nothing 'human' to be gained from such experiments and by scientists who say that instruments would record everything better than men in any case. The fact is that man must react, as man, to his whole environment. Nothing less will satisfy his hungry spirit. The future of poetry, like the future of the other arts, is bound up not only with the very slowly evolving nature of man but also with the very quickly evolving relation of man to his environment. Poetry today is in the process of recovering from an ambitious attempt – the attempt of Yeats, Pound, Eliot, Stevens – to separate its own artistic evolution from the general evolution of society. We must be able to admit that the poet's imagination, entering the operating

theatre or Brooklyn Bridge or a plane in wartime, allowing itself
to be guided by facts and truths which can be verified, and being
in this sense truthful, can still produce 'true poetry' in the old sense
of the term. We are often told that poetry has some higher truth
which is sometimes independent of the ordinary facts of life, and we
are told that the poet may be indifferent or partial with regard to facts
so long as he has this deeper kind of truth. I am not saying that there
is no poetry of this sort, or that all poets must turn over a new leaf
and verify the truth of their statements. What I want to express is a
concern about the very incomplete way in which poetry since the
nineteenth century has reacted to changes in society and in material
surroundings. It is because these changes have been so great that
I am made conscious of this strange communicative gap – which anyone will see who stands back to look at it – between poetry and life.
Our poetry needs greater humanity; but it must be the humanity
of man within his whole environment: not just the drop of dew, the
rose, the lock of hair, but the orbiting rocket in Anselm Hollo, the
lobotomy in Allen Ginsberg, the lunar mountains in Hugh Mac-
Diarmid. A glimpse of Petavius may not make the whole world kin
– yet. But it helps, and more eyes could well be scanning for what
the mind and heart might learn from it.

Gambit (Edinburgh University Review), Summer 1963.

The Poet and the Particle

WE seem to live, today, in many worlds rather than in one. There is the world of common sense and common experience, in which we catch buses, pour tea, see roughly the same face each time we look in the mirror, and know we can't walk on water. There is a world of metaphysics (whether philosophical or religious) which according to one's belief will bear a more or less clearly defined relation to the world of common experience. There is the world of international politics, working at a painfully low threshold of truth and morality, yet of necessity overlapping to some extent on the recognizable patterns of individual human experience. But it is the world of modern science, and particularly of physics, which appears to offer fewer points of contact than any other when we consider it at the level of theory. An uneasy dualism hangs over most of the writing on this subject, as if the natural laws governing the catching of buses and the pouring of tea – a good old coarse-grained Newtonian mechanics suited to the grossness of events in the human world – had nothing to do with the 'laws' or at any rate descriptive formulations which govern the subatomic world of the fundamental particles: a world not of things but of theoretical entities, unobserved, unpredictable, and unobservable. It is all very well for Schrödinger to tell us that 'quantum mechanics has nothing to do with the free-will problem' (*Science and Humanism*, 1951), or for Bernard Mayo to say (*Penguin Science News*, 1956): 'The constitution of cakes is an empirical question; the "constitution" of matter is a theoretical one.' With respect, we cannot believe either of these statements. It may be right for the physicist to deplore unrigorous extrapolations from physical theory by philosophers or thinkers in other disciplines – as in the wilder banner-wavings of the Indeterminacy Principle – but it can hardly be right for him to assume so readily that events in the subatomic world are essentially incapable of relation to events on the macrocosmic or human scale and must be thought of in a different way. Or so, to the outsider, it would seem.

Now if the poet is the man who traditionally finds links and resemblances, dissolves rather than erects barriers, moves among the various worlds of his time, often confronting one with another in such a way as to throw some light on both, what can he contribute to the present situation? Or, to put a slightly different question, why has the modern poet contributed so little? 'It is bizarre,' said C. P. Snow in his Rede Lecture on *The Two Cultures and the Scientific Revolution*, 'how very little of twentieth-century science has been assimilated into twentieth-century art.' And whatever reservations one may have about that lecture, Snow's implied and stated criticisms of modern poets were well justified. If it is not the duty, it should at least be the delight, of poets to contemplate the world of science. It is only indeed by an extraordinary ingrownness and wilful self-blinkering that modern poetry has managed to preserve its purity from contamination by the dominant interest of the age: like a man sitting at his window, refusing to admit that an elephant passing back and forward outside really is there, or thinking that if he just ignores it, it will go away and not worry him. The point is, however, that it *should* worry him. Also, it is not going to go away.

Robert Garioch's remarkable poem *The Muir* is one of the few recent attempts to do something about this situation. It is a poem which deliberately confronts the everyday world with the two worlds of physics and metaphysics. Previously, Garioch's rather elusive and scattered poetic work has restricted itself to occasional pieces dealing largely with Edinburgh life in a variety of moods from pathos to the satiric and the fantastic (*Seventeen Poems for Sixpence*, 1940; *Chuckies on the Cairn*, 1949; *The Masque of Edinburgh*, 1954; a fine commemorative address *To Robert Fergusson* (1952); and translations such as his Scots versions of George Buchanan's Latin plays *Jephthah* and *The Baptist* (1959). Most of this poetry is in Scots, and Garioch remains our most persuasive user of it, at any rate in poems of any length. He has a fine ear for what remains of spoken Scots, and has had more success than most modern Scottish poets in building unobtrusively on this speech basis, though not without some archaism: but at least the archaism is constantly being corrected by a nice colloquial accuracy, and the over-all tone is unusually acceptable.

It might seem the perversest of tasks to write a 'scientific poem', a non-two-cultures poem, in Scots (and using a difficult rhyme-scheme at that), but given the particular kinds of confrontation *The*

Muir wants to make, involving Scotland and Scotsmen as well as things more universal, the choice was not so perverse. Although most of the scientific terms are in their customary English forms (e.g. particle, electron, nucleus, radar, cathode-blips, quantum, orbit, trajectory, mass, velocity, antinomy, atomic, acausality, scientist, physicist, universe), and only a select few are Lallanated (e.g. haar-chaumer, licht, maitter, boomb), there is no doubt that something is gained by the mixture of English and Scots in a passage like the following, commenting on the idea that the natural laws of combustion will have to be suspended in Hell:

> And that's a ferlie that we never see
> even in nuclear physics; tho we read
> that atoms of Uranium can gie
> out energy a gey lang while indeed,
> they cheenge throu time and finish up as leid;
> echt-thousan million years or thereabout
> they hae a kind o life, and syne they're deid.
> An endless trauchle that wad seem, nae dout,
> to folk in Hell wha cudna manage out,
> but no the same thing as eternity
> wi flames imperishable as the soot
> they mak in brennin; maitter and energy,
> timeless, framed in perpetuity,
> aye unconsumed, an everlasting rot,
> an oxydising antisyzygy
> maybe a thocht congenial til a Scot.

The poem strides along upon a series of questions. If a great metaphysical vision like Dante's *Inferno* is and must be based on worldly experience and built up with worldly imagery, why can't we as non-believers in Hell and devils simply follow the liberating secular Rabelais' advice to 'Fay ce que vouldras' and enjoy our common-sense world? Yes, but have we got such a world – what has physics done to it? Particles which we 'know' only by their tracks in the cloud-chamber, light conceived sometimes as particles and sometimes as waves, causality lost in subatomic behaviour, particles 'unobservable' because mere observation imposes change on the object – how do we relate all this to the solid world of which electrons, atoms, and molecules are a part? When the poet Robert Fergusson in his last manic-depressive phase lay howling in the straw of a hideous Edinburgh madhouse in 1774, were his guilty fears of

Hell less real than our fears of an unintelligible unsolid core to our world? Did Hiroshima therefore prove that something can come of nothing? If this is absurd, can we grasp instead the straw of suba-tomic 'probability', evolving itself gradually into 'law' as events move up the scale of size into human experience in the macrocosm? If I walk on a Scottish moor on a brilliant summer day, surrounded by most real, tangible, sharply defined rocks and heather and grass, can I get at that reality any more closely than by the method my unaided senses allow? If I could scrape the very bowels of the hills, what would I learn?

Of these questions Garioch offers in the end only a dualistic resolution – which of course is not a resolution. Science must investi-gate, but man must be the judge of what is relevant to him as a human being. Science is necessary to discover the 'philosophic god', but only the heart can track down 'Jehovah'. So we are left with the classic modern dichotomy on our laps, and although many readers will find this an unexceptionable conclusion, humanist but not anti-scientific, I find it rather a disappointment, considering the tenor of the poem's questioning. This dichotomy belongs, after all, to a pre-cybernetic, pre-computer age, which will soon be rapidly receding from us. Robert Garioch still seems to have no doubt that

> It taks a human tongue to sing Amen
> in melody by whilk Man's hairt is mevit.

Well – maybe. But I wouldn't be too sure. Science and art may not yet be one flesh – but has an engagement not been announced?

New Saltire, 8 (June 1963).

Into the Constellation: Some Thoughts on the Origin and Nature of Concrete Poetry

As a conscious movement in the art of language, concrete poetry can be dated from 1955. In that year the Noigandres group of poets in São Paulo – Augusto de Campos, Haroldo de Campos, Décio Pignatari – used the title 'poesia concreta' for the first time, in an article published by Augusto de Campos and also in the exhibition held in November at the Teatro de Arena, where concrete poems were read aloud and simultaneously projected on a screen. In the same year Pignatari met the Swiss-Bolivian poet Eugen Gomringer at the Hochschule für Gestaltung in Ulm – a meeting which was to prove fruitful for the whole movement – and Gomringer, although he had used the title 'constellations' for the poems he himself had been writing in what later became known as the concrete movement, agreed with Pignatari that 'concrete poetry' was the best general term to use. As he wrote to Pignatari: 'Avant de nommer mes "poèmes" constellations, j'avais vraiment pensé de les nommer "concrets".'

Every movement has antecedents, which must be regarded as a proper object of investigation, but the prehistory of concrete poetry is already a thickly littered battlefield, with some heavily entrenched positions and a shortage of reasonable panoramic comment. The movement itself has developed in so many directions, some of them certainly unforeseen by the founders, that no conceivable definition could umbrella every example, and it is natural that some theoreticians should periodically try to plug the dyke, which involves among other things the insistence on a selective list of ancestors, if purity is to be maintained. Surely, however, it depends on the context in which one is writing. There is a place and time for didactic definition of a movement seen at its most central, but it is equally important, in a more discursive, wide-ranging, and generally communicative context, to trace analogues as well as connections, and to be prepared to admit surprising evidence even if this flutters the grid.

It is usual, because of the obvious and overriding importance of structure in a concrete poem, to relate concrete poetry to the work of constructivist artists and theorists, and to push the links back to the days of the Bauhaus and De Stijl and the Russian Suprematists but preferably not much further. The links are not hard to trace, and the influences are often acknowledged. Gomringer was Max Bill's secretary from 1954 to 1957, and Bill as creator, exhibitor, and critic of concrete art during the 1940s had been a key figure: taught at the Bauhaus by Albers and Kandinsky, later joining forces with artists like Mondrian, Arp, and Vantongerloo, Max Bill exemplified an almost classic search for some sense of order that would not be mere abstraction (hence not 'abstract art') but a positive alignment of forces, often mathematical, into a working harmony, a concretized statement of control, whether in sculpture, painting, or industrial design. In 1936 he wrote in his essay 'Konkrete Gestaltung': 'The term "concrete art" refers to those works that have developed through their own innate means and laws ... It must be clear, unambiguous, and aim at perfection ... The individualistic element is pushed aside for the benefit of the individual.' His own works show a striking combination of topological ingenuity and clear over-all impact. A painting like 'Integration of Four Systems' (1958–60), built up entirely of merging, flickering squares of subtle colour, seems very close in its construction to a concrete poem which might similarly 'integrate four systems' of words within a patterned background of letters. A sculpture like the extraordinary granite Moebius strip of 1960, or the even more eye-teasing gilded copper 'Surface Bounded by One Line' of 1948–9, offers a parallel to certain spiralling and reversed-letter effects quite often found in concrete poetry. But it is essentially the use of a principle of construction which makes common ground between concrete art and concrete poetry.

Ian Hamilton Finlay's poem 'Homage to Malevich' (in two versions, derived from Malevich's 'black square' and 'black cross' paintings) and Eugen Gomringer's 'Parafrase zu Josef Albers' (a permutation-piece paying ironical homage to Albers's 'Homage to the Square') serve to remind us of two other artists whose work and ideas have relevance. Albers, poet as well as artist, has a little poem which, though two-edged, expresses what many concrete poets would want to agree with:

Beruhige dich
das meiste was geschieht
geschieht ohne dich

lackblockblackb
lockblackblockb
lackblockblackb
lockblackblockb
lackblockblackb
lockblackblockb
lackblockblackb
lockblackblockb

lackblockblackb   lackblockblackb   lackblockblackb
lockblackblockb   lockblackblockb   lockblackblockb
lackblockblackb   lackblockblackb   lackblockblackb
lockblackblockb   lockblackblockb   lockblackblockb
lackblockblackb   lackblockblackb   lackblockblackb
lockblackblockb   lockblackblockb   lockblackblockb
lackblockblackb   lackblockblackb   lackblockblackb
lockblackblockb   lockblackblockb   lockblackblockb

lackblockblackb
lockblackblockb
lackblockblackb
lockblackblockb
lackblockblackb
lockblackblockb
lackblockblackb
lockblackblockb

Ian Hamilton Finlay: 'Homage to Malevich'

'Calm down/most of what happens/happens without you.' Such an anti-involvement aesthetics has a potential of bad consequences for society which needs no underlining, but its insistence on the value and importance of the work in hand in one's immediate environment, and its belief in a 'less means more' art, are a significant reassertion of core thinking as opposed to flux thinking, and whether disagreed with or not, this has to be grappled with in the aesthetics of concrete.

'In the art of Suprematism,' wrote Malevich in his book *From Cubism and Futurism to Suprematism* (1916), 'forms will live, like all

living forms of nature'. In the form of the square, man asserts something upon and against the superficial fullness and irregularity of
nature's flux, yet paradoxically he may be echoing what he feels to be
the necessary underlying 'constructedness' of the world of nature.
Things do not fall apart; the centre can hold. Instead of deep calling
to deep, economy calls to economy. Malevich again:

> I declare Economy to be the new fifth dimension which evaluates and
> defines the Modernity of the Arts and Creative Works. All the creative
> systems of engineering, machinery, and construction come under its
> control, as do those of the arts of painting, music, and poetry, for they
> are systems of expressing that inner movement which is an illusion in
> the tangible world. (*On New Systems in Art*, 1919)

And hence, to Malevich, as also I have no doubt to Albers, Gomringer, and Finlay: 'One could feel more sorry about a screw breaking off than about the destruction of St Basil's Cathedral.' ('On the
Museum', 1919.)

However, the fact that it is easier to apply a constructivist

Futurist typogram by Ardengo Soffici (1915)

aesthetics to sculpture and painting (and architecture and industrial design) than to an art working with language means that concrete poetry can never be in quite such a clearcut area of theory as expositors might wish. It may well be, in general terms, 'against a poetry of expression', as the Brazilians put it in their *Pilot Plan* of 1958, and it may well be regarded as representing 'polemically the search for a new metric pattern' as Mike Weaver has described it in his essay 'Concrete Poetry' (*Lugano Review*, Summer 1966). Yet expressionisms, individualisms, and romanticisms move in and out of concrete poetry and have to be reckoned with. As Mary Ellen Solt points out in her sane and balanced introduction to the special concrete number of *Artes Hispanicas/Hispanic Arts* (Winter/Spring 1968), theoretical classifications are all very well, 'but when we are confronted with the particular text or poem, we often find that it is both visual and phonetic, or that it is expressionistic as well as constructivist.' Nor should this be surprising, except perhaps in the corridors of Ulm. But how expressionistic may a constructivist poem be? Where must the axe fall? Mike Weaver, in the essay quoted above, took his position firmly, and it might be argued too firmly, when he wrote: 'Concrete poetry is an aesthetic movement in poetry, only indirectly concerned with moral, social, and psychological values. This is not to say that concrete art and poetry are not fully committed to the improvement of the environment, but only the Brazilians and Czechs have shown any inclination for social or political engagement.' Well, that 'only' is pretty bland, considering the very widespread impact and distinctive qualities of these two schools of poets, and in any case one cannot brush aside 'moral, social, and psychological values' so long as the medium in question is linguistic. Few of the poets themselves, indeed, would take the definition as far as Weaver does. Even Finlay's much-quoted statement of 1964, that concrete 'by its very limitations offers a tangible image of goodness and sanity ... very far from the now-fashionable poetry of anguish and self', is nothing if not a socially relevant comment. Positive through apparent negative is one way of proceeding, and may be more effective than positive reinforcing positive (Neruda on communism) or negative reinforcing negative (Lowell on America). Finlay's 'Acrobats' is certainly not swept under the table by (for example) Ted Hughes's *Crow*. Those who think that it is might ask themselves the question, whether they would prefer their children to go to a school where one external wall was carved with the poem 'Acrobats' or to a school where they were taught to admire either the view of life or the deployment of language we find in *Crow*? Eugen Gomringer, in an interview in *Zürcher Woche* (20 July 1962), answered a question about whether it was still the poet's job to draw a comprehensive picture of reality by claiming that: 'the complexity of the world – though I don't believe it's more complex today than at earlier periods – has entered into my "constellations". Also, looking back at earlier definitions of poetry I would say that both nature lyric and asphalt lyric are contained in the "constellations".' And eight years before, Gomringer had said in his article 'From Line to Constellation': 'The aim of the new poetry is to give poetry an organic function in society again, and in doing so to restate the position of poet in society ... The constellation is an invitation.'

Between these views of Gomringer and Finlay, and overtly political, socially committed concrete poems like Augusto de Campos's 'Cubagramma' or Décio Pignatari's 'beba coca cola', which are anti-posters or anti-advertisements attacking United States imperialism, there is a gradation rather than a gulf. The tighter the construction the better the poem, may still be the rule; but within the acknowledgement of construction on concrete principles, wit and satire and direct social comment are clearly not to be denied to the concrete poet – even outside Saõ Paulo and Prague. Of course the point may come where social reality presses so hard on the poet that concrete cracks and topples and can no longer be used, or if it continues to be used it is only on condition of transformations and accommodations that virtually overthrow the constructivist core. This is in fact what French concrete poets have been experiencing since the events of May 1968. Either they have rejected concrete poetry or they have tended to employ collage, photomontage, fragments of newsprint, and roughly written words and letters, in such a way as to fall back on concrete's secondary sources in Dada and Futurism, and hence to become involved with far more expressionistic data than constructivist-minded critics would allow. In the 'death of concrete' number of *Stereo Headphones* (Spring 1970) which addressed itself to this problem, Henri Chopin referred to the Paris and Prague of 1968 and said: 'I was and am opposed to concrete poetry, which concretizes nothing, because it is not active. It has never been in the streets, it has never known how to fight to save man's conquests: the street which belongs to us, carrying the word away from the printing-press.' In other articles, Julien Blaine

beba coca cola
babe   cola
beba coca
babe cola caco
c aco
cola
c l o a c a

Décio Pignatari : 'beba coca cola'

```
drink   coca    cola
dribble         colla
                      ge
drink   coca
dribble colla   collo
          ge      ps
collo
     ps
colla
   ge
      ps! cloacage
```
Translation of Décio Pignatari's 'beba coca cola' by Edwin Morgan

and Jean-François Bory expressed varying degrees of suspicion, Bory making the point that concrete poetry as what he called 'a human movement' was trying painfully to emerge, through an alliance of print and photomontage. The susurrus of constructivists turning in their graves can hardly be hidden. Yet the contrast between 'clean' and 'dirty' concrete (a useful distinction commented on in the article by B. P. Nichol the Canadian poet) points to something which is real and cannot be wished away. Too much Max Bill leads to graffiti. After a surfeit of gestalt we may begin to see more in the explosions of Marinetti, and to feel as he did that *parole* need *libertà*. (There is, unfortunately, a humourless academicism about some of the critical writing on concrete which provokes the very reaction it castigates.) All this is not to say, however, that a 'clean' or purist aesthetics necessarily pushes towards high-grade trivialization, any more than the 'dirty' or brutalist view is bound to result in a desired mindbending or in social action. Neither life nor art is so simple. Jean-François Bory is honest enough to admit – and adverse critics of concrete should consider the point – that 'clearly, the next artists will not write in a pre-concrete manner, just as it is impossible to write today as though surrealism never existed.'

Eugen Gomringer once saw concrete poetry as not merely international but supranational, with the possibility of now forming 'the nucleus of the future universal common language'. Through the principle of 'economy' and the study of information theory and the new language of signs and images in advertising, television, newspapers, the poet should be able to tap a Chomskian deep universal structure, with the smallest linguistic quanta made directly communicative and with poetry changed from personal buttonholing to what could be an 'indispensable auxiliary medium' for man.

La nueva poesía se funda en las relaciones internas de la estructura lingüística, en las reciprocidades fonológico-morfológicas. En la nueva literatura lingüística, la más mínima información posee un sentido comunicativo. A través de su valor de comunicación concentrado, la poesía NO es un sucedáneo de relaciones personales directas, sino un medio auxiliar indispensable. ('La poesía concreta como lengua supranacional', 1967)

It is true that much concrete poetry, whatever its language, comes across as a gestalt, or a gestalt that needs only a minimal lexical nudge towards clarity. An attractive example would be the Japanese poet

Seiichi Niikuni's 'kawa/sasu' ('river/sandbank'). (See page 29.) It is also true that concrete has cut across some surprising frontiers, geographically and politically. If Spain and Portugal have it, so do Czechoslovakia and Russia. Although the 'rediscovery' of constructivism has so far been sluggish in Russia despite the rich Russian contribution to its history, signs are not lacking that it is going on. The cleancut, functional, yet imaginative typography and layout of El Lissitzky were already on the verge of a visual poetry in 1920 (e.g. his delectable children's tale 'Of Two Squares'). At the opposite, non-didactic, 'magical' end of the proto-concrete spectrum, llya Zdanevich developed *zaum* ('transrational' language) into optophonic patterns in his remarkable 'Easter Island' (1919), where the letters are placed and designed to give the immediate double visual effect of the actual Easter Island script plus an imaginary inscription in

Eugen Gomringer   two poems

```
from deep
to deep
from near
to near
from grey
to grey
from deep
to near                          untracked
from near                        being trackless
to grey                          being trackless
from grey                        lightfoot
to deep                          lightfoot
from two                         being powerless
to four                          being powerless
from three                       dangerous
to one                           dangerous
from one                         being untracked
to four                          being untracked
from deep                        trackless
to two                           trackless
from four                        being lightfoot
to near                          being lightfoot
from grey                        powerless
to one                           powerless
                                 being dangerous
                                 being dangerous
                                 untracked
```

Translated by Edwin Morgan

Seiichi Niikuni: 'kawa/sasu'   kawa=river sasu=sand-bank

Old Church Slavonic, both being 'coded' messages where the visual and/or phonetic data remain talismanic. (See page 30.) And somewhere in between, one would unearth the prophetically so-named 'ferroconcrete poems' (*zhelezobetonnyya poemy*) of Vasily Kamensky which show even in 1914 the mingling of visual and sonic effects characteristic of the later genre. (See page 31.)

Andrei Voznesensky included a section of concrete poems in his latest book *The Shadow of a Sound* (*Ten' zvuka*, 1970), calling them 'izopy' (i.e. *opyty izobrazitel'noi poezii*, 'experiments in figurative poetry') and introducing them with bows towards Mallarmé, Apollinaire, Mayakovsky, Khlebnikov, cinema and TV, and the oriental ideogram. Russian *izopy* might be either Aesopic or isotopic, but there is a simple example in 'a Luna kanula,' a palindromic arc which says 'but then Luna disappeared'. The meaning is that after

аркестрам

ХАХАТУН. ЗАТ ОК
ХА ХАХА
ЩВ ОК

ЛУБ ЧУ Ш. абЖОлы. ФОДЯТ РАРЕЯ
УХАЧ ХА. ХААХЬЮ
СВАХА ЧушОаРЖО.

НАК ОНИ. КЛЕТЫ Л Н
Х ХОПЬ
ШЫВЫЙГОП. МЕТ. СВОЧЬ

ЛАБ Й ТУН
ПХАБА
ПХАБА

Н Г РЯЛА
ХАХ ХАВОР ТЫНЬ
ШАБАВОЙ ЬЯХА
С

Л Б Ь. ЛЕБ ЕДЬЮ. ВНЫЙ Я. РЯ
ХА ХЬЕШ ХАХ Ю ХАХАХА. СМО ХА
ПДАЕШЧЬ. ШТАК. ДОФ. ЛЧЬ

НИ ОМ НЫМИ З НАПЛОУ ХА УЧИТ: —
ИИ И НЫ. И АЛО А АХА
ХТОМ Б. ЖБАФЬ. Л АХА

Ilya Zdanevich : 'Easter Island'

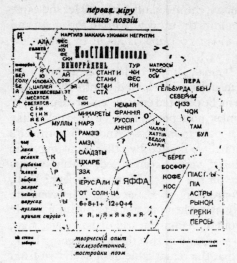

Vasíly Kamensky : ferroconcrete poem 'Constantinople'

Vasíly Kamensky : cover of book *Tango with Cows*

the first men walked on the moon, the moon of myth and legend came
to an end. The reader's eye follows the trajectory up to the moon and
back down; either way, the moon as 'Luna' is about to sink below
the horizon for ever. (See page 33.)

Can Voznesensky's calm 'Luna', Bory's raging 'Peste', and Finlay's three-dimensional poem-objects set lovingly into the grasses
and waters of his Dunsyre farm, be counted equally 'concrete poetry'?
Is Bory post-concrete, is Finlay post-poetry? Is Voznesensky, like
the cow's tail, too late on the scene to impress? And is Gomringer's
belief in a 'lengua supranacional' so limited by other, non-linguistic
tensions (as for example purist versus committed, 'clean' versus
'dirty') that it must founder on the facts of human society? Well,
without contraries is no progression, as Blake said. The concrete
movement considered merely as a phenomenon has forced a whole
new series of creative confrontations on the use of language, sign,
metaphor, typography, and space, and in this there is no going back.
While some would disagree that the remarkable designs drawn from
the sheer concrete thinginess of printers' type and typewriter type
(in e.g. Hansjörg Mayer and Dom Silvester Houédard respectively)
have anything to do with poetry, even if they do appear in concrete
poetry anthologies, no one surely would fail to accept that a revolt
in perception, or more properly a jolt into perception, has occurred,
and that this will increasingly affect publishing, education, art training, and many forms of design, quite apart from the impact on
aesthetics itself. There will be no more double-column Spensers
with every line turned over because there is 'no space' for it. And
perhaps we shall now get Ezra Pound's famous little haiku 'In a
Station of the Metro' printed as he intended it (and as it never is):

> The apparition of these faces in the crowd :
> Petals on a wet, black bough :

Poets have been the slaves of publishers and printers for far too long.
They are now beginning to assert themselves.

As for the tensions, accretions, and reneguings within the movement, in the 'death of concrete' number of *Stereo Headphones* already
quoted Gomringer stated simply that the scene had changed and
that typography had sometimes become too dominant a concern.
'But so has grown up something else and there is no sorrow.' This
is Blakean, and good. Mammoth international concrete exhibitions,
each aiming to be more definitive than the last, still trundle onstage

Луна канула

Andreї Voznesensky:
'a Luna Kanula'

in museums and galleries in many parts of the world, and although
these will at times make the judicious grieve in their holist voracious-
ness, they show, however imperfectly that the global village is not
just a figment grown in Toronto. The global village, in fact, may be
regarded in Gomringer's terms as a constellation, held together by
shuddering and whipping lines of force, or to jump back to Mallarmé
from whom Gomringer derived the word and idea, it is

A CONSTELLATION

cold from neglect and disuse
yet not so much
that it does not count
on some empty and superior plane
the next collision
sidereally
of a final reckoning in the making
watching
doubting
revolving
blazing and meditating
before it halts
at some final point which consecrates it

(*Un coup de dés*, 1897, trans. by Daisy Aldan)

Mallarmé in his preface to the poem foresaw a new, spatial development of poetry which would run parallel to, but not supersede, the
linear poetry of time and measure. His division of the natures of the
two poetries is strikingly prophetic:

The genre which this [i.e. spatial poetry] may become, little by little,
like the symphony compared to the monody, leaves intact the old style

JEAN-FRANÇOIS BORY

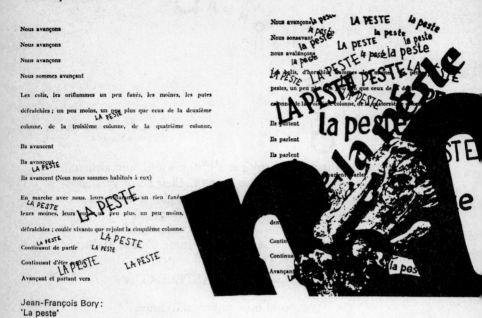

Jean-François Bory:
'La peste'

of verse, toward which I retain the greatest respect and attribute the sovereignty of passion and of dreams; while this would be the preferred manner for dealing (just as it follows) with subjects of the pure and complex imagination or intellect: which there is no reason any longer to exclude from Poetry – that singular well-spring.

The singular well-spring still plays.

Akros, VI, 18 (March 1972).

The Walls of Gormenghast:
An Introduction to the Novels
of Mervyn Peake

A WRITER who is also an artist, with a strongly developed visual imagination and a distinct flair for portraying the grotesque and the strange, tries his hand at the novel. He sees this literary form, this great tract so ill-defined in shape and purpose, apparently welcoming a lavish and indulgent play of imagination, a story-telling rich with fantastic incident, whose sole necessity is to enthrall. This is a freedom he will find deceptive, but only partly deceptive. He discovers that the 'necessity to enthrall' involves him willy-nilly with human feelings and experiences, and that the novel is oddly tenacious of its verisimilitudes, even when it is shading off towards fairy-tale or allegory. If he can learn this lesson, humanize his fantasy, localize his strangeness – he has the chance of proving how important the imagination is, in a form which is constantly being pushed towards documentation and naturalism. It would be wrong, certainly, to judge *Wuthering Heights* without reference to how life was lived in the north of England in the early nineteenth century; but the lack of imaginative life in the novels of, for example, C. P. Snow is a more serious fault than the lack of a minute realism in Emily Brontë, because it leads to dullness, and nothing is worse than dullness. Poetry has to be periodically brought down to earth; the novel has to be periodically lifted off.

Mervyn Peake is one writer who has made this experiment, and within fantastic narratives (I am thinking especially of *Titus Groan* and *Gormenghast*) that are superficially of great self-indulgence and escapism he has been able to show the emergence of a positive imaginative power of a peculiar and valuable kind. What I want to do is to try to define this peculiarity and this value.

Apart from his work as an artist (drawings, paintings, book-illustrations), with which I shall not be concerned here, Peake has produced two volumes of poetry, a play, four novels, and a long short story. Of these, it is only the novels and the short story that are important, though many an interesting and idiosyncratic touch will be found in his other writings. The poems (*Shapes and Sounds*, 1941; *The Glassblowers*, 1950) are romantic and exploratory, with some striking imagery, but for the most part they fail to achieve the necessary distinction of form. Often one feels the excitement that lies behind the poem, without feeling that the excitement has been made meaningful or fully worked out in poetic terms. Strong reactions to 'shapes and sounds' – as in the title-poem 'The Glass-blowers' – stamp his poetry with the fluent sensuousness that is found in all his work. His poetic comedy, *The Wit to Woo*, was produced at the Arts Theatre by Peter Wood in 1957. This, like the poetry, shows Peake using a medium where he cannot extend himself in the special way he requires. A fantastic love-story, set in the hall of a country house, with a good deal of verbal humour (e.g. four tipsy undertakers 'primed in our roles and rolling in our prime'), the play came too close in atmosphere and diction to the work of Christopher Fry, at a time when drama had moved away from the verbal-poetic mode, to have a full success on the stage. It has a nice lyrical feeling, but the 'reality' of the love theme is too flimsily illustrated by the dramatic action.

It is in prose that the 'literature of imagination' tends to be written – by Beckford or Bunyan, Poe or Kafka, Rabelais or Wells, Orwell or Asimov. The literature of imagination requires at least two things that prose can best command: strong pictorial visualization (for the strange has to be made credible), and dramatic action (since the author has a story to keep up). In his book-illustrations and original drawings Mervyn Peake had already shown his capabilities as a visualizer of haunting and penetrating images, both grotesque and realistic, and this power did not desert him when he turned to prose narrative: his descriptions are alive, and almost Dickensian in the way that they call out for illustration, and his often detailed accounts of physical action – a rare pleasure in an epoch of psychology! – appear as an extension of his artist's control of gesture, an animation of the tense but arrested movements of another medium.

Even his minor works of fiction succeed admirably on their own terms. *Mr. Pye* (1953) is a light and amusing novel about the sojourn of Harold Pye, a plump little 'sleuth of glory', on the island of Sark (where Peake himself has done much of his writing). Mr Pye, whose sole desire is to turn Sark into a paradise of goodness and love, finds that his missionary efforts result in his sprouting a rather troublesome pair of wings. To counteract the embarrassment he tries to do evil, but as the wings diminish on his back, horns push through on his forehead. At the end his good nature accepts the winged state, and on the last page we see Pye (rather like Wells's Pyecraft) becoming airborne and floating off from the island. As in many fantasies, a small island is chosen as a naturally isolated spot where marvellous events might be looked for; but the treatment here is gently humorous rather than seriously imaginative.

Boy in Darkness (1956) is very different: it is a *nouvelle*, a sinister epic incident, a reflection in miniature of the world of *Titus Groan* and *Gormenghast*. The story is separate from the two big novels, but has the same hero, the boy Titus. The Boy, aged fourteen, undergoes a testing allegory of adolescence, and successfully outwits the three horrible half-human figures of the Goat, the Hyena, and the Lamb, into whose country he strays. The blind, dead-white Lamb with his hyperacute hearing and soft musical voice is a more appalling Comus, transforming his human captives into a shape half-way towards the animal which their ruling passion or quality suggests. When the Boy kills him, he kills an enchantment. 'There was no blood, nor anything to be seen in the nature of a brain.' The danger had in one sense been real: he had experienced the first shock of identity, of being not a boy but a man, a free and individual soul whom others (including the most evil) would now begin to trouble, cover, touch, and attack. But the danger and the dread are presented as a dream, a nightmare which he himself will forget – or remember only as an unexplained strengthening of his courage in moments of temptation or terror in waking life.

With the long novel *Titus Groan* (1946) and its two sequels *Gormenghast* (1950) and *Titus Alone* (1959), we reach Mervyn Peake's major work. Here, the full range of his imagination rouses itself, from weird fantasy and farcical humour to horror, pathos, and moral and social allegory.

The action of the first two books of the trilogy takes place in or near the enormous ritual-ridden castle of Gormenghast, in a highly organized and ancient society. At the top of the hierarchy are the Earl and Countess of Groan, Sepulchrave and Gertrude; abstracted, solitary figures, Sepulchrave immured with his books, Gertrude with

her cats and birds. The family includes the Earl's twin sisters, Cora
and Clarice, single-minded in jealous hatred of the Countess; his
daughter Fuchsia, awkward, passionate, hungering for the love that
her remote parents have denied her; and his newly born son Titus,
who is still a baby at the end of *Titus Groan* but has already given
signs of an independent spirit by throwing certain sacred objects in
the lake. The privileged ranks of society are headed by the eccentric
but good-hearted Dr Prunesquallor and his man-hunting sister Irma.
Then come the vast array of servants, from the knee-cracking head
valet Flay down to the versatile but Machiavellian kitchen-boy
Steerpike who becomes the focus of interest in *Titus Groan*. Lowest
of all are the Outer Dwellers living in huts in the shadow of the
castle walls – a different race:

> Mrs. Slagg was never very tactful. 'You have some food thrown down
> to you from the battlements every morning, don't you?' She had pursed
> her mouth and stopped a moment for breath. A young man lifted his
> thick black eyebrows and spat.

The story, which is continued in *Gormenghast* to the point where
Titus is a young man, and in *Titus Alone* to the hero's first experience of life and love beyond the castle walls, presents a crisis in the
life of this society. Gormenghast is threatened, in the first place by
the coldblooded and ambitious Steerpike, who is willing to use
murder, arson, and seduction as stepping-stones to power, and hopes
for eventual dictatorship, replacing the Groan dynasty with an even
more rigid and frustrating régime. He overreaches himself, and is
killed by Titus. But Titus himself represents a second and perhaps
more serious threat. His motives for destroying Steerpike are personal
rather than public, and he becomes, ironically, the deliverer of a
society he is eager to reject. The laws and rituals of his forebears
('the traditional equine masks were being worn at the correct angle
of dejection'), with which he is bound to comply whatever the
heroism or indifference of his personal character, stifle his adventurous spirit. 'What do I care,' he exclaims to his mother, 'for the
symbolism of it all? What do I care if the castle's heart is sound or
not? I don't want to be sound anyway! Anybody can be sound if
they're always doing what they're told. I want to live!' His mother
assumes that this is the natural and temporary rebelliousness of
youth, and does not try to stop Titus when he rides off alone from
the castle on the last page of *Gormenghast* in search of a freer exist-

ence. 'There is nowhere else,' she tells him. '... There's not a road, not a track, but it will lead you home. For everything comes to Gormenghast.' But in this the Countess is over-confident. It is not just a matter of time's reconciling the stubborn idealism of Titus with the hard facts of human inertia and age-old tradition. Life in Gormenghast, as in many human communities, has become morbidly stiff and encrusted with meaningless ceremonies; Titus sees it not merely as the world of his boyhood which he must outgrow, but also as a world that has become unnaturally resistant to change. With Steerpike's death, Gormenghast has a breathing-space; but with Titus's departure – the defection of the heir – a criticism is made of the old ways which is deeper than the Countess knows. Like a spore of new life breaking off from some great colony in decay, Titus bears with him an impress of tradition and order and authority of which he is himself hardly aware, but he will not re-enter the ancient castle, and if some day he founds a castle of his own it will only be 'Gormenghast' as a man is the son of his parents, not as a king succeeds a king. At the end of the third volume, *Titus Alone*, the young hero returns to Gormenghast Mountain, after many adventures in an alien country where the people's mocking disbelief in his noble origin gave him an intense homesickness for the very things he had tried to escape from; but as soon as he hears a ritual salvo booming from the still invisible walls, his old rejection of Gormenghast is suddenly confirmed and strengthened, and he swings off in another direction, away from the castle. His mother's words have in a sense been fulfilled, but not to her comfort, or to the comfort of her house. As for Titus: 'He had no longer any need for home, for he carried his Gormenghast within him.'

These three novels are in fact commenting – neither directly nor by strict allegory but by significant juxtaposition and mingling of the grotesque and the human – upon society, upon the relation of the individual to traditional forms, upon what Guillaume Apollinaire called

> . . . *cette longue querelle de la tradition et de l'invention*
> *De l'Ordre de l'Aventure.*

They do this, admittedly, with a profusion of romantic, exciting, and sometimes lurid incident, but the point must be made that they are by no means 'Gothick' in their total effect. (The American edition of *Titus Groan* was sub-titled *A Gothic Novel*, against the wishes of the author.) The gradual emergence of full human qualities in Dr Prunesquallor and the Countess and Fuchsia and even Flay, as recognition of Steerpike's menace begins to dawn in *Gormenghast*, is beautifully managed, and their earlier grotesqueness is in keeping with the ossification of their still unshaken society. As life is threatened, feeling awakes. Before Fuchsia's drowned body

> The face of the Countess showed nothing, but once she drew the corner of the sheet up a little further over Fuchsia's shoulder, with an infinite gentleness, as though she feared her child might feel the cold and so must take the risk of waking her.

Far from 'having no more connection with the reality of living than *The Hunting of the Snark*,' as one reviewer* asserted of *Gormenghast*, the novels give an impression of relevance to life that is all the more extraordinary because it might seem incompatible with the undoubtedly 'Gothick' material – crumbling turrets, hooting owls, guttering candles – which Peake doesn't hesitate to incorporate. This material falls into a wider imaginative scheme: it is not at the centre of the novels. It is the almost wanton richness of the author's imagination that gives his work something of the richness of life itself. Images are thrown off which would be irrelevant to the more didactic and narrow fantasy of a William Golding or a George Orwell, but which here (rather as in Kafka and Melville) reinforce credibility with sudden pleasure. When Steerpike is exploring the tremendous ramifications of the castle roofs, he sees very far off in the sunlight a tower half-filled with rainwater.

> In this circle of water whose glittering had caught his eye, for to him it appeared about the size of a coin, he could see that something white was swimming. As far as he could guess it was a horse. As he watched he noticed that there was something swimming by its side, something smaller, which must have been the foal, white like its parent.

These horses are not like Chekhov's gun; they don't have to be there. But it is such details – details here of a world within a world – that make the fantasy leap into verisimilitude.

The novels are not without faults. The recapitulation at the beginning of *Gormenghast* slows up our entry into the main action. I am not quite happy about the position and meaning of the Outer Dwellers (it is hinted that they may be concerned in some way with

* Emyr Humphreys in *Time and Tide*, 21 October 1950.

the rejuvenation of Gormenghast), and the primitive simplicity of their portrayal was perhaps a mistake: they remain unassimilated. *Titus Alone*, which introduces a new set of characters, has some fine scenes but shows rather less certainty of purpose than the two earlier volumes. And there are, throughout, curious solecisms and mis-spellings which could have been tidied up.

But what matters is the many truly remarkable passages in these three books which are unfolded with a narrative energy and descriptive brilliance not commonly found among more conventional novelists today. Let me recommend in particular four scenes which show the unusual range of Peake's effectiveness: Steerpike's reconnoitring climb over the complex of the castle roofs and battlements (*Titus Groan*, ch. 18–21); the nightmarish duel between Flay and Swelter in the Hall of Spiders (*Titus Groan*, ch. 61); Irma's soirée with the Professors and her dallying with the Headmaster in the moonlight arbour – surely one of the funniest scenes in modern fiction (*Gormenghast*, ch. 33–6); and the ghastly Dostoevskian throngs of the Under-River (*Titus Alone*, ch. 47–51). A man climbs over a roof. Two men fight. A woman holds a party. A man explores a sewer. This basis in recognizable experience, highly particularized and circumstantial, is what preserves Peake's grotesque from whimsy and from crude melodrama. Yet his greatest quality is the sweep of free imagination with which he fills a large and tumultuous canvas. In his finest pages he leaves the grotesque behind. At the climax of *Gormenghast* there is a deluge which almost ruins the castle physically at the moment when Steerpike is striking at its soul. The description of the storm, the evacuation of the vast crowded mass of buildings floor by floor as the floodwaters rise, the final stark encounter of hero and villain when Titus hunts Steerpike among the ivy, and the eventual receding of the water and re-emergence of the castle, and the return to everyday life – all this has an epic quality of multitudinousness and grandeur and inevitability of action. The dead Fuchsia is ferried across the water to her burial-place on Gormenghast Mountain, and Peake gives us a last look at his creation from that vantage-point.

> From this location the castle could be seen heaving across the skyline like the sheer sea-wall of a continent; a seaboard nibbled with countless coves and bitten deep with shadowy embayments. A continent, off whose shores the crowding islands lay; islands of every shape that towers can be; and archipelagos; and isthmuses and bluffs; and stark

peninsulas of wandering stone – an inexhaustible panorama whose every detail was mirrored in the breathless flood below.

Artist and writer, outward and inward eye, combine to produce an image which is in its own way an image of the world.

Chicago Review, XIV, 3 (Autumn–Winter 1960).

Three Views of Brooklyn Bridge

I

HART CRANE'S long poem *The Bridge* was written in the six years from 1923 to 1929 and published in 1930. Its distinctive, and distinctively modern, feature is that it attempts to build up a myth which is focused on a recent man-made object: the Brooklyn Bridge. The obvious romantic appeal of a bridge, and the deep and ambiguous psychological attraction that large bridges have (joyful suspension among the elements; setting out; landfall; suicide; vantage-point; thrills and stunts), are added here to one of the specific achievements of nineteenth-century engineering, a splendid structure that combines massive solidity (the huge stone towers) with the beauty and lightness of its suspended curves and tracery (the cables). But splendid or not, a physical object presents problems to the poet who wants ambitiously to draw large conclusions. Crane was interested in this bridge both as a universal symbol of union and aspiration (aspiration towards 'the other shore') and as a possible symbol of the American consciousness which could be used because it showed a successful linking of bold vision and untried technology. But a bridge is steel and stone. Can these stones live?

> What bridge? Great God, the only bridge, the bridge of power, life and joy, the bridge that was a span, a cry, an ecstasy – that was America. What bridge? The bridge whose wing-like sweep that was like space and joy and ecstasy was mixed like music in his blood, would beat like flight and joy and triumph through the conduits of his life for ever. What bridge? The bridge whereon at night he had walked and stood and watched a thousand times, until every fabric of its soaring web was inwrought in his memory, and every stone of its twin terrific arches was in his heart, and every living sinew of its million cabled nerves had throbbed and pulsed in his own spirit like his soul's anatomy.
>
> 'The – the Brooklyn Bridge,' he mumbled. 'The – the Bridge is good.'
>
> (Thomas Wolfe, *Of Time and the River*, 1935)

Wolfe's ecstatic prose does at least make the point clear, that this particular bridge easily gathered human associations and was readily metaphorized (its cables becoming 'sinews' and 'nerves', itself becoming a 'cry' of joy signalling 'America'). Yet the metaphors arise out of the physical reality of the bridge and of the feet that have 'walked and stood' on its span. If it has magic, the magic comes from use, and is a magic of time and place. The same unusually swift transition from artefact to symbol is seen in Henry Miller, who says in his essay 'The Brooklyn Bridge':

> For me the Brooklyn Bridge served very much as the rainbow did for Lawrence. Only whereas Lawrence was seeking the bright future which the rainbow seemed to promise, I was seeking a link which would bind me to the past . . . Walking back and forth over the Brooklyn Bridge everything became crystal clear to me. Once I cleared the tower and felt myself definitely poised above the river the whole past would click. It held as long as I remained over the water, as long as I looked down into the inky swirl and saw all things upside down. It was only in moments of extreme anguish that I took to the bridge, when, as we say, it seemed that all was lost. Time and again all was lost, irrevocably so. The bridge was the harp of death, the strange winged creature without an eye which held me suspended between the two shores.

(The Cosmological Eye, 1939)

Crane (who died in 1932) would no doubt have appreciated these extensions of his own feelings and concerns. He was excited to discover a kindred spirit in the artist Joseph Stella whose painting 'Brooklyn Bridge' he wanted to use as frontispiece for the Black Sun Press edition of *The Bridge*. Stella had written about the 'massive dark towers dominating the surrounding tumult of the surging skyscrapers with their gothic majesty sealed in the purity of their arches, the cables, like divine messages from above, transmitted to the vibrating coils, cutting and dividing into innumerable musical spaces the nude immensity of the sky', and he regarded the bridge as a 'shrine containing all the efforts of the new civilization of AMERICA'. The cathedral-like towers, the divine messages, the music, the shrine, the identification with America – all these are found in Crane too. But where he differs slightly from Stella is in the essential point of the actuality or historicity with which he partly keeps apocalypticism at bay. It may well be that Crane was more deeply committed to the industrial and commercial values of

American capitalism than he knew. He had worked in his father's factory (the Crane Candy Company!), he had been an advertising copywriter, and (the deepest irony) he sought and obtained financial support from the banker Otto H. Kahn, as good an exemplar of successful materialist America as could be found. In his first letter to Kahn in 1925, he described how his poem aimed 'to enunciate a new cultural synthesis of values in terms of our America'. Our America! But to some extent Crane was only developing something that goes back to Whitman – a prophetic pride in the achievements of industry and science and a conviction that poetry's job was to encompass that area of experience as well as experience of nature or love. What Whitman said in 'Crossing Brooklyn Ferry' to the city and its harbour and ships and foundry chimneys – 'bring your freight, bring your shows ... we use you, and do not cast you aside ... we love you' – reflects the same outgoingness of feeling towards the inanimate and the man-made as Crane expressed later in *The Bridge*, especially in those sections of the poem where Brooklyn Bridge itself is in the foreground.

The most notable locus for this spiritualization of the material is of course the opening section, called 'Proem: to Brooklyn Bridge'.

> How many dawns, chill from his rippling rest
> The seagull's wings shall dip and pivot him,
> Shedding white rings of tumult, building high
> Over the chained bay waters Liberty –
>
> Then, with inviolate curve, forsake our eyes
> As apparitional as sails that cross
> Some page of figures to be filed away;
> – Till elevators drop us from our day . . .
>
> I think of cinemas, panoramic sleights
> With multitudes bent towards some flashing scene
> Never disclosed, but hastened to again,
> Foretold to other eyes on the same screen;
>
> And Thee, across the harbour, silver-paced
> As though the sun took step of thee, yet left
> Some motion ever unspent in thy stride, –
> Implicitly thy freedom staying thee!

Out of some subway scuttle, cell or loft
A bedlamite speeds to thy parapets,
Tilting there momently, shrill shirt ballooning,
A jest falls from the speechless caravan.

Down Wall, from girder into street noon leaks,
A rip-tooth of the sky's acetylene;
All afternoon the cloud-flown derricks turn . . .
Thy cables breathe the North Atlantic still.

And obscure as that heaven of the Jews,
Thy guerdon . . . Accolade thou dost bestow
Of anonymity time cannot raise:
Vibrant reprieve and pardon thou dost show.

O harp and altar, of the fury fused,
(How could mere toil align thy choiring strings!)
Terrific threshold of the prophet's pledge,
Prayer of pariah, and the lover's cry, –

Again the traffic lights that skim thy swift
Unfractioned idiom, immaculate sigh of stars,
Beading thy path – condense eternity:
And we have seen night lifted in thine arms.

Under thy shadow by the piers I waited;
Only in darkness is thy shadow clear.
The City's fiery parcels all undone,
Already snow submerges an iron year . . .

O Sleepless as the river under thee,
Vaulting the sea, the prairies' dreaming sod,
Unto us lowliest sometime sweep, descend
And of the curveship lend a myth to God.

In this poem, a strong impression of actuality (Wall Street, the
Statue of Liberty, the North Atlantic, elevators, cables, piers,
cinemas, subway, girder, acetylene, derricks, traffic lights) is bled
out into romantic and symbolic properties (accolade, harp and altar,
choiring strings, prophet's pledge, prayer, sigh of stars, iron year),
and with a rough hopeful stitch in the middle ('How could mere toil
align thy choiring strings!') the poet pushes his central point through
in the form of a rhetorical question. How could danger-harried and

unskilled labour (twenty men died during the building of the bridge, and others, to quote one account, were 'permanently paralyzed as they returned to the normal air from the pressurized caissons in which they had to work under the river') produce an object that utterly transcended its mundane purpose of linking Brooklyn to Manhattan across the East River? And Crane would not be satisfied with the answer that John and Washington Roebling were, as bridge-builders, men of genius and vision. The world is modern. Science itself has leaked through into nature, as in Crane's poem the noonday sun leaks down into Wall Street, 'a rip-tooth of the sky's acetylene'. Man creates, whether by accident or design, a new and startling beauty, a new 'curveship' which might even 'lend a myth to God' – Promethean no doubt, and raising works of use and material mastery to the full level of either God's nature or man's art. Art – and how clearly this poem, in part wonderfully expressive and in part forcedly poetical, shows it! – must pant after the acetylene. And who holds *that* torch?

II

'Proem: To Brooklyn Bridge' was completed (apart from later minor change) in July 1926. About a year before this, between July and November 1925, Crane's Russian contemporary, Vladimir Mayakovsky, visited America and wrote his own poem 'Brooklyn Bridge'. So far as we know the two poets never met, nor did they know each other's work, though Mayakovsky held many public meetings and poetry-readings in New York and elsewhere, and Crane was living in Brooklyn at the time. If they had met, they would have discovered that they both admired Whitman and were both keenly aware that poets were living in a world being rapidly transformed by science and technology. But there were two big differences. Mayakovsky was shaped by politics and believed that political matter had as much right to be in poetry as matter from any other source; to Crane, politics was of minimal concern. And although both poets were loners, outsiders, Mayakovsky had an ebullient sense of comedy and the grotesque that is lacking in Crane.

The Russian poet wrote a batch of poems about his American experience, and also a prose work called *My Discovery of America*. He saw himself as a Columbus with a difference: entirely typical of the peripatetic Soviet writer (Voznesensky and Yevtushenko are two more recent examples) was his ambivalent sense of being both emissary and rubberneck. He came to the New World from one that was still newer (born in 1917) and yet much older too. He came to the most industrially advanced country from a country engaged in belatedly furious industrial emulation. As far as poetry was concerned, he came from a twentieth-century tradition that was different but of equal inventiveness and vigour.

In *My Discovery of America*, which is essentially a travel diary, he shows the Russian love/hate reaction to America very clearly. He was fascinated by Broadway and gives a lyrical paragraph on the 'light, light, light' of the Great White Way, but immediately contrasts it with the poor quarters which are 'filthier than Minsk – and Minsk is pretty filthy', and with the pervasive dry, dusty, carbonladen air which keeps windows closed and nostrils stuffed. The dollar is Father, Son, and Holy Ghost, yet to the American its green has a vernal and poetic look, very simpatico. He laughs at Chicago's superlatives but admires its energy. In his summing-up he attacks the 'rapacious character of American life' and its 'bivouac-like structure' and says America will become 'entirely a country of finance and usury' (shades of Ezra Pound!), but he also admits that

> The futurism of sheer technology, of the external impressionism of smoke and cable-strands, which has had the huge task of revolutionizing the ankylosed, fatty-degenerate, rustic-slumbering psyche – this basic futurism has been conclusively affirmed by America.

And he adds a definition of his own task as a Soviet writer, finding a parallel which is not quite a parallel:

> not the celebration of technology but the harnessing of it in the name of the interests of humanity – not the aesthetic enjoyment of iron fire-escapes on skyscrapers but the simple organization of living quarters.

This last recommendation is in fact not very far from Hart Crane's remarks in his essay 'Modern Poetry':

> Machinery will tend to lose its sensational glamour and appear in its true subsidiary order in human life as use and continued poetic allusion subdue its novelty. For, contrary to general prejudice, the wonderment experienced in watching nose dives is of less immediate creative promise to poetry than the familiar gesture of a motorist in the modest act of shifting gears.

Such excellent intentions, however, are borne down when both poets are confronted with the masterpiece of the Roeblings. Mayakovsky's 'Brooklyn Bridge' is very much a 'celebration of technology' and it is his chief and ungrudging tribute to the American genius.

      Coolidge ahoy!
      can ye shout wi joy?
      This makar'll no be blate
                  at namin
      what's guid.
             Blush rid
                  at my praises, you s-
uperunited states-man –
                    rid
                      as the flamin
flag o Sovetsky Soyuz.
Like a cracked sanct
             hirplin
                  to his kirk,
to some stere,
             semple
                  Culdee wig-
wam o stane,
          here
               in the grey dwam and mirk
o gloamin
             I set fit doucely on Brooklyn Brig.
Like a conqueror
             enterin
                the toon he has taen,
the swanky
           ridin his cannon-rig
its giraffe-snoot cockit,
                I'm fu wi glory, I'm fain
o life,
      I'm prood
            to sclim on Brooklyn Brig.
Like a daft penter-chiel
              that digs an auld-maister's
madonna wi his sherp lovin een,
                I trig-
ger my sicht
         fae the airy
             starn-thrangsters
doon
      through aa New York
            by Brooklyn Brig.

New York,
          pechin
                    in daylang ure and stour,
pits by
          its trauchle noo,
                    and its giddy waas
shaw nane but freely spooks
                    that skoor
the lichtit windaes
                    wi hamely-glintin claws.
Ye can juist hear
          the grummle
                    o the rummlin El,
and up here
          there's naethin
                    bar that laich grummle
to tell
          hoo trains
                    are traipsin, clatterin fell,
like ashets in a press
                    flung thegither in a tummle.
See the shopkeeper
                    humphin his sugar fae
a mill
          that seems
                    to loup oot o the stream –
while
          masts gang furrit unner the brae
o the brig
          nae langer nor preens.
It's prood I am
                    o this
                    wan mile o steel,
my veesions here
                    tak vive and forcy form –
a fecht
          for construction
                    abune flims o style,
a strang
          trig-rivetit grid,
                    juist whit steel's for!
And if
          the feenish o the warld

                              sud come
and chaos
              clout the planet
                              to smithereens
and the wan thing
                       left staunin
                              in the sun
sud be this brig spreedeaglt owre the reeky stanes –
then,
        as a hantle
                      o puir peerie banes
swalls
        to a curator's
                      vaudy dinosaur-chaumer,
sae
      fae this brig
                    some faur-aff geologist yonner
in the centuries'll
                      bigg up
                              the haill warld o oor days.
He'll say:
            'See thon
                      muckle steely paw –
it jyned
          the prairies to the seas; fae this end
Europe
          breenged Westwart, Westwart,
                                        blawin
a flaff
        o Indian fedders
                          doon the wind.
See
      the rib therr –
                      minds me o a machine;
I wunner,
            staunin wi a steel-fit grup
in Manhattan,
                  wid the hauns rax
                                    steeve and clean
to hook and rug owre
                      Brooklyn
                              by the lip?
And see

                    the electric cable-strands – we ken
          it's eftir
                    the James Watt era,
                                        that here
          the radio
                    hud fouth
                              o bummin
                                        men;
          and planes
                    were fleein
                              through
                                        the atmosphere.
          Here,
               some folk
                         fund life
                                   a gairden-pairty,
          ithers
               a lang-drawn
                         tuim-wame
                                   granin-time.
          Doon therr,
                    the workless pairted
          fae it,
               heid first
                         into the Hudson's slime.
          And noo . . .
                    noo the eemage
                                   gaes sae clear, sae faur
          it skimmers on the cable-strings
                                   richt to the feet o the starns.
          Here in my een
                    I can see
                              Mayakovsky staun –
          he stauns as a makar,
                              the syllables jow in his harns –'
          – And I'm gawpin still
                              like an Eskimo at an injin,
          like a cleg at the neck-band
                              drinkin it aa in.
          Brooklyn Brig –
          man . . .
               that's BIG!

(Vladimir Mayakovsky, translated into Scots by Edwin Morgan)

Mayakovsky presents himself setting foot on the bridge in a series of analogies: a believer entering a church, a conqueror taking over a town, an artist appreciating a madonna, an Eskimo gawping at a train, a tick fastened to an ear. The extravagant variety of the comparisons helps to emphasize the *bouleversant* nature of the new experience, and the mixture of humility and pride the poet feels. As in Hart Crane, there is a lyrical reaction to the sheer physical presence of the bridge, and sometimes, though only in touches, the lyrical moves out into the visionary, as towards the end when the geologist from the future watches the cables stretching to heaven. But mostly Mayakovsky is more down-to-earth, and keeps bringing the bridge back to man and society where Crane keeps making it grow myth like a pearl. Crane gives a vivid sketch of a suicide but describes him as mad, a 'bedlamite', part of the life/death mythology of bridges; Mayakovsky also brings in suicides, but they are unemployed men and starving, they are a part of his social comment on America. And whereas Crane watches the beauty of the traffic lights 'condense eternity', and the bridge lift night in its arms like some extraordinary steel Pietà, Mayakovsky's central vision of the bridge is constructivist rather than suggestional, it reminds him of his own struggle as an artist, 'the struggle for construction instead of style'.

Mayakovsky's poem fairly crackles with life and invention, so much so that even the highly improbable initial buttonholing of President Calvin Coolidge (described by Irving Stone as 'the epitome of the joyless soul' who took with him to the White House 'a political kerosene lamp with which to light his way in an age of vast electro-dynamics') seems right and proper.

III

Coolidge addressed Congress at the end of 1928 as if history held no surprises. 'No Congress of the United States ever assembled, on surveying the state of the Union, has met with a more pleasing prospect than that which appears at the present time.' But the business boom of the twenties, if he had known it, was stretched to breaking-point, and the Wall Street stock-market collapsed in October 1929 and the Great Depression began.

That desperate autumn and winter of 1929–30, when Hart Crane was putting finishing touches to *The Bridge*, was the unlucky time chosen by Federico García Lorca to visit America. He never read or met Crane, as far as is known. New York made a tremendous impact on him, as well it might, and like Mayakovsky he wrote a number of poems about the experience which were later collected as *Poeta en Nueva York*. These poems are very different from the main body of Lorca's work, and to some critics they seem like an aberration which they prefer to forget. Lorca with guitars and gypsies in Andalusia is all right, but not Lorca howling like Ginsberg in the slums of Harlem. The situation is complicated by the fact that before coming to America Lorca had been interested in surrealism and had friendly connections with Dalí and Buñuel, so that even without the traumatic trip to the States he is hardly likely to have continued writing within the song and ballad forms that had made him famous. But the anguish and painful excitement and sense of terrible alienation that came to him during his transatlantic months gave his surrealism a use and a meaning: his American poems are not strictly surrealist, but employ some surrealist techniques to convey his nightmarish, almost hallucinatory feelings about American society during the crack-up of 1929–30. From dusty Spanish roads and olive groves to Wall Street and Harlem was a contrast of the kind the twentieth-century specializes in, and it would have shaken up a less sensitive and solitary voyager than the Englishless Lorca wandering into a first-class national crisis.

Yet it was not all nightmare, or if it was, then the nightmare could fascinate as well as repel – as Mayakovsky had found. In Black America, Lorca saw, prophetically enough, great and explosive qualities of life that were still denied outlet.

> Oh, Harlem! Oh, Harlem! Oh, Harlem!
> There is no agony like your beaten-down rubies,
> your blood buffeted in dark eclipse,
> your garnet rage deaf and dumb in the penumbra,
> your great king imprisoned in a janitor's suit!

('The King of Harlem')

Also he was aware, as Crane and Mayakovsky were, of the optimistic tradition of Whitman, and like Crane he uses Whitman as a mythical figure whom he can bring into his poetry and address directly, as he does in the 'Ode to Walt Whitman'. In that poem he contrasts Whitman's rare ability to praise both industry and loafing with the modern world's furious devotion to the former and loss of the latter. Along East River, in the Bronx and Queensborough, he says, young men were wrestling with industry, but 'no one wanted to

be a river ... no one wanted to be a cloud.' He waits for Whitman,
like Blake's Albion, to waken again. Business and technology between
them have parched the fluid spirit of the country.

In the meantime, it is 'the moment of dry things', 'the cruel
silence of money', 'hurricanes of gold and groans of paid-off work-
men', 'the Market a pyramid of moss', 'little swallows on crutches',
'the obscene threat of a science without roots', 'the false dawn of
New York', 'boys trembling under the chalky terror of directors',
and everywhere 'The moon! The police! The transatlantic sirens!'

In this nightmare world many places are mentioned by name, and
there are poems devoted to 'Landscape of the Vomiting Crowd:
Coney Island Twilight', 'Landscape of the Urinating Crowd:
Battery Place Nocturne', 'Murder: Two Voices at Dawn on River-
side Drive'. But unlike Mayakovsky, Lorca is not an observer with a
notebook, and is scarcely concerned with any kind of verisimilitude.
These are merely places where things happen, where the spirit grows
stunted or desperate, where indefinable and terrible forces are at
loose and can only be indicated through recurrent imagery, often
non-realistic. So that when Lorca, like Crane and Mayakovsky,
comes to Brooklyn Bridge, and writes his 'Sleepless City: Brooklyn
Bridge Nocturne', he shares none of their elation of mind, or wonder-
ment at the engineering triumph of the bridge, or interest in either
its history or its myth.

Sleepless City: Brooklyn Bridge Nocturne

No one sleeps in the sky. No one, no one.
No one sleeps.
The moon's creatures prowl and sniff round their cabins.
Living iguanas arrive to gnaw the insomniacs
and the heartbroken man on the run will meet at streetcorners
the quiet incredible crocodile beneath the soft protest of the stars.

No one sleeps in the world. No one, no one.
No one sleeps.
There is a dead man in the farthest-off graveyard
who for three querulous years
has grumbled at the shrivelled landscape fixed to his knees;
and the boy they buried this morning cried so much
they had to call out dogs to give him his quietus.

Life is no dream. Watch out! Watch out! Watch out!
We fall downstairs to eat damp earth
or climb to the snowline with a dead dahlia chorus.
But there is no oblivion, no dream, only
living flesh. Kisses bind mouths
in a maze of fresh veins
and the one whose pain vexes him will be vexed without rest
and the one whom death terrifies will be bowed under it.

One day
horses will neigh in taverns
and rabid ants
will attack the yellow skies lurking in crows' eyes.

Another day
we shall see a resurrection of dissected butterflies
and then as we stroll through a sponge-grey boat-still scene
we shall see our rings flash and our tongues spill roses.
Watch out! Watch out! Watch out!
For those who still guard the claw-tracks and the cloudburst,
that boy weeping because the invention of the bridge is beyond him
or that dead man left with a head and a shoe,
they are all to be taken to the wall where iguanas and snakes are waiting,
where the bear's teeth are waiting,
where the mummied hand of the child is waiting
and the camel-skin bristles and shivers in raw blue fever.

No one sleeps in the sky. No one, no one.
No one sleeps.
But if any eye should shut –
lash him awake, boys, lash him!

Imagine a panorama of staring eyes
and bitter sores kept flaming.
No one sleeps in the world. No one, no one.
No one sleeps.
I say it here.
No one sleeps.
But if anyone should find a glut of night moss on his temples –
open the trapdoors and let the moon look down on
the sham wineglasses, the poison, and the skull of the theatres.

                    (Federico García Lorca, translated by Edwin Morgan)

To Lorca the bridge is the natural centre of a 'nocturne', a brooding meditation on insomnia and death that makes New York like James Thomson's 'City of Dreadful Night'. Beyond the single reference to the boy crying 'because the invention of the bridge is beyond him', the great bridge itself is a mere locus and has no need to be described: it is simply the place where a solitary sleepless man might stand at night, looking over the lights and darkness of New York. What Crane had seen as a divinely imperturbable vigilance ('O Sleepless as the river under thee') is now a bleak neurosis ('No one sleeps in the world. No one, no one'). The city is seen as a centre of ultimate restlessness. Lorca's favourite sinister animals prowl and crawl, harass and wait: the iguanas, the crocodiles, the snakes, the dogs. Not only can the living get no sleep, but even the dead will not rest. Love, pain, and the fear of death are all raw and perpetual, like wounds perpetually re-inflamed. It is as if all eyelids had been removed, as if everyone was forced to stare, and run, and shudder, and stare again. To try to escape from the nocturne is futile: everything is false, vicious, or empty; the sham wineglass and the theatre skull are no nearer true humanity than the iguanas and crocodiles. In Lorca's Aspirin Age there are not even any aspirins, only the fever that wants them.

This poem in its very lack of clarity seems an apt comment on the chaotic situation Lorca was pitchforked into in the fall of 1929. Unhampered *laissez-faire* had murdered sleep; rugged go-getting had released the iguana. *Poeta en Nueva York*, for all its surreal effects, was a political poem that Mayakovsky would have understood, and it extended Lorca's range in unforeseen ways. The poet from unindustrial Spain recorded a greater shock than Mayakovsky or Crane did, and because of his personal alienation and unhappiness he missed the enormous resilience of America which the other two poets recognized. But the Brooklyn Bridge stopped all three in their travels, and like the Ancient Mariner held them till a tale was told.

Akros, III, 9 (January 1969).

Introduction to *Wi the Haill Voice: 25 Poems by Vladimir Mayakovsky Translated into Scots*

ALTHOUGH it is now nearly half a century since the death of Vladimir Mayakovsky (1893–1930), his work still keeps a springy and accessible vitality, and his ideas and feelings about the relation of poet to society are as relevant and controversial as they ever were. He took enormous risks, throwing hostages to time in his devotion to transitory issues, and some commentators have accused him in this of a paradoxical foolishness, a perversely wilful stifling or mis-direction of his admitted genius. 'He wasted his talent,' wrote Patricia Blake,* 'drawing posters, and composing thousands of slogans and "agitational" jingles that urged the Soviet people to drink boiled water, put their money in the bank, and patronise state stores.' But who is to say that these activities, which to Mayakovsky (and he was artist, editor, playwright, film-writer, as well as poet) were an important part of the cultural midwifery of the new Soviet state, can only be regarded as a 'waste of talent'? *Ex ungue leonem.* Here is one of the 'agitational jingles', written in 1920 during the civil war period, and saying roughly 'Wrangel – out!':

> Vrangel – fon,
> Vrangelya von!
> Vrangel – vrag.
> Vrangelya v ovrag!

The marked beat, the word-play, the popular mnemonic patterning all speak Mayakovsky. The pleasure he took in writing the jingle is clear, yet it is also the useful little snap of Bolshevik polemic it is

* In V. Mayakovsky, *The Bedbug and Selected Poetry*, ed. P. Blake (Weidenfeld & Nicolson, 1961).

designed to be. Of course a man so strongly individual and original as Mayakovsky could not transform himself into the spokesman of a new and tough-minded social order without cost. He was entitled to say, in his late poem 'With the Full Voice' (1930), that he was 'fed up with agitprop' and had 'trampled on the throat of (his own) song', but at the same time, and equally, he is proud of the fact that he was able to mould himself in accordance with the demands of a Revolution he wholeheartedly believed in, and he claims that his verse will reach and affect posterity – *because* of the honesty of its pain and its cost, is what one might add – when life itself has moved on and the art-works of our struggling age are dug up like arrow-heads and antediluvian bones.

When Mayakovsky read 'With the Full Voice' in the House of the Komsomols in Moscow in March, 1930, the poem was well received, and he obviously felt encouraged at that moment that such a com-plexly-textured poem should have broken through the audience barrier. He commented: 'The fact that it got across to you is very very interesting. It shows that we must, without impoverishing our technique, work devotedly for the working-class reader.' In the more-proletarian-than-thou word-battles of the later 1920s, Mayakovsky was often under attack for his difficulty, or for what was regarded as the lingering bad legacy of futurist extravagance in his work, or for what seemed to some an insufficient identification with workers' problems and aspirations. Many of the attacks were unjust, and distressed him greatly; the philistines, gaining confidence and power, certainly contributed to his eventual suicide, whatever more personal causes were at work. Resilient, if not resilient enough in the end, Mayakovsky had made more than one spirited reply to his enemies. In particular, his article 'Workers and Peasants Don't Understand You' (1928) gave this interesting defence of a Soviet artist's position:

'A genuine proletarian Soviet art must be comprehensible to the broad masses. Yes or no?'
– Yes and no. Yes, but with a corrective supplied by time and propa-ganda. Art is not born mass art, it becomes mass art as the result of a sum of efforts: critical analysis to establish its soundness and use-fulness, organised diffusion of the work through party and state chan-nels if its usefulness is agreed, good timing of mass diffusion of the book, no clash between the question raised by a book and the maturity of the questions of the masses. The better the book, the more it outruns events.

The last sentence seems almost to show Mayakovsky as Machiavelli. At first it clinches the argument for state supervision which the previous sentence unfolded, and then by a species of double-take you find that he has left behind, after all, a classic little time-bomb from the *avant-garde*. The ambience is going to have its work cut out to catch up.

It was Mayakovsky's unenviable dilemma to feel obliged, by his own conscience, to attempt the transition from a brilliant, explosive, tormented, and largely subjective futurism to a more outward-looking, more comprehensible and more comprehensive, yet not self-compromised poetry. The polarization between those who extol the early poetry for its expressive freedom (and this includes Boris Pasternak as well as many Western critics) and those who suspiciously walk round it because futurism is pre-revolutionary and has sinister connections such as Marinetti (and many Soviet critics are still in this position), has been unfortunate. Mayakovsky's work is in fact more of a piece than is often admitted. Although his poetry became less dependent on startlingly unexpected sequences of imagery, he never gave up his belief in innovation; and conversely, Soviet critics rightly point out that even in the pre-1917 poems like *A Cloud in Trousers*, *I*, and *The Backbone Flute* the poet's concerns often reflect society at large although dealing with themes of personal alienation and erotic hang-up. In 1918 – post-Revolution but only just – Mayakovsky wrote: 'Revolution in content is unthinkable without revolution in form.' For content he was thinking about 'socialism-anarchism', and for form 'futurism'. Nevertheless, the statement stands as a general position which he kept, with very few qualms or qualifications, even when Lenin and Lunacharsky thought otherwise. In his poem 'A Talk with the Taxman about Poetry' (1926) he still writes, in the midst of a most entertaining defence of the hard work of a professional poet: 'Poetry – all poetry! – is a journey into the unknown.' And in the long essay 'How Verses are Made' (also 1926) he repeats: 'Innovation, innovation in materials and methods, is obligatory for every poetical composition.'* In that essay, innovation joins careful craftsmanship, a feeling for the age, the use of the spoken language, and a commitment to social struggle as one of the prerequisites for modern poetry.

But what were the innovations? There was a turning away from nature (which bored Mayakovsky) and an attempt to incorporate

* Quoted from the translation by G. M. Hyde (Cape, 1970).

into verse something of the urban, industrial, and technological dynamism of the modern world – hence the importance to him of Brooklyn Bridge as a symbolic object, and hence the imaginary Wellsian workers' palace of the poem 'Versailles', with its million rooms of glass and steel so bright that they hurt the eyes. There was a determination to refresh and revive language, not only in the post-Revolution sense of a newly liberated popular speech which must find its way into art (though ironically, when Mayakovsky says 'whore' or 'shit' his Soviet editors trot out a Victorian dot-dot-dot) but also at the aesthetic level of mind-bending imagery and juxtaposition, and an acutely inventive use of word and sound in every device of onomatopoeia, alliteration, assonance and dissonance, pun and palindrome, and perhaps above all (and in the spirit of the highly inflected Russian language) morphological play and dislocation.

Mayakovsky was one of the signatories of the 1912 futurist manifesto 'A Slap in the Face of Public Taste', which said among other things:

> The past is crowded . . . Throw Pushkin, Dostoyevsky, Tolstoy, *et al.*, *et al.*, overboard from the Ship of Modernity . . . All those Maxim Gorkys, Kuprins, Bloks, Sologubs, Remizovs, Averchenkos, Chernyis, Kuzmins, Bunins, etc., etc. need only a *dacha* on a river . . . We look at their nothingness from the heights of skyscrapers! . . . *We decree* that the poets' *rights* be honored:
>
> 1) to enlarge vocabulary in its *scope* with arbitrary and derivative words (creation of new words).
> 2) to feel an insurmountable hatred for the language existing before them . . .
>
> And if *for the time being* even our lines are still marked with dirty stigmas of your 'common sense' and 'good taste', there tremble on them *for the first time* the summer lightnings of the New-Coming Beauty of the Self-sufficient (self-centred) Word.*

This iconoclasm was in the mood of the time and Mayakovsky went along with it. Three years later, in his own little manifesto 'A Drop of Tar', he had backpedalled sufficiently from futurism to agree that the movement was dead but at the same time he argued that its effects lived on and were now generally diffused: 'Today we are all futurists. The people are futurist.'

In fact Mayakovsky's solidity and authority seem to be shown in

* Quoted from V. Markov, *Russian Futurism: A History* (MacGibbon & Kee, 1969).

the fact that for all his originality and formal brilliance as a writer, he was essentially less extreme than fellow-theorists like Kruchonykh, Khlebnikov, and Kamensky, and their work remains of great interest but more narrow and obsessed. Experiments in Russia at this period included visual poetry, sound-poetry, and combinations of the two. All these experiments find some reflection in Mayakovsky's work, but it is others who take them further. With visual poetry, it is not surprising that Mayakovsky should be interested, given his own artistic leanings and his close friendship with a number of well-known artists. His revolutionary play *Mystery-Bouffe* (1918) had set designs and costumes by the suprematist painter Malevich. His long poem *About This* (1923) was illustrated by the remarkable photo-montages of his friend, the constructivist 'artist-engineer' Rod-chenko. His collection of poems *For the Voice* (1923) was designed and given a stunning typographical layout in black and red by El Lissitzky – constructivist again, and as fresh and eye-catching today as if no fifty years had intervened. Mayakovsky himself, in his first book, *I*, hand-lithographed in 1913, showed his own interest in the visual possibilities of poetry, as may be seen in this translation of the opening section:

> Along the pavement of my soul
>   worn out by feet
>   the steps of madmen beat
> their hard-heeled sentences
>   where
>   cities
>   are hanged and steep-
> les congeal with their twisted necks
>   in the noose
>   of clouds
> I go alone and shriek that on cross-
>   roads
>   they are cruc-
>   ifying po-
>   lice

Even in that early poem, we see the interaction of eye and ear – the line-breaks doing a certain amount of visual 'enacting' of the meaning but also suggesting that the poem must be read aloud in a certain way – and this looks forward to the almost paradoxical volume *For the Voice* (dominantly visual in appearance, yet with poems designed for public performance) and also the general later Mayakovskian habit of 'stepping' the lines to indicate a reader's phrasing, though again not without a degree of meaningful stimulation of the eye.

When it comes to the ear, we know from many reports and observers that Mayakovsky was a spellbinding reader, who regarded the auditorium as both challenge and reward. Something of the quality of his voice can still be heard, on what is apparently the only recording commercially available,* where he reads from 'An Extraordinary Adventure' ('Vladimir's Ferlie' in the present volume), and although the recording is so bad that the words are often hard to follow, some impression can be got of his scooping and pouncing mastery of pause and emphasis. 'Vladimir's Ferlie' is interesting to hear as well as see, because it has a hidden regular stanza-structure counterpointed by a continuous narrative-style printing with the lines broken up into irregular lengths. Only the pattern of the rhymes, caught chiefly by the ear, gives away the underlying stanzaic grid; by disguising the grid (which is nevertheless felt) the poet achieves all sorts of subtle free-verse effects that are not really *vers libre* at all.

Mayakovsky deploys aural resources inventively and lavishly, throughout his poetic career. But he never followed his friend Alexei Kruchonykh (whose work he admired and publicly defended) into *zaum*, the 'transrational' sound-poetry which involved, in effect, the creation of an imaginary language. Kruchonykh believed that *zaum* could produce 'a universal poetic language, not artificially created like Esperanto, but organically born'.† Both Kruchonykh and Mayakovsky were agreed about the immense power mysteriously inherent in language, but Kruchonykh's splendidly unWittgensteinian slogan SLOVO SHIRE SMYSLA (his capitals!)‡ – 'the word is broader than its meaning', i.e. a word contains but is not merely coextensive with its so-called meaning, and the glory is in the overlap not the template – must increasingly have seemed to Mayakovsky to burke the problems of the auditorium and of communication.

In the same way, he would accept but not imitate the experiments of his co-futurist friend Vasily Kamensky in visual poetry. Kamensky's 'ferroconcrete' poems (the name curiously prophetic of the

* *Govoryat pisateli*, Melodiya 05592(a).
† In his manifesto *Transrational Language Declaration*, 1921.
‡ In his essay 'New Paths for the Word', 1913.

concrete poetry of recent years) were to him a concentrated but restricting parallel to his own interest in the visual presentation of poetry as a means of increasing impact. And again, the move towards riddle and enigma in the ferroconcrete poems would hamper communication.

What gives Mayakovsky's work its peculiar character, and I think also its peculiar value, is its unusual combination of wild *avant-garde* leanings and flashes and something of central human concern. A grotesque and vivid comic fantasy is never lost; neither is the sense of pain, of loneliness, of longing, sometimes disguised by creative exhilaration; neither is the sense of history and the role and duty of the poet. He wrote too much, and there is in his long poems some tedious rhetoric and breast-beating. But the tribute of Boris Pasternak, describing his reaction to seeing the self-shot poet in his coffin in April 1930, stresses his remarkable significance.

> Other people by now had taken the place of those who had filled the room earlier in the day. It was quite quiet. There was scarcely anybody crying now.
>
> All at once, down under the window, I thought I saw his life, now utterly a past-tense life. It sidled away from the window up a quiet street, like Povarskaya, tree-lined. And the first person to be met there, huddling to the wall, was our country, our incredible, impossible country, for ever knocking at the centuries, now accepted in them for ever. There it was, just below me, within earshot. One could have taken its hand. The bond between them was so striking that they might have been twins . . . Of all men, he had the newness of the age climatically in his veins.*

Very Russian, and very modern, is Pasternak's verdict. The two things no longer go naturally together, but they certainly did in the years from 1910 to 1930. What is perhaps strange is that Mayakovsky still seems modern. Ezra Pound was once, like Mayakovsky, extremely active in telling people to 'make it new', yet with the passage of time Pound's work seems more and more to be being sucked back into the late Victorian romanticism it tried to burst out of. Pound, of course, although he contributed to Wyndham Lewis's vorticist, sub-futurist magazine *Blast* in 1914–15, was no futurist, and Wyndham Lewis's description of him as 'demon pantechnicon driver, busy with removal of old world into new quarters', is a telling pointer to the gulf between Pound's modernism and that of his Russian contemporaries.

* *Safe Conduct* (1931), translation by Alec Brown (Elek, 1959).

Mayakovsky was not looking for new quarters for an old world. He had a new world.

At the time of his death he left some verse fragments which movingly bring together the personal and public concerns of the poet. Usually called love poems, they are only partly that. They speak of ageing, of history, of the universe; of poetry and the power of words. They even – Shakespearian touch – have a pun. 'Tragic' seems an insulting term to apply to them, and they are best left to find their own way and make their own points:

1
Loves me? loves me not? I wring
my hands
            the broken fingers drift away
like petals of roadside daisies
                        withering
plucked to tell fortunes in May
The grey my barber sees is there all right
but even if it all bursts out
                        like silver
I hope—I believe—you'll never find
shameful good sense has sold me down the river

2
Past one already
                you must be in bed
Yet I wonder
            if you too are –
I'm in no hurry
                And why should I send
express telegrams
                to wake you
                        with fear

3
the sea withdraws to its deeps
the sea withdraws to its sleep
As they say the incident is cloves
the love-boat wrecked on reality
You and I are quits
And why again expose
mutual pain affront and injury

4
Past one already you must be in bed
In the dark our Galaxy like Oka's flare
I'm in no hurry and why should I send
express telegrams to wake you with fear
As they say the incident is cloves
the love-boat wrecked on reality
You and I are quits and why again expose
mutual pain affront and injury
See how still now this world is
Night has paid the sky its due of stars
in such an hour we rise we speak to eras
to history to the created universe

5
I know the force of words I know the tocsin of words
I don't mean words for plushy claques in stalls
I mean the kind that clatter coffins forward
on to their four oak legs and walk them off
Oh yes they reject you unprinted unpublished
But the cinch tightened the word bolts away
saddle-bells for centuries and trains crawl up and
snuffle the calloused hands of poetry
I know the force of words It hardly shows
more than a petal kicked by dancers' heels
But man within his soul his lips his bones . . .

The translations which follow are in Scots. There is in Scottish
poetry (e.g. in Dunbar, Burns, and MacDiarmid) a vein of fantastic
satire that seems to accommodate Mayakovsky more readily than
anything in English verse, and there was also, I must admit, an
element of challenge in finding out whether the Scots language could
match the mixture of racy colloquialism and verbal inventiveness in
Mayakovsky's Russian. I hoped Hugh MacDiarmid might be right
when he claimed in 'Gairmscoile' that

> . . . there's forgotten shibboleths o the Scots
> Hae keys to senses lockit to us yet
> – Coorse words that shamble thro oor minds like stots,
> Syne turn on's muckle een wi doonsin emerauds lit.

From *Wi the Haill Voice: 25 Poems by Vladimir Mayakovsky
Translated into Scots*, Edwin Morgan, Carcanet Press, 1972.

Zbigniew Herbert

NEITHER aerial warfare nor civil aviation has made much difference to the concept of frontiers. The joke about the American tourist stepping off the plane and asking 'What country is this?' is only a joke because those who spend most of their time on the ground rather than in the air are still perfectly aware that countries have boundaries and are not provinces or regions. On the world's central land-mass, the fact that you can walk from Lisbon to Vladivostok, or fly the same route without the break of any sea, can even now only wheedle a ghostly idea of 'Eurasia' out of the tense welter of states that are the reality. To live on this land-mass is to undergo an experience of a different sort from the experience of the Americas, or Australasia, or island appurtenances like Britain and Japan. Frontier-consciousness comes with the territory. History does not come with geography, geography comes with history. The Americans, reaching the Pacific, turned 'frontier' into a metaphysical conception, but to Europeans it is still the check-post, the watch-tower, the alien tongue. Irredentism, lebensraum, occupation, refugees, liberation, dismemberment, protection, alliance, union, national resurgence – these are the realities, and old Rome or new Russia could only stretch over them a film of roads, a film of revolution. Offshore, British Quant and Apple, Japanese Yashica and Honda. In the heart-mass, tanks and delegations, 'frank and comradely' talks, suppurating historical sores, ashes and diamonds, involvement of writers.

Involvement: in Poland surely, in that Catholic atheist Communist film-making poster-proud history-conscious country: above all, in that *country*, that centre of relationship, to Russia, Germany, France: a nation oppressed, subjugated, renewed, defined and redefined: of national and prophetic poets, of the smoking shell of Warsaw, of the Auschwitz ovens, of *Two men and a Wardrobe*.

But there is involvement and involvement. The work of Zbigniew

Herbert,* born in 1924 and one of the best postwar Polish poets, emerges with great clarity out of one, precarious, post-rhetorical solution to the problems of involvement. Herbert, who fought in the Polish resistance in his teens, studied law and philosophy and the history of art during the Stalinist years, and only began publishing the volumes of his poetry after the 'thaw' of the mid-1950s, grew up with war and politics as elements of the air – frontiers crossed, cities flattened, edicts proclaimed, art censored. But if there is any lesson that European poets have learned, it is the lesson that patience, irony, deliberation, cunning, and an anti-hysterical and even anti-indignant art are more likely to make their points for them than a romantic grasping of lapels, poets' or readers'. Herbert's art is intelligent, reflective, dry. History, both modern and ancient, is there; but it has been shaken out, hung up on the line: it is shirts and dusters, rather than flags and plumes. The Langobards flock into the valley 'shouting their protracted nothing nothing nothing'; the Polish general boasts that the Germans shall have not one button, and the buttons mock that no one shall have the soldiers 'sewn flatly on to the heath'; of five men executed at dawn, two very young and the others middle-aged, 'nothing more/ can be said about them'; even in paradise there is a work week of thirty hours, and few see God, 'he is only for those of 100 per cent pneuma'; while on earth, in contemporary Europe, fear is not the unknown or the supernatural but 'a scrap of paper /found in a pocket /"warn Wójcik /the place on Długa Street is hot"'.

A sense of history does pervade Herbert's work, in prose as in poetry. In the essays in *Barbarzyńca w ogrodzie* ('The Barbarian in the Garden', 1962), themes of art or religion wind out into historical meditation. Van Gogh's Arles is traced back in history and out into a consideration of Mistral and the problems of regional and national identity. Talking of the Albigenses and of Montségur: 'A sick heavy smoke rolls down the valley and vanishes in history.' Noting how certain methods used against the Templars were added to the natural repertory of power: 'In history nothing is ever finally closed.' And in prehistoric Lascaux human history becomes basic: 'Colours: black, bronze, ochre, vermilion, crimson, mallow, and limestone white ... Colours of earth, blood, and soot.'

This earth, blood, and soot; scrap of paper; button on a soldier's

* *Selected Poems*, translated by Czesław Miłosz and Peter Dale Scott, Penguin, 1968.

blouse; torture of a heretic: all this wrung-out, dry-eyed evidence of
the reality of danger and suffering and the inescapability of the
socio-political order will tend to imply a certain view of the poet's
function.

The poet is to be wary, precise, concrete, hard, impersonal, un-
lyrical, unpretentious.

> my imagination
> is a piece of board
> my sole instrument
> is a wooden stick
>
> I strike the board
> it answers me
> yes – yes
> no – no   ('A Knocker')

In 'Tamarisk', a poem used in his radio play *Reconstruction of a Poet*,
the Homeric bard confesses how in his emphasis on battles and
heroes and storms at sea he had forgotten the tamarisk, a 'common
plant, prolific and useless', cousin perhaps to Robert Graves's
common asphodel – the tough, unscented reality that lies at the
heart of both history and poetry. The poet strikes the board, praises
the tamarisk, praises a pebble because it is 'mindful of its limits' and
'cannot be tamed', humorously strokes an oaken stool because it is
'genuine'. Yet he knows that poems are not made from oaken stools,
but from language, and in 'Study of the Object' he struggles, like a
pared-down Wallace Stevens, to accommodate an inversion of the
Platonic to an acknowledgement that 'the most beautiful is the object
/which does not exist'. Like Stevens with his jar placed in the
wilderness of Tennessee, Herbert wants the poet to extract from the
shadow of a non-existent object seen by the inner eye

> a chair
>
> beautiful and useless
> like a cathedral in the wilderness
>
> place on the chair
> a crumpled tablecloth
> add to the idea of order
> the idea of adventure

– the apparent quotation from Apollinaire ('La jolie rousse') helping to qualify any mere rage for order and beauty with a nod towards the principle of contradiction or the fact of strangeness.

The incongruity of a tablecloth on a chair, and the ideas of order and adventure, come back to mind in the fine poem 'Elegy of Fortinbras', where the surviving and successful man of action addresses the dead Hamlet who 'believed in crystal notions not in human clay'. To Fortinbras Hamlet was 'not for life', and although he accomplished what he had to accomplish, it was an accomplishment in the realm of death, 'but what is heroic death compared with eternal watching.' Fortinbras and Hamlet are both heroic, but whereas Hamlet knows about this majestical roof fretted with golden fire, Fortinbras knows about frontiers. Fortinbras's case is put as the case of a vigilant man who will see how to rule, and do it. His limitations are clear, even to himself, but Herbert is writing at a time and in a world where survival has pushed itself up in the scale of values and tragic heroism has slipped down. This gives an edge of sympathetic understanding to the portrait, even while the man's bluntness might make us despair of a society composed of Fortinbrases.

> Adieu prince I have tasks a sewer project
> and a decree on prostitutes and beggars
> I must also elaborate a better system of prisons
> since as you justly said Denmark is a prison
> I go to my affairs This night is born
> a star named Hamlet We shall never meet
> what I shall leave will not be worth a tragedy

This is beautifully poised, and the balance between the incongruous extremes of 'a sewer project' and 'a tragedy' – both of them excellent things – has something about it that is typical of Herbert and his wry, ironical probing of both life and art.

The translations are clean-cut and close to the text, and read well. Occasionally a sound-effect has been lost (e.g. the echo *doradza/ odradza* in 'Inner Voice', or *obraca/obraz* in 'Wooden Bird'). Once or twice there is a slightly skittish extension ('parkers quink' and 'cooks tour' for 'ink' and 'excursion'). A few awkward inversions could have been avoided ('where stood the object', 'where persists the continuous', 'on which splash the shadows'). But this is an admirable addition to the Penguin Modern European Poets, and Herbert's voice is well worth listening to.

Heraclitus in Gorky Street: The Theme of Metamorphosis in the Poetry of Andrei Voznesensky

THE HONOUR of a poet may be said to subsist in a double commitment. Towards defined values he reacts with a vigilant curiosity that can still acknowledge dependence, kinship, stance, era. For undefined values he reserves his deepest receptiveness, prepared to take on boarders, fight fires, or abandon ship as the case may direct. Since the 'case' can only be whatever is, the poet is as likely to come back at reality through the revolving doors of Montale's Eastbourne hotel –

> all flashing leaves and facets –
> another picks up the signal and flashes back –
> so am I twirled in a roundabout that traps
> and sweeps up everything it whirls

– as through the 'concept of progress' without which Yevtushenko's Bratsk Station hums and pounds in vain. This is not said in order to upgrade doors and downgrade concepts, but only to give a reminder that a poet may find himself committed to a flash of glass. It would be his prerogative to deny that such commitments were mindless. 'For instantly a light upon the turf/ Fell like a flash, and ...' and changed the grass, and itself, and Wordsworth's observing eye, into something both more and less palpable than the 'case' of a moon over Snowdon; more, because netted by awed human experience; less, because intellectualized by the equally human desire to 'take over' and 'make over' nature in metaphor or metamorphosis.

Yet we too are being taken over and made over. Values invade us as we them. A poet may have to bury and hide himself like a bulb, for anything to grow. Distraction is continuous, enormous, fascinating, and frightening. Roles are adopted and discarded. The self shrinks, shudders, makes covert decisions, asks terrible questions. A poetry which wants meaningfully to interlock with this age must be prepared to be vulnerable, fluid, various, adventurous, and searching. It is in connection with such speculations and demands as these that the poetry of Andrei Voznesensky seems to be both diagnostically and absolutely of great interest. I would like to start discussing it from an example, an extract from a long poem included in his volume *Akhillesovo serdtse* (1966):

* * * * *

Everything flows. Everything changes.
                                        One thing passes into another.
Squares go slipping into ellipses.
Nickel-plated bedstead-ribs
        flow like boiling macaroni.
Dungeon portcullises dangle
                    like pretzels or shoulder-knots.

Henry Moore
            red-cheeked English sculptor,
                drifted over the billiard-cloth
                    of his well-trimmed lawns.
The sculptures gleamed like billiard-balls,
but sometimes they swam off like a flux, and sometimes
                took jewel-shapes of pelvic joints.
'Stay still!' Moore cried. 'You are beautiful! . . . '
They never stayed still though.

A flock of smiles swam through the streets.

In the world's ring, two wrestlers embraced panting.
Orange and black.
Their breasts pressed hard together. They stood moving sideways
                on vertical pliers.

Bu-ut how horrible!
        Menacing black stains began to spread on the orange back.
Something was seeping through.
                With a neat ruse, orange twisted his rival's ear
                and howled with pain –
                        from his own ear.
It had flowed across to its antagonist.

* * * * *

Sentences unstable. Wordspressedtogetherinonephrase.
Consonants dissolving.
Only vowels left now.
'Oaue aoie oaaoeaia! . . .'

> That's what I'm screaming.
> They wake me up. They thrust the icy thermometer under my
> > armpit.

> I look up in terror at the ceiling.
> It's square.

* * * * *

('Sketch of a Long Poem')

Voznesensky's concern with the theme of metamorphosis, which
this passage brings out fairly clearly, has three aspects. It reflects the
quite real blurring, overlap, interchange, and evolution of forms
which fast travel, cinema and television, modern art, and newspaper
and advertising techniques have made a familiar part of experience;
it has, in its Russian context, a quasi-Aesopian function in that without lifting the blunt instrument of allegory it helps to recommend
disavowal of the monolithic; and perhaps most important, it tries to
resurrect the creative imagination through a development of that
linguistic *ostranenie* ('dislodgement', 'alienation', 'making strange')
which the Russian formalist critics of the 1920s saw as central to
poetic vigour. In the poem, instability and paradox are shown as
features of modern life that are at least as unavoidable (if one is open
to the signs of change) as dogma and explanation. This is expressed
partly by hyperbolic and often comic imagery (metal bedsteads
flowing like macaroni), and also by the references to art and ideology.
The name of Henry Moore is carefully chosen – the English words
having a functional 'strangeness' in their Russian context, his works
having that combination of 'flow' and hardness which the poem is
concerned with, and Moore being recognized as an influence on a
Soviet sculptor like Neizvestny whom Voznesensky and other poets
admire despite official disapproval. Many of Moore's sculptures are
unusually variable as you walk round them, and photographs of them
taken from different angles can be almost unrelatable. Voznesensky
presents the sculptor himself as being humorously exasperated, but
also pleased, by this fluidity, and one remembers the rather similar

attitude of the poet himself to architectural forms in his poem 'New York Airport at Night', where he talks in terms of a 'mastery of immaterial structures', and sees the airport as advancing far beyond the beauty of stone:

> Instead of a stony mass
> like an idol,
>   a cool
> glass of dark blue – without the glass.
> With its hushed grilles and counters
> it's like a vapour
>   of anti-matter.

And if stone becomes flux, and matter looks like anti-matter, how can ideologies remain pure? Mao Tse-tung would make short work of the little fable of the black and orange wrestlers. It could only confirm him in his suspicion that one touch of revisionism makes the whole world kin – in unprincipled cosmopolitanism. There is no need of course to interpret so specifically as to say that Voznesensky is speaking about Russia and America. At the same time one is aware of how often the theme of America recurs in his poetry, and of how deep and confused his feelings about America are.* The politically dangerous metamorphosis of becoming what you begin by sympathetically observing is what lies behind some Soviet criticisms of Voznesensky's American poems. It might be all right to have airports like New York's, but not the beatniks and striptease as well, though the poet presents these with equal vividness. This criticism is misplaced, since if Voznesensky trails his American coat a little, this is done largely as part of a broader strategy, in which he can see himself and Robert Lowell, and poets in other countries too, as the necessary gnoseologists of 'this age' in its non-ideological aspect, post-Stalin but also post-Kennedy, post-Hiroshima but also post-sputnik, post- so many things that for all its baffling malaise and hideous Vietnams it seems like an age about to be one of extraordinary beginnings. Where Lowell cries out like a glowing cinder someone has driven a poker into, Voznesensky is the light dancing flame on the cinder which is ready to spring to the new wood.

* Among many poems showing these ambiguities, one of the most remarkable is the 'Poem with a Footnote', dedicated to Robert Lowell, which was printed in *The New York Review of Books* on 18 May 1967 in a translation by Louis Simpson. It is almost an illustrative expansion, in movingly personal terms, of the fable of the wrestlers.

But not easily, not obviously. 'Words strain,/ Crack and sometimes break, under the burden .../ Will not stay still.' It is both ironic and yet only true that Voznesensky of all people – a master of poetic language – should claim to find words failing him ('only vowels left now') when he tries to make language accompany and define the transformations of the world. Perhaps, like Kafka's Gregor Samsa, the speaker is 'sick', but he does not wake up one morning transformed into a gigantic insect – he is wakened from a nightmare of the dissolution of language into the simple daylight terror of looking up at a square ceiling. The terror of the rational square is worse than the irrational metamorphoses of bedsteads, sculptures, ears, sentences, and words.

This would suggest that 'flowing' is almost a metaphor for change, seen under the double aspect of the upsettingness of anything new and the attractiveness of any reversal of roles. On balance, the attraction is greater than the upset, because of the rigid cultural context the poet works in and seeks to prise open through exaggeration and fantasy.

Many poems take up this 'prising open' process, from different angles. In the simplest ones, a slightly startling but naturalistically based analogy is used. The leather-clad Amazon of 'Motorcycle Stunts on the Vertical Wall' is bored with 'living vertically' on the ground and as soon as she steps off her motorcycle her eyes are filled with 'horizontal nostalgia'. Here, the hazardous but thrilling human displacement of the wall-of-death ride is allowed to reverberate as an idea without being pushed into any statement about the restricting verticality or uprightness of conventional life. The rider has been metamorphosed, through habit, into a creature living at right angles to the norm, but the poem surrounds her with a grotesque humour which salts away any straightforward recommendations.

In 'Wings', a similar idea is developed farther.

> The gods are dozing like slummocks –
> Clouds for layabouts!
>
> > > What hammocks!
>
> The gods are for the birds.
> The birds are for the birds.
>
> What about wings,
> all that paraphernalia?

It's too weird, I tell you.
What did the ancients see in these things?
Nearer
    and nearer
        to the fuselage
clouds press them in,
        to a vestige-
ality of winginess on our things,
our marvel-machines, strange
to them. Men have unslung
something new, men don't hang
out wings, men are with it, bang.
Man, men are winged!

In the ages of time, men become the gods they once adumbrated. The wings they gave deities they take to themselves, but in the process of becoming truly 'winged', men go through the meta-morphoses – from Leonardo to the Wright Brothers to Gagarin – of inventing, developing, and then discarding actual wings. The light, buoyant tone of the poem is not too light to conceal the joy of tracing an enormous, but enormously slow, change in human exploratory capability. And who is to say whether Gagarin was living vertically or horizontally?

In two poems, 'Foggy Street' and 'Earth', Voznesensky presents first a naturally and then an imaginarily transformed environment. In the former poem, the poet delights in the confusions and errors induced by fog – bumping into people, mistaking men for women, interpreting or misinterpreting disembodied objects like car-lights, a glimpse of a cheek or a moustache, everything 'in pieces, dis-connected as delirium'. At the end rationality returns and he wishes he could send the fog packing, but only after he has given us, in the main picture, the pleasures of distorted perception. 'Earth', on the other hand, combines a strong feeling for the actuality and thinginess and inescapability of our planet as it is, with a Chagall-like dream of what it might be. The second half of the poem projects two futures – or perhaps they are the same future, seen in a science-fiction aspect – in which change is beautifully balanced between surreal fantasy and scientific progress, but in both cases tied to and emerging from and acknowledging the familiar and the old. Man transforms both him-self and his world, and what characterizes Voznesensky is the joy he takes in envisaging the transformations; but there is nothing vapidly optimistic about the joy. Wherever he goes and whatever he does, man takes with him his handful of earth, his handful of pain, of history and remembrance.

> An earth in dreams appeared to me, without trenches and chains,
> without detonation of mines: a dream of telescopes,
> of lime-trees, eucalyptus, peacock rain-
> bows, lifts on crazy ropes
> and showers of aluminium!
> A world of seas, of trains, of women –
> a world all puffing and
> > fructifying,
> > > marvellous as man! . . .
>
> Somewhere on Mars he goes, a visitor from Earth.
> He walks. He smiles. He takes out a handful of earth –
> a tiny handful of that burning,
> half-bitter, homely,
> far-whirling,
> heart-catching earth!

Transformation of environment can of course be used for satirical purposes, and Voznesensky is not lacking in satire. But he has evolved a peculiar brand of metasatire where the social, aesthetic, or moral criticism is so closely plaited with comic, lyric, and hallucinatory elements that to speak of reformism or didacticism would be well off the mark. In 'Paris without Rhyme' he starts off by observing how clean Paris is becoming, building after building being sandblasted under M. Malraux's instructions until a new city seems to be emerging. But why stop there? Why not blast the walls away altogether, see what the city is really like under the protective shell of architecture? So there is a sudden transformation-scene: Notre Dame minus its walls is only a rose-window hanging over the square like a traffic-sign, in a room a teapot-shaped mass of tea stands without a pot, people whose heads have been screwed off walk about with their thoughts 'whistling there like birds in wire cages', an OAS man's mad pate holds Sartre smouldering away in a frying-pan, a striptease girl starts to peel off not her clothes but her skin until the poet is sent shuddering back to normality at the moment of horror when he sees nothing but the whites of her eyes 'dead and blank like insulators, in that dreadful howling burning face'. He is sitting in the world of solid walls; with his friends; eating a melting ice. Yet

the poem ends with a curiously disturbing transfusion of Hieronymus Bosch into the normal city of 1962:

> But through the window and through the centuries
> motorcyclists race
>   in their white helmets
> like fiends from hell with chamber-pots.

This extraordinary poem, reminding us of some of the difficulties of
interpreting Swift's 'woman flayed', shows a complex irony at work,
and also something which is not irony at all. The woman peeling off
her skin 'like tights' is beyond being a comment on the decadence of
striptease, even though the juxtaposition of 'dead eyes' and 'howling
face' at once suggests some such deadening of the spirit, a silent
screaming from some accepted indignity that only a poet can hear
and report. Since the poem runs the gamut from playfulness to
horror, it may be that Voznesensky, like Swift, is pointing out both
the necessity and the dangers of 'stripping off appearances' and
trying to reach the raw truth. The woman was screaming, certainly;
but why should Mass not be celebrated in a cathedral without walls?

In a sensitive and beautiful love-poem, 'Autumn in Sigulda',
Voznesensky describes a parting and separation, and in doing so he
makes metamorphosis a central feature of the interdependence of life –

> but o you are going away, going away,
>   as a train goes, you are going away,
> out from my empty pores you are going away,
> each of us goes, we separate, we go on our way,
> was this house wrong for us, who can say?
>
> you are near me and somewhere far off,
> Vladivostok is no farther off,
> I know our lives come round again
> in friends and lovers, grass and grain,
> changed into that, and those, and this,
> nature abhorring emptiness . . .

the old saw about nature reflecting here a Pasternakian sense of the
dissolving of the artist into the lives of others, a perpetual renewal
under perpetual conditions of change, the lost and mysterious seeds
of the personal life transformed into a general standing grain in the
fullness of time. Not only from, but to, everything flows.

Part Two

Dunbar and the Language of Poetry

I

'OF what we call genius', wrote Matthew Arnold, 'energy is the most essential part.' Energy in poetry, however, is compelled to manifest itself through form, not simply or necessarily metrical structure but a continuous inevitability of movement from word to word ('continuous' ideally, or only in the greatest poetry, but the sense of control of direction must be interrupted as little as possible), startling the reader's mind into considering something which the poem follows to the end of consideration and closes with a satisfaction. If poetry is the manifestation of energy in order, Arnold's statement is still the backbone of the argument; we are dealing with ordered energy, not with energetic orderliness. The final reflection we make on a great passage of Shakespeare is that his feeling for control and pattern has been *adequate* to the demands so peremptorily made on it by the majesty of his energy. Energy without order usually gives us the feeling that we are in touch with a poet but not with a poem: the forges clang, the air is thick with the spark and fume of production, but in the end nothing is made, no object is presented to us that we can grasp and appraise. Such is Whitman's 'Song of Myself'. Order without energy is exemplified by the poet whose inspiration is fitful and less than a match for his knowledge of what effects poetry can produce – as in Robert Bridges's sonnet-sequence *The Growth of Love*. Of the two imperfections, the first takes us nearer the fountainhead, and no amount of that virtuosity which may be the complement of the second's deficiency will atone for the lack of Arnold's 'most essential part'. But there is a complication, which Arnold did not consider. Energy may be felt by the poet primarily *as order*. A poet with a strong sensuous and linguistic tone to his imagination can find himself inspired within his own concern with words, with rhythm, with shape, with concatenations that are audible as well as thematic: elements which would normally be a hazard, a mere snare of formalism. Verbal energy of this kind is well exemplified in Hopkins, and it occurs to an important extent in the poet about to be considered here as well as in some of the poetry which influenced him. Where a major writer like Shakespeare will most commonly keep his sound-effects mysterious, contributory to a more salient preoccupation –

> Ensear thy fertile and conceptious womb,
> Let it no more bring out ingrateful man*

– the poets who are attracted by the 'energy as order' mode try to make of such half-felt and unanalysed word-linkages something concrete, basic, and sustaining, by opening up the way to them more externally and consciously; and they are helped by our stubborn alliterative tradition, in Middle English a dying alternative to the imported syllabic verse of France, and later absorbed by it, though breaking out periodically from it. This tradition, which influenced Dunbar, must now be looked at more closely.

II

It is well known that Dunbar and his fellow-poets in fifteenth-century Scotland wished to repay their literary debt to Chaucer. Chaucer was the 'rose of rethoris all', the 'horleige and reguleir' for the future movements of poetry. But their references to Chaucer's 'sugurit lippis', 'aureate termis', and 'eloquence ornate' rather than to his pathos, his simplicity, or his narrative gift help to betray the background of their eulogies, where Chaucer is set as an inescapable yet partly alien figure. The poets did not refer to the northern alliterative poetry as they referred to Chaucer – with the respect and enthusiasm of the disciple and imitator; but their practice proves that the older tradition was very pervasive and very congenial to the Scottish spirit, and they pay it that debt of exemplification which is often more revealing than their addresses to Chaucer. We do not find acknowledgements of the great alliterative poems which have been preserved from the North Midlands and the North-West of England, of *Pearl* or of *Sir Gawain and the Green Knight*; instead we have passing references to the more popular developments of this way of writing, especially to the romances and the farcical or fantastic alliterative and semi-alliterative poems composed in Scotland as the

* *Timon of Athens*, IV, iii, 188–9.

influence spread north and received its disequilibrating infusion of forthright zestful topsyturvydom. We may take a glance at some of these once widely-known and still interesting productions. The following stanza (LII) from an anonymous poem mentioned by both Dunbar and Gavin Douglas, *Rauf Coilyear*, shows the more serious use of alliteration in romantic description, partly brilliant and pictorial, partly an eking out of narrative with conventional alliterative phrases. The uncouth hero of the romance, Ralph the Collier, enters the great hall of Charlemagne in Paris, and is dazzled by its array:

> Thocht he had socht sic ane sicht all this sevin yeir,
> Sa solempnit ane semblie had he not sene;
> The hall was properly apperrellit and paintit but peir,
> Dyamountis full dently dentit betwene;
> It was semely set on ilk syde seir,
> Gowlis glitterand full gay, glemand in grene,
> Flowris with flourdelycis formest in feir,
> With mony flamand ferly, ma than fyftene;
> The rufe reulit about in reuall of reid,
> Rois reulit ryally,
> Columbyn and lely,
> Thair was ane hailsum harbery,
> Into riche steid.

Apart from the alliteration, this stanza-form, with its closing 'wheel' of short lines which comes in with a light dancing rhythm and ends on a little eddy or turn back into the state of rest, had a special attraction for the Scottish poets; Henryson, Dunbar, Douglas, and Lyndsay all have their examples of it.

Rauf Coilyear combines the alliterative rhythm with regular rhyme. In other poems we have, as a further stage, a fairly regular syllabic verse with rhyme and irregular alliteration: the poet has perhaps half an intention of trochaic tetrameters or trimeters rhyming in pairs, but any excitement in the writing breaks the structure down into a loose alliterative swing, and usually where this is allowed to happen and the older non-syllabic rhythms prevail, the verse takes on a flailing verve and momentum, and if it is satirical or fantastic, as it often is, an effect is produced which is a notable Scottish characteristic of the period – wild, flamboyant, ludicrous, and 'fouthy' with words. Here are some lines from *The Cursing of Sir John Rowll* (33–50), one of the most popular of those poems, which was referred to by Lyndsay and probably by Dunbar. Sir John calls down anathema on certain persons unknown, 'resettaris and preve steilaris', who have pilfered from his yard 'fyve fat geiss' and many another bird of his owning. (The reader is invited to make use of the appended glossary.)

> Now cursit and wareit be thair werd
> Quhill thay be levand on this erd,
> Hungir, sturt, and tribulatioun,
> And nevir to be without vexatioun,
> Of vengance, sorrow, sturt, and cair,
> Graceless, thriftles, and threidbair;
> All tymes in thair legasie
> Fyre, sword, watter, and woddie,
> Or ane of thir infirmeteis
> Off warldly scherp adverseteis,
> Povertie, pestilence, or poplecy,
> Dum, deif, or edroposy,
> Maigram, madness, or missilry,
> Appostrum or the perlocy,
> Ffluxis, hyvis, or huttit ill,
> Hoist, heidwark, or fawin ill,
> Kald, kanker, feistir, or feveris,
> Brukis, bylis, blobbis, and bleistiris . . .

It is said that fashions change preferences beyond recognition, but the modern reader who may be dismayed by Rowll's *Cursing* should compare the kind of gusto which blows through it, and the cataloguings and word-linkages that its gusto takes, with similar outbursts in Rabelais, Skelton, Urquhart, or James Joyce – passages of

> such a climacterical and mercurially digested method, that when the fancy of the hearers was tickled with any rare conceit, and that the jovial blood was moved, he held it going with another new device upon the back of the first, and another, yet another, and another againe, succeeding one another for the promoval of what is a-stirring into a higher agitation; till in the closure of the luxuriant period, the decumanal wave of the oddest whimzy of all, enforced the charmed spirits of the auditory, for affording room to its apprehension, suddenly to burst forth into a laughter.*

Another very popular poem, *Colkelbie Sow*, mentioned as a famous anonymous romance by Douglas, is referred to more than once by Dunbar, who was greatly taken by the highlight passage of

* Sir Thomas Urquhart, *ΕΚΣΚΥΒΑΛΑΥΡΟΝ*, Maitland Club edn., p. 229.

its first 'fitt', the hilarious and satirical feast where the 'merry man' Colkelbie's pig is to be served. Dunbar likens the fools and rogues who gain preferment at Court to the select list of invited guests at this banquet. The list is in what James VI would have called 'tumbling verse'; it tumbles at its best, and stumbles at its worst. Dunbar would see the ideal form or latent possibility of a poem relatively without art but containing this appealing virtue of rhythmically underlined verbal proliferation in the easy pell-mell helter-skelter of its 'tumble' down the page.

Finally, Dunbar was familiar with the last stage of the absorption of alliterative writing by syllabic and rhyming modes as exemplified in some of the best passages of Henryson. Here there is nothing to distinguish the structure of the verse from that of Southern Chaucerian poetry except the frequency and the heightening descriptive use of alliteration (as, for example, in *The Testament of Cresseid* or *The Garmont of Gud Ladies*).

The poet of *Sir Gawain and the Green Knight* told his readers that he was going to give them the romance

> As hit is stad and stoken
> In stori stif and stronge,
> With lel letteres loken,
> In londe as hatz ben longe.

– 'as it is firmly set down in story, bound together with true letters, the ancient practice of this land'. Here is the Old English tradition, struggling to maintain itself against changes in the language, yet admired and used by a master who is invoking the past at a time when Chaucer was already writing his *Canterbury Tales*. And this is the tradition which forms the basis of alliterative writing in Scotland. But the 'locking of true letters', the far-off 'word gebunden' of the Anglo-Saxon *scop*, must be seen as supplemented in Scotland by other influences, and it is these in combination that would perhaps yield, if fully investigated, some of the secrets of the sudden superiority of Scots verse at this time as well as a description of its characteristics. Alliteration on the 'popular' side of poetry recommended itself to the Scots because it was an apt medium for racy narrative, because it established an immediate link between verse and the fund of alliteration in common proverbs, tags of speech and phrases from ballads and songs, and because it encouraged the peculiar Scots leaning towards the wild and the outspoken, the vituperative and the incongruous. Alliteration on the 'art' side of poetry is one aspect of a larger movement which affected all the poets of the time: the wakening consciousness of language as a ground open to deliberate enrichment and of literature as a growth springing from that prepared soil. We find in Scotland at the end of the fifteenth century a brilliant, optimistic, zealous, unhappy, and premature attempt to produce what England successfully developed later in the next century – an instrument of expression that would fuse what was most valued and accessible in popular speech with an immense body of reference-extending terms built up mainly from Latin and Greek. Douglas tells us in his Prologue to Book I of Virgil's *Aeneid* how hard it had been to translate the classical Latin into a worthy modern utterance:

> Besyde Latyne our langage is imperfite,
> Quhilk in sum part is the caus and the wite
> Quhy that of Virgillis vers the ornate bewtie
> Intill our toung may nocht observit be.

He complains bitterly of his 'bad harsk speche', his 'lewit barbour tong', his 'rurale vulgar gros', and his 'corruptit cadens imperfyte'. He warns the reader that his Scots has been abundantly fortified and broadened from Latin, French, and Southern English –

> Nocht for our toung is in the selfin scant,
> Bot for that I the foutht of langage want.

'Fouth' is to Douglas what 'copie' – *copia verborum* – became to the Elizabethans, the quality of meaningful variety, and with variety subtlety, both intellectual and musical, such as classical poetry was felt to possess. Liberty of experiment, importation, invention, and revival were wanted to widen the range of expression and to increase the possibility of those striking original collocations of words where poetry begins to jet out of the melting-pot, with new life whirling in the very materials it springs from. It can easily be seen what latent power there would be in the adding of this specific linguistic ferment and expansion of vocabulary to a writing tradition derived from both alliterative and Chaucerian sources, the alliterative source being itself both 'popular' and elaborately artistic. Some of the distinctive resulting forms may be noted and illustrated.

First there is the simple 'aureate' style, Latin-influenced but not extravagantly or emptily, the faint sense of formalism giving a stateliness and assurance to the verse, the suggestion of consonantal pattern inclining description towards a very makar-like onomatopoeia. So Douglas in his 'lusty crafty preambill' to Book XII of the *Aeneid*:

> For to behald it was a gloire to se
> The stabillit wyndis and the cawmyt see,
> The soft sessoun, the firmament serene,
> The lowne illumynat air and fyrth amene . . .

Douglas will also supply an example of the second important development, which might be called the 'anti-aureate' style. Here the lesson of latinism was shown to have been learned: the effect of culture, of authority, of the hieratic, of clarity and resonance, which a due latinizing supplied in descriptive passages where beauty, brilliance, splendour, and pleasure were involved, gave place at other points to an equally typical effect of deliberate harshness, apparent uncouthness, surface obscurity, and greater onomatopoeic emphasis, and for this the poets had recourse to Anglo-Saxon and Scandinavian rather than to Latin and French components, to the tough, concrete, and actively sensuous rather than to the tranquilly majestic, however gleaming and marmoreal. This experimental differentiation of vocabulary is striking and original, but not unexpected at that period of linguistic awareness. It is only in part a conscious artistic device; it is just as much a natural turning to the older Germanic in dealing with the physical, and especially the disagreeable-physical, where its words retain great force and have powerful non-literary associations, the Romance elements having on the whole weaker physical associations and a more literary and cultivated field of reference. This is how the Scottish winter sets in in Douglas's 7th Prologue, the *tristis prologus*:

> Dym skyis oft furth warpit feirfull levyne,
> Flaggis of fyir and mony felloun flawe,
> Scharp soppis of sleit and of the snypand snawe.
> The dowy dichis war all donk and wait,
> The law vaille flodderit all wyth spait,
> The plane stretis and every hie way
> Full of fluschis, doubbis, myre, and clay;
> Laggerit leys wallowit farnys schewe,
> Broune muris kithit thair wysnit mossy hewe,

> Bank, bra, and boddum blanschit wolx and bair;
> For gurll weddir growyt bestis haire;
> The wynd maid wayfe the reid weyd on the dyk;
> Bedovin in donkis deyp was every syk,
> Our craggis and the front of rochis seyre
> Hang gret isch-schoklis lang as ony spere . . .

A third characteristic of much of the makars' poetry is a lyrical run or lilt of a peculiar kind which comes from a nice fusion of native alliteration and French-based verse-form. The fact that the alliteration does not always coincide with the syllabic accent but leads the reader on with a sinuous stress of its own gives the writing a chatoyant and dance-like quality which is very attractive. A good example is the anonymous *Peblis to the Play*, or *Tayis Bank*, or the lyric *My heart is heich above*. In the last stanza of *Tayis Bank* the alliteration binds the lines in couplets, while the repeated rhyme draws on the couplets to the end of the verse, the whole being alive with movement and lightness:

> The rever throw the ryse cowth rowt
> And roseris raiss on raw;
> The schene birdis full schill cowth schowt
> Into that semly schaw:
> Joy wes within and joy without
> Under that wlonkest waw,
> Quhair Tay ran down with stremis stout
> Full strecht under Stobschaw.

Lastly, there should be mentioned the chief Scots development of the alliterative habit – satirical invective and 'flyting', with many variants from the norm of harmless 'aesthetic' *tour de force* improvising to the two extremes of serious denunciation and outspoken bawdiness. The force here is in the combining of the alliteration of old verse-forms with the alliterative tendencies in vehement and vulgar speech; rhyme, often internal as well as final, is a spice in a total flavour which will not be to everyone's taste. The form, however, is both interesting and important in Scots writing, and particularly in Dunbar, as will be seen later.

III

> Than cam in Dunbar the mackar,
> On all the flure thair was nane frackar . . .

These lines from Dunbar's *Dance in the Quenis Chalmer* might well describe his equally nimble and lively entry into poetry. What is immediately noticeable in his work is the *display* of *poetic energy* in forms that have considerable technical and craftsmanly interest, rather than the *distillation* of *poetic situation*, in personal emotional encounters. His first mark is a certain effectual brilliance that may commend him more keenly to the practising poet than to the ordinary reader – an agility, a virtuosity in tempo and momentum, a command of rhythm. His poems were produced by cooperating with and transforming the linguistic trends of his age rather than by relying (as Henryson did) on the ancient common fund of human situation and story from which poetic feeling can be summoned with less expenditure of the specifically poetic verbal gift. If Dunbar has at times 'words with no matter', Chaucer and Henryson in their less satisfactory passages have matter (the story) and form (the careful metre) but no word-energy. These are complementary wants; and if we sometimes sigh for a Henryson-leavened Dunbar we can also wish, more heretically perhaps, for a Langland-leavened Chaucer. The fusion of the two elements had to wait for Shakespeare. Dunbar's character as a poet – his wild imagination, his quickness of response to particular situations in a humorous and mocking spirit and to general ideas in a serious spirit, his evident delight in gesture, in presentation, in fanfare and march and rout and climax – fitted hand-in-glove with all those tendencies which in Scotland supplemented the influence of Chaucerian poetry. His work shows how far a writer could go at that time whose poetic energies could be released so largely by formal preoccupations.

The most general effect of the various echoic combinations of alliteration and rhyme Dunbar used (with internal rhyme often acting as an additional, vocalic alliteration) was to accentuate the movement and increase the speed of the verse. Like sounds draw the ear forward, sometimes before it has assimilated the sense, and encourage it to participate in the poet's glancing and headlong jugglery as a delight in itself, and not only that, but to see how from this delight he was more able to work up the fiery poetic object. Not only does the verse dance, but in many of the best poems this rhythmic success bears its fruits within the subject-matter, where either dancing or some other vivid movement is described, and the approach towards such a scene is one of Dunbar's greatest pleasures.*

* A recurrent pleasure in Scots verse, as witness *Colkelbie Sow*, *Tam o' Shanter*, and *The Witch's Ballad*.

Thus we have the free and hilarious *Dance in the Quenis Chalmer*; the *Dance of the Sevin Deidly Sinnis* with its sombre nightmare processional of the involuntary revellers of Hell and its sweep-the-board ludicrous catastrophe in the 'Highland pageant' called up and dissipated by Satan; the strange tale of the *Fenyeit Freir of Tungland*, which can hardly wait to describe the charlatan aeronaut's 'flight' from Stirling Castle, pursued and mobbed by all the birds of the air, attacking and crying alliteratively and cumulatively according to their characters; or the concluding blow struck in the *Flyting* with Kennedy, where he conjures up a vision of Kennedy the 'Carrick cateran' entering Edinburgh, fleeing through the streets with dogs at his heels, boys and old women shouting after him, fishwives throwing their baskets, horses running away with their carts – and a vale-dictory word-drubbing in the clattering last two stanzas when even the preceding movement is speeded up by the device of three internal rhymes to each line in addition to the normal end-rhyme and allitera-tion:

> Loun lyk Mahoun, be boun me till obey,
> Theif, or in greif mischeif sall the betyd;
> Cry grace, tykis face, or I the chece and sley;
> Oule, rare and yowle, I sall defowll thy pryd;
> Peilit gled, baith fed and bred of bichis syd,
> And lyk ane tyk, purspyk, quhat man settis by the!
> Forflittin, countbittin, beschittin, barkit hyd,
> Clym-ledder, fyle-tedder, foule edder, I defy the.
>
> Mauch-muttoun, byt-buttoun, peilit gluttoun, air to Hilhous;
> Rank beggar, ostir-dregar, foule fleggar in the flet;
> Chittirlilling, ruch-rilling, lik-schilling in the milhous;
> Baird rehator, theif of natour, fals tratour, feyindis gett;
> Filling of tauch, rak-sauch, cry crauch, thow art oursett;
> Muttoun-dryver, girnall-ryver, yadswyvar, fowll fell the:
> Herretyk, lunatyk, purspyk, carlingis pet,
> Rottin crok, dirtin dok, cry cok, or I sall quell the.

Next we may notice how Dunbar was able to use and improve on the effects of the semi-alliterative 'popular' verse like Rowll's *Cursing* and *Colkelbie Sow*. The subject-matter of such poems was congenial to him, and the form was one which particularly suited his combina-tion of word-linkage and rhythmic liveliness. Here again his poetic feeling is stirred up by the movement of the verse; cataloguing becomes denunciation, reporting becomes satire. But he ends more seriously than jocularly, applying the lesson in presentation he gained from the 'popular' verse to a different purpose. The motley swarm of adventurers and climbers Dunbar watched at James IV's court through the eyes of slighted merit might have been dealt with in the uproarious mode of the *Flyting*, but this time, when he came to write his *Remonstrance* and his *Complaint* to the King, the poetry raised through the rushing form took on a harshness and gravity which may be felt to reach nearer the personal than the quite spiteless dismissal of Kennedy. In the *Remonstrance* these are his enemies:

> Fenyeouris, fleichouris, and flatteraris;
> Cryaris, craikaris, and clatteraris;
> Soukaris, groukaris, gledaris, gunnaris;
> Monsouris of France, gud clarat-cunnaris . . .

And this is his conclusion:

> My mind so fer is set to flyt
> That of nocht ellis I can endyt;
> For owther man my hart to breik
> Or with my pen I man me wreik;
> And sen the tane most nedis be
> In to malancolie to de
> Or lat the vennim ische all out
> Be war anone, for it will spout,
> Gif that the tryackill cum nocht tyt
> To swage the swalme of my dispyt!

The piling up of defamatory variants is of course an ancient method of satire, based on the invective of vulgar speech; its tendency is towards humour, in literature as in life, because of the element of fantasy or incongruity which increases the longer the variation is kept up. Here we have rather the semi-realistic catalogue than the list of variants, and the choice of tone is more at the will of the artist. He describes actual groups of people in a way which shows his contempt for them; they come tumbling out into the metre, flung together unceremoniously in the levelling process of sound-echo, *soukaris* with *groukaris*, *gunnaris* with *clarat-cunnaris*, and they are left to stand long enough for the writer to knock them down with his comment. The theme of broad inclusive denunciation by an onlooker whose attitude sways between simple scorn and the epi-deictic, half-ethical, half-aesthetic, was one Dunbar liked and returned to; it gave him the double opportunity he desired to exploit vocabulary on the technical level and to ride on Urquhart's 'decumanal wave' on the emotional level, the emotion coming largely from and through the technique.

Another of Dunbar's methods of raising pleasure and excitement formally may be seen in his uses of Latin, as in the *Testament of Andro Kennedy* and the *Dregy of Dunbar*. Macaronic intermingling of English and Latin was an old tradition, going back through Middle English to Anglo-Saxon times, and it was extended greatly during the fourteenth and fifteenth centuries, often admitting French as a third language. It was naturally associated with the ritual and especially with the hymns of the Church; many religious poems in English had a Latin refrain which gave the recurrent gesture of authority and devotional remembrancing; *Piers Plowman* has much Latin interpolation, often within a half-line of verse; and it was obviously a usage which would offer itself to the consideration of a formal artist like Dunbar for purposes of unexpected contrast, the ancient religious echoes being made to apply to things the most profane and reprobate. To weave Latin, not tags but original phrases, into a body of rhyming verse was a challenge to his dexterity; in the feat itself was pleasure, and in the result humour. So he sets off in his *Testament of Andro Kennedy*:

> I, Maister Andro Kennedy,
> Curro quando sum vocatus,
> Gottin with sum incuby,
> Or with sum freir infatuatus;
> In faith I can nought tell redly
> Unde aut ubi fui natus,
> Bot in treuth I trow trewly
> Quod sum dyabolus incarnatus.

The extreme improbability of the statement's ever being made, coupled with the neat light assurance of its utterance, produces an attractive ludicrous effect which is kept up for fourteen stanzas, the half-Latin and half-Scots terms of his legacy bolstering up a continual expectation and quasi-secretive unfolding of the testamentary revelations. In the *Dregy* Dunbar enjoys himself even more. This parodies the 'dirge' or office for the Dead, and is ritually arranged with readings, responses, and final prayer. It is for the soul of the King, 'exiled' in the purgatory of Stirling from the heaven of Edinburgh, and all the saints and fathers are invoked to permit his quick release and return with his company: 'Requiem Edinburgi dona eis, Domine'. Here, in a parody of the liturgical form, Dunbar has found his aesthetic form ready to hand. The humour of this cleverness, this adaptiveness of his in the sudden taking up of an unusual structure, begets an enthusiasm which explodes all its force within a relatively narrow compass, so that the feeling for form has little chance of being dispersed, and the joke retains its point along with the poetry. Dunbar also made a more serious use of Latin, however, in the refrain-lines of his religious poems, in his *Lament for the Makaris*, and in such a poem as 'Into this warld may none assure'. In this poem the same use of close contrast is made as had appeared in the *Testament*, but with exactly opposite effect. Now the Latin offers no element of surprise, brings in no ridiculous finishings of the sense of the Scots, but strengthens, emphasizes, continues, and sharpens the already serious meaning, and gives it an impressive background or harmony of old non-poetic admonitory reference. Here the Latin breaks in at the end, as the poem's formal climax. It had been preceded by a growing amount of alliteration with the measured return of a refrain-line bringing each stanza nearer the concluding burst of energy. The verses mount towards a scene of breaking and loosening commotion, not (this time) a dance or a flight or a chase, but the tumult of the Judgement. Form pounds on till imagination rises and sees its object, and, with its warning Latin voice, the poem rings out and subsides:

> O quho sall weild the wrang possessioun,
> Or the gold gadderit with oppressioun,
> Quhone the angell blawis his bugill sture,
> Quhilk onrestorit helpis no confessioun?
> Into this warld may none assure.

> Quhat help is thair in lordschips sevin
> Quhone na hous is bot hell and hevin,
> Palice of lycht or pit obscure
> Quhair yowlis ar with horrible stevin?
> Into this warld may none assure.

> *Ubi ardentes animae*
> *Semper dicentes sunt Vae! Vae!*
> Sall cry Allace! that women thame bure,
> *O quantae sunt istae tenebrae!*
> Into this warld may none assure.

> Than quho sall wirk for warldis wrak,
> Quhone flude and fyre sall our it frak,
> And frelie frustir feild and fure,
> With tempest keyne and thundir-crak?
> Into this warld may none assure . . .

Something like the obverse of Dunbar's vituperative legacy may be examined in the formal usages of his religious poems, notably the *Nativitie*, the *Resurrection*, and the *Ballat of Our Lady*. The force of exultation which distinguishes these poems from the rest of his religious work matches exactly the decrying and demolishing gusto of the *Flyting* and the *Fenyeit Freir*. The utterance is high-pitched; there is an accumulation of similar views or variants of an idea, giving the reader no breathing-space and gathering him up with its momentum (and, in the last of the poems at least, almost dazzling him with sparks in a pyrotechnic ascent); and we have a brief refutation of Dr Johnson's dictum that 'the topicks of devotion ... can receive no grace from novelty of sentiment, and very little from novelty of expression'.* The all-importance of the formal foundations is strikingly confirmed if these three successful religious poems are compared with Dunbar's other attempts – the *Passioun*, the *Table of Confession*, and the *Maner of Passing to Confession*. In each of the first three there is a most distinctive use of several kinds of pattern (cataloguings and collections of variants, alliteration and assonance, extensive and often significant or stressing rhyme, Latin liturgical lines), and in the other three the absence of such components accompanies and accounts for their lack of expressive vehemence.

Finally, for the combining of many of these formal usages to produce effect in a relatively long and ambitious poem, there is the excellent and remarkable *Tretis of the Tua Mariit Wemen and the Wedo*. The workmanship of this poem, which is in rhymeless alliterative lines, is pleasant and easy, and shows that this experiment in structural archaism was congenial, a narrative medium loose and smooth enough to keep the story moving for several hundred lines and yet interesting enough formally to hold him always on the threshold of poetry. Chaucerian couplets would have told the story for him, but failed to draw fire; rhyme added to alliteration in syllabic verse would have served his poetry, but failed to keep the narrative on its necessarily low level of general intensity. The metre was therefore convenient; it was also a source of pleasure, along

* *Life of Waller*

different lines. It is a late-flowering growth of a very old tradition, which pleases by showing what it sprang from – and its author's awareness of this: the ghostly prevalence of Anglo-Saxon rhythmical types, seen through the lighter and longer Middle English line, links it with the medieval alliterative romances and behind them with the more heroic poetry of Old English – not in any more than a suggestive way, but with recurring hints and recollections in the fall of the words and in the use of old alliterative phrases, sometimes transformed, sometimes consciously taken over. It gave scope for that lavish and glittering scenic description Dunbar required as a contrast to his ladies' revelations when they spoke up and 'sparit no matiris':

> Quhyt, seimlie, and soft, as the sweit lillies
> New upspred upon spray, as new spynist rose;
> Arrayit ryallie about with mony rich vardour,
> That nature full nobillie annamalit with flouris
> Off alkin hewis under hevin, that ony heynd knew,
> Fragrant, all full of fresche odour fynest of smell.

What has its basis in the conventional May-morning vision of the romances becomes with Dunbar an instrument of sharp descriptive clarity and ringing verbal beauty. The care with which he has composed is reflected in a passage like the following, where the repeated alliteration clings to the sense-division of the lines into pairs:

> Thus draif thai our that deir nyght with danceis full noble,
> Quhill that the day did up daw, and dew donkit flouris;
> The morow myld wes and meik, the mavis did sing,
> And all remuffit the myst, and the meid smellit;
> Silver schouris doune schuke as the schene cristall,
> And berdis schoutit in schaw with thair schill notis;
> The goldin glitterand gleme so gladit ther hertis
> Thai maid a glorius gle amang the grene bewis.
> The soft sowch of the swyr and soune of the stremys,
> The sueit savour of the sward and singing of foulis,
> Myght confort ony creatur of the kyn of Adam,
> And kindill agane his curage, thocht it wer cald sloknyt.

Thirdly, and as the converse of this, it suited equally well Dunbar's purpose in the loose-tongued satirical part of the narrative where something of the spirit of the flytings was needed. When the first wife says of her husband,

> I have ane wallidrag, ane worme, ane auld wobat carle,
> A waistit wolroun, na worth bot wourdis to clatter;

or when the widow tells of her aged first husband how she would

> kemm his cowit noddill,
> And with a bukky in my cheik bo on him behind,
> And with a bek gang about and bler his ald e;

or says softly of herself

> I wes dissymblit suttelly in a sanctis liknes:
> I semyt sober, and sueit, and sempill without fraud,
> Bot I couth sexty dissaif that suttillar wer haldin:

we can see that the alliterative form of writing was no strain on the range and resource of Dunbar, nor on the other hand was it an excuse for mere wordy excess, with epithets empty of everything except the requisite sound. Both the artistic control and the eager verbal impetus are present, as they are in the descriptive passages at the beginning and end.

The dance and lightness of the verse, typical of most of Dunbar's best poems, need little emphasis here. These lines, however, might be quoted to show the variety and surefootedness of rhythm obtained. The widow, in mourning 'as foxe in a lambis fleise', goes to church:

> Full oft I blenk by my buke, and blynis of devotioun,
> To se quhat berne is best brand or bredest in schulderis,
> Or forgeit is maist forcely to furnyse a bancat
> In Venus chalmer, valyeandly, withoutin vane ruse:
> And, as the new mone all pale, oppressit with change,
> Kythis quhilis her cleir face through cluddis of sable,
> So keik I through my clokis, and castis kynd lukis
> To knychtis, and to cleirkis, and cortly personis.

She concludes her long discourse with a joyous recollection of the gatherings of young gallants at her house, a lodging amorously hospitable, situated apparently on the Venusberg,

> quhen baronis and knychtis,
> And othir bachilleris, blith blumyng in youth,
> And all my luffaris lele, my lugeing persewis,
> And fyllis me wyne wantonly with weilfair and joy . . .

After which the medieval Anna Livia Plurabelle rests her defence – 'I am so mercifull in mynd, and menys all wichtis' – and the three ladies join in laughter and concord and pass the cup round 'with confortable drinkis' until dawn. The festive scene at the widow's lodging melts into the summer night fantasy-scene of the ladies in their own festive arbour, and these figures themselves are then melted into the gradually lightening real landscape of the May morning, their laughter becoming birdsong, their voices the 'soft sowch of the swyr', and the gold and green and silver of their garments and goblets the dewy glitter of wood, field and burn in the first sunlight. These are masterly transitions, and nowhere in Dunbar is stylized language so keenly felt to be appropriate – for the return to that almost onomatopoeic descriptive reality the setting demanded, and for the conveying of this curious poet's word-conducted energy to its earth, safely reached after the long stretch (for him) of over five hundred lines.

Dunbar's restless and nervous force and his darting quick-silver personality almost invite the impatience with his writing he so often receives. It is only when his limitations are realized, when we no longer look in him for the particular kind of great poetry we have become over-accustomed to by Burns's lyrics and songs, when we make the effort to find his own individual value, that we can see him undistorted by not a little irrelevant prejudice. As has been indicated, his is not the singing voice which celebrates the perennial relations of the sexes in heartfelt immediacy and simplicity. Lacking this gift, he disturbs us by a startling indifference to theme in poetry; we are uneasy as we watch him turn from the Rabelaisian endearments of 'In secreit place' to a religious *Nativitie* or *Resurrection*, from a mocking address to a Negro lady to his 'Quhat is this lyfe bot ane straucht way to deid', from fantasy to ethics, from ethics to satire, and from satire to stately elegy and eulogy, with no category botched, no nonchalance of treatment, however he may have alighted on his subject. The answer to such half-formulated queries of his 'sincerity' or his 'seriousness' is that Dunbar's main interest in poetry was a formal one, that he succeeded in writing poems of great worth *because* his energies as well as his literary preferences were canalized verbally. In saying this the distinction must be repeated – with its bearing on Dunbar's real limitation as a poet – between the stylized language that carries its own evidence in alliteration or anaphora or rhetorical cataloguing or any other device and the more usual language of the greatest poets where created meaning rises out of the relations between words *unlikely* from the immediately rhetorical or resonant point of view to be fruitful. Here Dunbar does not escape from the still primitive, however struggling, example and conception of his period's poetry, and it is the pity or tragedy of his achievement, if I may speak for Scotland, that his genius had to write under dawn's left hand. But with a little adjustment on our part, a tackling of the vocabulary, a tolerance of tastes and pleasures which much of the poetry we know best has not shared, and a realization of how frequently the effects in Dunbar belong to something permanent in the spirit of the language, manifesting itself at different times in different disguises, he can be appreciated for the fine energy issuing through all his works in forms as dexterously wrought as they may be superficially extravagant.

GLOSSARY (of less familiar words)

Alkin: every sort of
Amene: pleasant
Appostrum: abscess

Barbour: barbarous
Bedovin: immersed, lost
Bewis: boughs
Bler: deceive
Blynis: leave off
Brand: brawned
Brukis: tumours
Bukky: (quasi) shell

Carlingis: crones
Cawmyt: becalmed
Chalmer: chamber
Chittirlilling: (?) manikin
Clarat-cunnaris: wine-connoisseurs
Coilyear: 'collier', charcoal-burner
Cok (cry cok): admit defeat
Countbittin: infected
Cowit: sparse-haired
Crauch (cry crauch): admit defeat
Crok: old ewe

Decumanal: 'tenth-wave', culminating
Dentit: inserted
Dispone: give away, dispose
Doubbis: puddles
Dowy: dreary

Edroposy: dropsy

Endland: along

Fanyeit, fenyeit: false
Farnys: ferns
Fawin ill: epilepsy
Feir (in feir): together
Felloun: fierce
Flaggis: flakes
Fleggar: flattering beggar
Fleichouris: fawners
Flet: house
Fluschis: water-overflows, slush
Flyt: quarrel
Fouth(t): fullness, richness
Frackar: more spry
Frak: run, rush
Frustir: devastate
Fure: furrow
Fyle-tedder: gallows-bird
Gett: offspring
Girnall-ryver: granary-robber
Gled: kite
Gledaris: (?) shifty-eyed characters
Gowlis: red
Groukaris: (?) time-servers
Gunnaris: (?) chatterers
Gurll: stormy, angry

Harbery: lodging
Having: demeanour
Heidwark: headache
Heynd: person

Hoist: cough
Horleige: clock, dial
Huttit: abominated, horrible

Isch-schoklis: icicles

Kithit: showed

Laggerit: muddied
Leid: man (sg.), folk (pl.)
Levyne: lightning
Lewit: unlearned
Lik-schilling: chaff-eater
Lowne: tranquil

Mahoun: Satan
Mauch-muttoun: maggoty mutton
Menys: take pity on
Missilry: leprosy

Ostir-dregar: oyster-dredger

Perlocy: palsy
Poplecy: apoplexy

Rak-sauch: gallows-bird
Rare: roar
Reguleir: standard, model
Rehator: enemy
Rethor: 'poet', master of eloquence
Reuall: boss, round ornament
Roseris: rose-trees
Rowt: run
Ruch-rilling: rough-shod

Ruse: boasting

Seir, seyre: separate, several
Selfin: same
Sloknyt: quenched
Snypand: biting
Sowch: murmur
Spynist: blown, flourishing
Steid: place
Stevin: sound
Sture: stern
Sturt: strife, trouble
Swalme: mass, swelling
Swyr: pass, glen
Syk: burn, stream

Tauch: tallow
Tholl: bear
Tryackill: remedy
Tyt: soon

Wallidrag: sloven
Wallowit: withered
Warpit: cast
Waw: wall, bank
Wite: blame
Wlonkest: fairest
Wobat: 'caterpillar', unkempt old man
Woddie: hanging
Wolroun: mongrel
Wysnit: shrivelled

Yadswyvar: mare-rider (obscene)
Yowle: howl

Dryden's Drudging

Thy Genius, bounded by the Times, like mine,
Drudges on petty Draughts, nor dare design
A more exalted Work, and more Divine.
(*To Sir Godfrey Kneller*, 1694)

I am still drudgeing on: always a poet, and never a good one.
(Letter to Mrs Steward, 2 February 1699)

I

WHATEVER homage may have been paid to John Dryden in the last
thirty years, there is little doubt that his poetry is neither widely
read nor greatly enjoyed. It is easy enough to become convinced of
his historical importance, but there comes the point at which every
reader of Dryden's verse stops and asks himself, 'What would
happen if I were to read this as a human being? Can I find out what
sort of poetry it really is, if it is poetry?' If the reader then disjects
what Mayakovsky called the professorial bicycle-spectacles in order to
see at a more natural and human rate, he may well find it still none
the simpler to pick out the poetry as he goes along, or to be surer of
its value than he was before. Poet and period seem here to be unusually inseparable. For this reason it is not merely the romanticist
who is worried by the unsolved question of Dryden's stature as a
poet; there is a general interest in asking how far the quality of his
verse requires to be either explained or excused (as he himself
excused it) by reference to environment rather than to innate
capacity. The question may also claim to have some relevance at the
present time, since the combination in Dryden of vigour, hardness,
and clarity is something that contemporary poets are likely to take
an increasing interest in, as the suggestional-exploratory-ametrical
mode begins to have completed its work.

Why, then, these 'petty Draughts'? Milton wrote his own epic;
Dryden wished to, but only translated the *Aeneid*; Pope contributed
a *Dunciad*; Cowper sang the Sofa; and Blake and Wordsworth, in

the total absence of great subjects at the end of this deterioration, had
to try creating great subjects for themselves. Dryden, we may feel,
was uttering in 1694 a timely complaint. But against the complaint
we must set the complacence. The century from Dryden to Johnson,
though shot periodically by regrets or velleities after the manner of
these lines to Kneller, expressed consistently its deeply-felt sense of
advances gained, culture retrieved and anarchy dispelled. To grasp
the one virtue of stability, it sold many others, and finally forgot
the price it had paid. 'There was therefore before the time of
Dryden', Johnson wrote in his Life of the poet, 'no poetical diction,
no system of words at once refined from the grossness of domestick
use, and free from the harshness of terms appropriate to particular
arts ... To him we owe the improvement, perhaps the completion
of our metre, the refinement of our language, and much of the
correctness of our sentiments.' That Dryden would have agreed with
this, substituting Waller perhaps for his own name, is evident from
many references in his essays. He regarded the times, from the point
of view of language, as entering into a period of civilization and
grace after the harshness and barbarity of Elizabethans, Jacobeans,
and metaphysical wits. Donne received his praise as a monarch of
wit, but, as he says, would the satires not appear 'more charming,
if he had taken care of his words, and of his numbers?' We cannot
but feel, too, that his praise of Shakespeare is very different from
ours, and very much a part of his time, when he says: 'Never did
any author precipitate himself from such height of thought to so low
expressions, as he often does'. The truth seems to be that the age
thought itself blessed and propitious in a threefold sense, which at
first glance might indeed pass for an admirable benefit but which
proved a dangerous and insensitive circumscription of the poetic art.

The first aspect was metrical: Dryden, said Dr Johnson, improved
and perhaps completed our metre. As Dryden wrote both blank
verse and stanzaic metres in addition to heroic couplets, we must
assume that Johnson really did mean metre in general, and not
simply rhyming pentameters; and the apparent absurdity of his
remark (paralleled elsewhere, as in his Life of Pope) will be dimin-
ished only when we remember the paramount importance to him
and to his period of standards, and of the idea of achievement. In
its extreme form this sense of having arrived at a happy stability
after a long period of lawlessness is expressed by Dryden in the
epilogue to *The Conquest of Granada* (Part II), when he says:

If Love and Honour now are higher rais'd,
'Tis not the Poet, but the Age is prais'd.
Wit's now ariv'd to a more high degree;
Our native Language more refin'd and free.
Our Ladies and our men now speak more wit
In conversation, than those Poets writ.

Dryden's age looked back on the break-up of the Elizabethan and Jacobean poetry from a much closer viewpoint than ours, and with a very marked difference of emphasis on individual writers. To them it was much easier to dwell on the gradual degeneration and virtual eclipse of blank verse in the first half of their century, which we ourselves do not deny; and we must also concede that they would not have been true to themselves had they not condemned the metrical irregularities of a Donne, which apparently belonged to a careless use of language and which might have been 'improved' by taking thought, without an essential alteration of the sense. We can see that the rhyming couplets of 'The Second Anniversary' would be openly vicious in effect on following writers unimbued with the force to drive them continually yet not casually forward in defiance of the recurring rhyme, and that Dryden's age, laying down a stricter and a smoother measure in its couplets, was striving to make a standard, parallel to the classical hexameter, against which it would be possible to criticize such excesses as had passed muster in a less solicitous period. Such a standard would even supplant the blank verse which in the Jacobean dramatists had seemed to break metrical bounds and become altogether too loose for dignified utterance; and in fact we notice in the blank verse of the period, except of course in Milton and in Dryden at his best, an unmistakable and adulterating infusion of the heroic measure.

For the second aspect (closely linked with the first), we must consider what Johnson called 'the refinement of our language'. Here again we have to be quite certain of what was meant by 'refinement' in the ideas of the time. From many remarks on Shakespeare, we infer that Dryden would have thought more of him had he admitted fewer low expressions, or, as Johnson further defines them, too common or too technical terms. When we take a different view today, and look on the heroic style itself as one of a particular emptiness and absurdity, largely because of its generalizing vocabulary and windily 'high tone', we have to remember that at the time an important stop seemed to have been put to the intolerable congestion and obscurity of metaphysical conceits on the one hand and to the prevailing Elizabethan and Jacobean fondness for vivid concrete but 'vulgar' terms of description in both prose and verse on the other hand. Refinement carries its own dangers (always how unexpected by the refiners!), and is paid for by two unwanted effects, the lifeless and the ludicrous. But it was perfectly characteristic of the period to congratulate itself on the exercising of proper control here as in the question of metre, and demanding a standard of vocabulary for poets who wished to write within the newly narrowed gamut of public taste and propriety. It was chiefly an avoidance of the obscure, and of what was thought to be the incongruous, and its claim was to have produced a general vehicle of expression, which by means of slight and regulated modulations could serve for the utterance of almost the whole variety (but see Dr Johnson on Thomson and Young) of what was the poet's proper material.

The third advance concerned 'the correctness of the sentiments' of poetry. Much more anxious than we are about the ideas and themes and statements proper to poetic expression, the Augustan period believed strongly in a limiting of these within bounds suggested by the more general temper of the times. (Typical, perhaps, are Johnson's very careful remarks about the character of Milton's Satan, and his condemnation of Pope's *Unfortunate Lady* for the 'illaudable singularity of treating suicide with respect'.) It was assumed that the previous century had been reprehensible in encouraging a steady widening of the allowable subject-matter and consequently the expression of many things which it was not the business of the poet to meddle with: the feigner of beauty being a juggler with truth. For example, the free treatment of virtue and vice in the great dramas with their obviously open and imaginative approach to moral problems, and the uninhibited and often extra-moral sense of the divine among the metaphysical wits, seemed to have been happily superseded by the insistence on a scheme of morality, and the exclusion or distortion of themes and expressions calculated to upset it. In this sense *All for Love* had its own boldness, which we are apt to overlook; though it rested, perhaps, safely enough in the shadow of Shakespeare. We are given another indication of the meaning of 'correctness of sentiments' by the prevalence of satire. Just as there were a few subjects and ideas now encouraged which before had received little attention (for instance theological, moral, political, and literary argument in specific and up-to-date terms) as matters for a poet's consideration, so also the demands of 'correctness' led to an oblique treatment of many subjects which had formerly been open. Satire is characteristic of a period which prides itself on standards, both of conduct and of language; it is hardly necessary in a society where wide variation is not frowned on. It tends to become a stick for the back of eccentricity, and at last for mere individuality, since massive denunciations of perennial viciousness are suited only to the largest spirits, and may occur in any age, but departures from norms of civilized and regulated conduct, instead of receiving the humorous toleration of an individualistic period, irritate the sensibilities of these times, and are treated satirically, to put them out of countenance and send them packing from gracious intercourse.

It will be seen at once that disadvantages, some of them not suspected by the Augustans themselves, accompany this threefold progression.

The hypnotic ubiquity of the heroic couplet need not, of course, blind us to the wide variety of successes it achieved. There is a world of modulation between Dryden's prologues and the couplets of Katherine Philips, or between either of these and *Peter Grimes*. We should also remember the possible influence of the splendid (if banished) tradition of the couplet which ran through Marlowe, Chapman, and Donne. But against the successes must be set the limitations which by the end of the eighteenth century had become painfully obvious: a stiffening of the sense of rhythm, a loss both of subtlety in verse construction and of an interest in the possibility of subtle effects, and a deadening leaning towards certain grammatical and verbal formulas encouraged by the necessity of the rhyme, under which it became very difficult to make a unit larger than the couplet cohere (triplets and alexandrines being little more than a confession of the failure of the medium). Also, the refinement of diction by the excluding method of constant general censure of uncouthness is useful only in as much as it purges language of real coarseness in situations where coarseness is not apt; its use by the age of Dryden stands as a warning to future attempts. It is a common criticism that the admired 'poetic diction', with its habit of demanding the general, the moderate, the 'proper' description, in place of the startling, the more distantly metaphorical, the inevitable-only-on-second-thought description of the preceding period, was symptomatic of a certain decline of poetic sensibility, and permitted the writing of verse tautological, inane, inert, and unoriginal in the extreme. The greater poets such as Dryden and Pope had therefore subconsciously to modify that very diction which their period thought it was extracting from their works as an ideal. In the third place, we need only note that any command laid on poets (or implied, in the existence of satire) to manage their sentiments with 'propriety' is dangerous. There is nothing more ridiculous than the proper improperly introduced, just as there is often nothing finer than the improper properly introduced. Shakespeare's verbal wit in serious contexts angered Johnson; but Johnson's remark that '*Cordelia, from the time of Tate, has always retired with victory and felicity*' would make the stones of Stratford tremble.

In a more general and comprehensive way, how helpful or inimical was the theory of poetry emerging at that time? A key-phrase, repeated with many variants, is certainly 'proper Thoughts in lofty Language drest'. This, taken at its face value, and as it was written and intended to be read, might well apply to the *Aeneid*, to the *Divine Comedy*, or to *Paradise Lost*, but as we can see today, when the words have separated themselves from the immediate linguistic consciousness and become objects of historical contemplation, it might equally well be descriptive of *Don Sebastian*, *Venice Preserved*, or Pope's Homer, and is in fact the justifying aegis under which these latter examples foregather. It is possible now to understand in such a phrase what could not then be apparent, that it rested on a basically pernicious, if specious, division of the creative faculty. We cannot say that the poetry was a poetry of theory, since the style appeared first, and has its natural roots and growth, but the development of the theory (largely by Dryden himself) confirmed its use and blessed it for a hundred years. What sort of poetic composition does it in fact describe? It applies obviously enough to those passages, which in deference to the theory we might instance from Lucretius and Dante, not the least sleepless of poets, wherein we see the poet failing between bouts of inspiration and beating up his verse by just such mechanical means as the 'dressing' of thoughts in language suggests. But can it be said to apply except in flagging, laboured, transitional passages or in imaginationally undernourished verse? It recalls *An Essay on Man*; *Night Thoughts*; *The Course of Time*; *Merope*; *Festus*. The poet at his happiest will not be found selecting fine thoughts and then scouring his memory for expressions which will show off these thoughts to the best advantage ('like a dog out of the water, with a duck in his mouth', in Dryden's favourite image). He has no time for that, were he not under a profounder compulsion. He thinks in and through language: thinks words; his 'thoughts' are not nearer thought than these inverted commas allow, and to him a tear may be an intellectual thing. The greatness of his work is sealed by language rather than by thought because poetry is an utterance, and nowhere is falseness of speech for the sake of thought more instantly detectable, or loftiness for the sake of propriety more suspiciously examined. The most moving of poetic statements, which we might be tempted to classify under 'thoughts on life and death', may be expressions of language far removed from the magnificent, and are distinguished from other kinds of human utterance only by their quality of holding meanings and values that we never wholly expound. Thoughts we may and do trawl up from these depths, yet at the moment of being divided from their element of words they perish and their virtue which we had hoped to capture becomes a dead thing unsupported by its unique context. Were it otherwise, if the Augustan theory of writing gave a true description of the best practice, poetry would be little more than an elaborate game with dictionaries and history-books and moralists' vade-mecums, and that peculiar fusing, centripetal, focusing, meditating quality of creative writing, which is not thinking, or feeling, or speaking, or singing, or dancing, but something of all these, and an activity complete and distinct in itself from all others, however feebly it can be described from outside, would appear to be productive of an unreasoned beauty at best, and at the worst of dithyrambic unintelligibility. But we know that the age of Dryden was determined to avoid at all costs the obscurity it saw (and of course rightly saw) in the metaphysical poets and also in the Elizabethan and Jacobean dramatists, and to this end welcomed a scheme of writing which demanded first a perfect comprehensibleness, and then a succession of thoughts worthy of the comprehending faculty. Such writing is obtained by the method they described: proper ideas are selected, words recognized to be proper to the expression of these ideas are dug out of the poet's recollection, and, intellectually correct, down goes the expression, perhaps frigid in its generality, or threadbare by unconcernedly repetitive usage, but, as it seems, proper for the matter in hand. It is scarcely surprising that the eighteenth century should find it so necessary to satirize dullness, or that it should have added new meanings to that word. It failed to see how steadily (and with what self-acclaim!) it was marching down a well-built cul-de-sac.

II

It is now to be asked how far the work of Dryden, within such an environment as has been indicated, owes its virtues and deficiencies to the literary background.

When we look at the heroic plays, we may seem to see merely the exploiting of a genre that has proved to have no lasting appeal. Yet in spite of the declamatory method, the generalizing epithet, the mind's first verb, the punch-and-judy couplets, we are offered a progression which argues the Dryden working with unworthy materials, though not acutely or perseveringly conscious of their inadequacy. This progression is seen in the unquestioning acceptance of the heroic couplet in *The Conquest of Granada*, a sense of its drawbacks by the time of *Aureng-Zebe*, and its abandonment in *All for Love*; and in these plays a corresponding advance in dramatic power. We are forced to admit, however, that this is too simple, and that we owe the solitary outstanding play of *All for Love* rather to a fortunate group of circumstances than wholly to trends mounting up through the earlier dramas. The most fortunate of these circumstances was doubtless the amplitude of the theme, particularly as already announced by Shakespeare, a theme which might be expected to produce a poetic drama if any in the heroic style was in fact possible. Dryden, however, was wise in not relying on the theme itself to carry him through the arid heroic wilderness, and decided on the dangerous plunge into blank verse which did in fact save the play.

I have called the circumstances fortunate because of the considerable success of the style, heroic not in the narrow but in a general sense, quite distinctive at the time it appeared in 1677 and distinctive among Dryden's poetic work. On the normal working level it can be seen to derive almost equally from the rhetoric of the heroic drama and from Shakespeare; that is, it appears as an unusually dignified and solid rhetoric ('scarce rants at all', as the prologue says) eminently suited to the noble characters of the theme. But Dryden has made use of his blank verse to express something more important than this, significant though it is. As if with restraint and care unwilling to dissipate the dignity along a fatally easy torrent of formless verse, attractive enough after the heroic pinfolding, he goes exactly as far as dignity will allow along the road of metrical emancipation, permitting himself a thinly sown variety of enjambment, and discovering without being intoxicated by the aptness of occasional short lines in blank verse which he had introduced with bathetic and ludicrous effect among his earlier couplets; and the result, in many remarkable passages, is a style which no one seems to have used before, grave, often simple in the extreme, relying on scant or everyday metaphor, clear, escaping from the echoes that haunt the heroic play as a species, most fitted for the undertones of passion, the reverse of the heroic coin, a rumination on certain aspects and causes of feeling where the diction itself has managed to separate its existence from the more resonant but more common body of the oratory. Perhaps the best-known example of this style is Dolabella's speech in Act 4 Scene 1 beginning 'Men are but Children of a larger growth'. But the essence of simplicity which Dryden seems to be extracting in this play is perhaps best seen at two other points of the action. There is Antony's dying speech to Cleopatra in Act 5 Scene 1, niggardly of epithets, of imagery, even of metrical feet – but not niggardly of tragic feeling:

> But grieve not, while thou stay'st,
> My last disastrous Times:
> Think we have had a clear and glorious day;
> And Heav'n did kindly to delay the Storm
> Just till our close of Ev'ning . . .

Equally persuasive in this serious, quiet, self-sustaining style is a speech of Cleopatra's in Act 4 Scene 1, relying again on what is only one image, worked out slowly and as if reluctantly into its full meaning, becoming gradually of great imaginative weight:

> Like one, who wanders through long barren Wilds
> And yet foreknows no Hospitable Inn
> Is near to succour Hunger, eats his fill,
> Before his painful March:
> So would I feed a while my famish'd Eyes
> Before we part; for I have far to go,
> If Death be far, and never must return.

This, it seems to me, is far removed from the frequently admired 'When I consider Life' speech in *Aureng-Zebe*, and is perhaps as much an advance upon that as the *Aureng-Zebe* speech is itself an advance on four other lines which occur in the same scene:

> Oh, I could stifle you, with eager haste!
> Devour your Kisses with my hungry taste!

> Rush on you! Eat you! wander o'er each part,
> Raving with pleasure, snatch you to my heart!
>
> (*Aureng-Zebe*, Act 4 Scene 1)

To explain the success of *All for Love* we may go to Shakespeare, to the theme, or to Dryden's twenty years of experimenting; but we can scarcely deny that the effectiveness of the verse, which is at many points a new kind of effectiveness, quite opposed to the gorgeous and rondure-sweeping poetry of *Antony and Cleopatra*, must be the responsibility of the adapter.

From plays to their prologues and epilogues. Of these Dryden himself made the interesting remark:

> Expect no more when once the *Prologue's* done;
> The Wit is ended e'r the *play's* begun.
>
> (Prologue to *The Rival Ladies*, 1664)

This is of course only too often true, but in Dryden's case the emphasis is to be put not on 'plays' but on 'prologues', and these contain some of his most vigorous writing in a style very different from the grave manner of *All for Love*. Again posing the query, how far this vigour can be accounted for by reference to the general framework within which he wrote, we find an easy adherence to the metric, apart from a more frequent use of double and false rhymes, but an individual treatment of diction and 'sentiments' by means of which Dryden made these prologues and epilogues a characteristic and legitimate form of expression. 'Proper' diction he keeps for the plays, or for the prologues spoken at Oxford; elsewhere he admits a wide vocabulary, harking back to the Elizabethan in general effect though strictly contemporary in details, for the sake of a lively, colloquial, humorous, and satirical railing at the audience by sections, pit, wits, cits, and critics. The 'sentiments' are often improper enough, and the bantering sometimes flogs itself into invective, but wit, a very sparkling and biting wit, plays over and lightens and sustains everything, and there is not often a fall into either dullness or prurience. To be noted here is the expansion of his imagery, much more varied than it is in the plays themselves, and contributing most to the swiftness and vivacity and realism of these prologues. The imagery is, as we might expect, of shops and trades, of citizens and players, of card-games and bear-gardens, of masquerades and rope-dancing, judges and punks, Whigs and Tories, clubs and courts, quacks,

coxcombs, cannons, coffee-houses, and conventicles. But not only
is vigour drawn from a busy and complex urban environment. In
the combining of words Dryden has here, in spite of the theory,
recaptured some of the stinging freshness of the preceding age,
and he very seldom uses the stereotyped phrase when a more
vivid one presents itself. Thus he often seems to gain his effect by
speaking familiarly, if satirically, of contemporary events, and his
language owes its reality to that direct touch:

> 'Twas a sad sight, before they march'd from home,
> To see our Warriours, in Red Wastecoats, come,
> With hair tuck'd up, into our Tireing-room.
> But 'twas more sad to hear their last Adieu,
> The Women sob'd, and swore they would be true;
> And so they were, as long as e're they cou'd:
> But powerful *Guinnee* cannot be withstood,
> And they were made of Play house flesh and bloud.

(Prologue to *Marriage A-la-Mode*, 1672)

Of the more mordant and indeed thoroughly roused invective in this
style, a strong example is:

> The Clergy thrive, and the litigious Bar;
> Dull Heroes fatten with the spoils of War:
> All Southern Vices, Heav'n be prais'd, are here;
> But Wit's a luxury you think too dear . . .
> There needs no care to put a Play-house down,
> 'Tis the most desart place of all the Town.
> We and our Neighbours, to speak proudly, are
> Like Monarchs, ruin'd with expensive War.
> While, like wise *English*, unconcern'd, you sit,
> And see us play the Tragedy of Wit.

(Prologue to *Aureng-Zebe*, 1675)

And an example of a lighter, fantastic humour, extremely neat, a
snap rather than a bite:

> Next summer *Nostradamus* tells, they say,
> That all the *Criticks* shall be shipt away,
> And not enow be left to damn a Play.
> To every Sayl beside, good Heav'n be kind;
> But drive away that Swarm with such a Wind,
> That not one *Locust* may be left behind.

(Prologue to *Limberham*, 1678)

In the prologues and epilogues, then, there is little to which the self-exculpatory lines of Dryden need be applied. The fact that their success is a success in satirical writing leads now to a consideration of his poems.

But first, of those poems which are not satirical, the following may be said. Dryden's approach to the correspondences that exist between outer nature and human feeling was purely conventional: he possessed only in very undeveloped form the interests which would have made possible a love-poetry, a nature-poetry, a religious or mystical poetry: he drew no inspiration from the outer world except when it impinged on his civilized consciousness through the limited externals of London society, and he did not have that curious openness and simplicity of personal emotion in the face of the normal crises of the heart which could lead even the cool and ironical spirit of Marvell into lyricism.

The songs scattered through his plays have found their admirers, and it has been suggested that we read them before we condemn them. It might rather be suggested that we *hear* them before we condemn them, since they have surely little to recommend them as poems. Their effectiveness as songs is a different matter; transplanted from their context, they betray their frigid and factitious metrical sprightliness and their convention-ridden courtoiserie, in comparison with which the airiest air of Campion is an item to be handled with delicacy and respect. The best of the songs is perhaps the simplest, 'Young I am, and yet unskill'd' (from *Love Triumphant*, 1693). As for the Odes (*St Cecilia's Day*, *Mrs Anne Killigrew*, *Alexander's Feast*), these have been often enough and highly enough praised for a caveat of dispraise to be entered against them here. They have at best, in my experience of them, a glinting and baroque impressiveness, and at the lowest estimate they could be called laboured, ungainly, heteroclite, and flashy, in a half-hearted and mechanical fashion. *Mrs Killigrew* contains some of the worst diction in Dryden, to the tune of 'sylvan scenes' and 'lofty trees', 'blooming grace' and 'beauteous face'. The two musical odes are remarkably coarse-textured and rhythmically unskilful for poems of that kind, which should either arise exuberantly out of an expressional need like Milton's *At a Solemn Musick* or be fabricated with careful and constant artistic brilliance like Crashaw's *Musicks Duell*. Dryden's odes do not touch our feelings, nor do they much gladden our intellectual ear. It may be said here in extenuation that the use of the 'ode' in its

English variants between the times of Cowley and Gray was an unfortunate enthusiasm in an age of heroic couplets, because the heroic couplet, cultivated with fanaticism, overshadowed all lyric verse-forms so completely that the subtleties of their construction were forgotten, and in its 'odes' that period was producing merely chopped-up and adjectivally-heightened fragments of heroic verse which only very rarely assumed any life after Cowley had left the best examples, still fixed in a diluted metaphysical solution. It is a point of some interest, I think, that odes like *Alexander's Feast* do not really show us a brighter side to the constantly satirical picture, or another verse facet of Dryden's genius, but on the contrary are clear indications of the unique superiority of the heroic couplet in the late seventeenth century, and of the decline of the lyric forms which Herrick and Milton and Marvell had tempered to virtuoso pitch.

In *Religio Laici* and *The Hind and the Panther* we have Dryden 'hatter'd out with drudging works of grace'. The former poem, a low-toned disquisition where the language is seldom interesting enough to redeem the intractable matter, need not long detain the literary critic, whom Dryden has already forestalled in his preface. *The Hind and the Panther*, especially in its satirical parts, has a great deal more vigour, and some striking lines and couplets, but the absurdity of its animal fable is too great for it to be taken as seriously as it would have to be. The poetry of theological disputation is of course an all-but-impossible kind of poetry, and it was not helped here by being given such an uneasy and intermittently-remembered embodiment in a honey-tongued hind and a grumbling panther. In the two poems Dryden is obeying the 'language-as-dress-of-thought' heresy of his time, and making the best of an extremely difficult job: the desire to be lucidly didactic leading out towards prose (*Religio Laici*), the desire to sugar the pill leading to fantasy and incredibility (*The Hind and the Panther*).

Of the other non-satirical poems, there is a somewhat perverse satisfaction to be obtained from those early verses where we see the metaphysical influences of his 'darling Cowley' giving place gradually to the normal poetic diction of the unastonishing metaphor. There is a certain attraction in the *Elegy Upon the Death of the Lord Hastings*, with its grim echoes of the superseded microcosm, its Ptolemy and Archimedes, spheres and astrolabes, rosebud blisters and universal metempsychosis, and the massive fall of the closing couplet. In *Annus Mirabilis* the poetic diction, 'the feathered train', 'the first blushes of the morn', 'the melting breast', 'the watery field' and 'the scaly herd', may have the upper hand and account for the prevailing tone-lessness of the poem, but some fine stanzas and images appear when the eye of the poet seems really to be on its object, as in

> The utmost Malice of their Stars is past,
> And two dire Comets, which have scourg'd the Town
> In their own Plague and Fire have breath'd their last,
> Or, dimly, in their sinking sockets frown.

I turn now to the satirical poems, in which Dryden excelled. In his *Discourse concerning the Original and Progress of Satire* (1693) he distinguished clearly between satire which, called forth by the general badness of the times, expressed invective unsweetened, and that milder sort which aimed to laugh a vice or folly out of countenance and entertain as well as condemn. Of the first type are his translations of Persius and Juvenal, of the second his *Absalom and Achitophel*, *The Medall*, and *Mac Flecknoe*.

To consider the more suave chastisement: three remarks made by Dryden will help us to understand his aim in this method. 'The nicest and most delicate touches of satire consist in fine raillery.' 'Satire is a poem of a difficult nature in itself, and is not written to vulgar readers.' 'They are not the violent, whom I desire to please.' These statements give us pleasure, I think, because we realize that Dryden did have the peculiar gift of being able to direct his raillery, sharply pointed as it was, against individuals who are in themselves, or in their aspects as presented to us by him, perpetual subjects of raillery to be found in every civilized society. To Dryden himself this was evidently an idea of some importance. Many times he expresses concern about the proper object of wit, and about the misdirected energies of some of his contemporaries in letting fly denunciatory boomerangs. For the same reason he insisted on the value of a continually witty and entertaining treatment, realizing that, for poetry, such is the only alternative to the purely indignant and serious outcry. The poetry is there because Dryden felt with vigour what he was expressing, because he was using his considerable power to galvanize a fairly knowledgeable audience, and because his objects are readily set up in the imagination of succeeding readers. Satire is to bring folly into disrepute: but should it also exhort to virtue? It it does, the wit vanishes, and it was perhaps the wit that made the poem. The attempt to turn a satirical 'petty Draught' into something semi-heroic and positive can rarely be successful, and it is this attempt that makes *Absalom and Achitophel* less satisfying as a whole than the best parts of it suggest. There is a similar weakness in *The Medall*, and in *Mac Flecknoe* the problem is avoided. The satirist is seldom constructive or realistic; he will disguise a jeremiad as a blueprint, but his visions of good tend to be as unpersuasive as a Shelley's visions of evil. In *Absalom and Achitophel*, the series of dull and fulsome hyperboles relating to David and the state of kingship have in them something contemptible and are far from spreading a sense of the order Dryden no doubt had in mind to oppose faction and sedition. He rightly admired his portrait of Zimri; but what are we to say of David's long speech 'Thus long have I by Native Mercy sway'd'? Not only is the tone different, but the wit which sustained the portrait has quite fallen away, and the language is lifeless in comparison. The light touch has been lost, and the heavier substitute fails to impress, though it might be expected to carry a greater significance. This would suggest that the definition of a 'fine raillery' is insufficient for a satire of any considerable length or ambitious form (unless of course literary parody, as in *The Rape of the Lock*, is involved), and that *Mac Flecknoe* is Dryden's masterpiece in the genre. Here he is thoroughly at home with his subject from beginning to end; his enemy is the arch-enemy of all writers who attempt Dryden's own two particular virtues of clarity and forcefulness; setting and action are perfectly suited to the matter; and there is no deadening or inhibiting compulsion to exhort.

Yet satire was in some sense, in the theory and tradition which Dryden accepted, 'a species of heroic poetry'; and there are other indications that he finally favoured the definition of 'fine raillery' much less than the original and sterner one of invective or denunciation – a different approach to the heroic from that of *Absalom and Achitophel*. In the *Discourse* he makes the comparison of Horace and Juvenal favourable to the more rigorous master. While admitting Horace to be the greater poet over the whole of his work, he finds that Juvenal exceeds him in the force and brilliance of his satires, and these satires are of the severe kind where those of Horace are mild and (as Dryden says) 'insipid'. Juvenal is praised, it should be remembered, not as a satirist but clearly as a poet making of satire something equal in value to other forms of 'heroic' writing. 'We cannot deny', Dryden says, 'that Juvenal was the greater poet, I mean in satire. His thoughts are sharper; his indignation against vice is more vehement; . . . he treats tyranny, and all the vices attending it, as they deserve, with the utmost rigour.' It is after these statements that Dryden speaks of the 'nicest and most delicate touches' of satire as in Horace which he says show a greater triumph of art, but we are concerned here rather with his practice than with his judgement, and we can see from his own work that his praise of Juvenal's 'more vigorous and masculine wit' comes from his heart more immediately than his intellectual admiration of the 'fine strokes' of Horace. He seems to be recognizing a principle which may help to account for the success of his translations, by linking the severity, swiftness, and deadliness of Juvenal's style with the seriousness of his subject-matter, and suggesting that while raillery suits folly, no castigation can be too violent for the general vices of a society. In this we are brought up against the question in his own work, whether the more delicate thrusts of wit or the annihilating attacks of these late poems are farther removed from the status of 'petty Draughts'.

The unsatisfactory compromise that had to be effected in *Absalom and Achitophel* with material on which wit could scarcely work has already been noticed. May it not be that in the translations, where the necessity for such a compromise, in the continuous rigour of the condemnation, disappears, he found a more congenial form of utterance, and that he was able in them to preserve the usages of wit on a higher level, without descents to the makeweight of 'virtuous' commentary? Certainly he himself spoke elsewhere of the viciousness of the times and the aptness of heavy satire, and in these translations we feel that here alone has his wit attached itself to an object both speedy enough and massive enough to bear it. Here he employs the heroic couplet with a perfect realization of its capabilities; the rhyme is no setback but performs again and again the office of a double blow or of the epigrammatic sting in the tail of a two-line statement: the vocabulary escapes from 'diction' into very free and 'improper' usages often startling and vivid, helped to this freshness no doubt by the fact that Dryden was trying to make Juvenal and Persius speak as they would had they lived in Dryden's England; and in the matter of the denunciations, with which of course we credit the originals, he appears to have found subjects, often unpleasant enough but clamouring for 'strong lines' in the translator, to which his pen warmed with alacrity.*

* Wordsworth, who understood Dryden well although he opposed him in his critical writings, saw that 'whenever his language is poetically impassioned, it is

As an example of the imagery, which is immediate and 'free' in a sense not recommended by the theories of the time, the following lines from Persius (4th Satire):

> Him, do'st thou mean, who, spight of all his store,
> Is ever Craving, and will still be Poor?
> Who cheats for Half-pence, and who doffs his Coat,
> To save a Farthing in a Ferry-Boat?
> Ever a Glutton, at another's Cost,
> But in whose Kitchin dwells perpetual Frost?

And this, to show the extension of vocabulary, the liberty of approach it signified, and the richness of effect it made possible within the heroic couplet (5th Satire):

> Art thou of *Bethlem's* Noble College free?
> Stark, staring mad; that thou wou'dst tempt the Sea?
> Cubb'd in a Cabin, on a Mattress laid,
> On a Brown *George*, with lowsie Swobbers, fed,
> Dead Wine, that stinks of the *Borrachio*, sup
> From a foul Jack, or greasie Maple Cup?

Or from Juvenal, some lines which show the considerable musical and evocative power he was able to summon from this admission of Johnson's 'low expressions' (6th Satire):

> Who lewdly Dancing at a Midnight-Ball,
> For hot Eringoes, and Fat Oysters call:
> Full Brimmers to their Fuddled Noses thrust;
> Brimmers the last Provocatives of Lust,
> When Vapours to their swimming Brains advance,
> And double Tapers on the Tables dance.

And finally, the beginning of the powerful description of the bleakness of old age which has the intensity of Swift (10th Satire):

> Mistaken Blessing, which Old Age they call,
> 'Tis a long, nasty, darksom Hospital,
> A ropy Chain of Rhumes; a Visage rough,
> Deform'd, Unfeatur'd, and a Skin of Buff . . .

may be instanced as proof of the congenial nature of such graver and darker thoughts to Dryden in this period of his writing.

---

mostly upon unpleasing subjects, such as the follies, vices, and crimes of classes of men, or of individuals.' (Letter to Scott, 7 November 1805.)

I have indicated the successful emergence of at least three different styles: the serious, simplified, humane 'thinking-aloud' of *All for Love*; the light, brilliant, familiar, entertaining wit of the prologues, epilogues, and satires; and the later enriched, emancipated, vulgarized, less subtle but more passionate style of the Juvenal and Persius translations. With the exception of the single play *All for Love*, these successes took place within the accepted mediums, made use of contemporary material, and might have Dryden's disclaimer to Kneller applied to them by extension: they owed their vitality indeed to the ever-active mind of Dryden, but to that mind working in full co-operation with the tendencies of the time, and achieving distinction, by its own superiority and by a certain 'belated-Elizabethan' independence of approach, only within a restricted sphere. When we come to apply the disclaimer, however, as it stands, to the 'more exalted work' we know he desired, and to his existing essays in the lyric and dramatic fields, it seems less true to agree with him in this excusing of his deficiences by reference to the age he lived in (though it might well have been true!) than to say that he was constitutionally and inherently unsuited for any such designs. Many people, I think, have sought to praise Dryden for the wrong reasons, endeavouring to find some plausibly attractive resting-place for their general feeling of 'force' or 'greatness' in his work. He has suffered where lesser poets have not, by excelling in subjects and styles often disagreeable, hard, and unsympathetic to the ear, and from the fact that he has a difficult and elusive personality. But the qualities of his verse are worth study, as poets themselves have usually recognized, and in addition to the interest that should attach at the present moment to his unprofound but unyielding poetry of discourse and scorn, he offers peculiarly the poetry of a period in history, and evidence of the varieties of effect possible within a narrow and unpromising critical view of the poet's function, at a point just before that critical view had had time to harden into dogma and self-love.

Cambridge Journal, VI, 7 (April 1953). Reprinted in *Dryden: A Collection of Critical Essays* (Twentieth-century Views Series), ed. B. N. Schilling, New Jersey, 1963.

A Prelude to *The Prelude*

IN his letter of 1 May 1805 to Sir George Beaumont announcing the completion of *The Prelude* Wordsworth wrote of the work: 'Here, at least, I hoped that to a certain degree I should be sure of succeeding, as I had nothing to do but describe what I had felt and thought.' This, as he realized, was a most unusual way of proceeding in any long and important poem; the apparent baring and simplifying of poetic activity implied in the mere description of things previously felt and thought does in fact bristle with hazards and difficulties. What Wordsworth was to do was to take poetry one step further back into the creative chaos, or to make poetry out of material one step nearer the original mass of all his experience. His task was not to describe the growth of a poet's mind, but to make poetry, using as material his recollection of the growth of a poet's mind. 'Il n'est pas une recherche du temps passé, mais une œuvre d'art dont la matière-prétexte est ma vie d'autrefois', as Jean Genet says of his *Journal du Voleur*. However important it may have seemed to him intellectually to be setting down this record, as something significant in itself, it is obvious from the completed work that *The Prelude* came alive under his hands and in the end gave him and us a new kind of poetic utterance in addition to the unprecedented material.

I have called Wordsworth's method a seeming simplification, as compared with the methods the great poets have normally followed, because at first sight his proposed activity looks like a concession to weakness: he is not going to exert himself till his imagination 'bodies forth the forms of things unknown' but simply to tell his readers what he has been feeling and thinking, and how it has come about, for the past twenty years. We recall, in support of this initial suspicion, how other great poets begin, as it were, where Wordsworth leaves off. They take for granted, as something superfluous to discuss, the fact that their minds have known a steady, enriching, and interesting growth in power and sympathy, and they lose little breath or time in reminiscence over the incidents which have made them what they are, because they know that all these incidents have become a part of their whole consciousness, and must of themselves issue out and rise up in the creative action of writing, causing and forming their similes and metaphors, and giving their style the stamp of the past man plunged in the wax of the present. The material of each individual poet's experience is accepted merely as the rich ground from which new and hitherto unexperienced forms will arise; it shapes these forms, even in the dramatic poet, but it is the new forms themselves which are of the first importance to him, not the scattered experiences lying behind and through them.

To take an example of this: when Milton, speaking of the heavenly hosts round God in *Paradise Lost*, says

> About him all the Sanctities of Heaven
> Stood thick as starrs, and from his sight receiv'd
> Beatitude past utterance,

> (III. 60–2)

we know that what empowers the statement is its simple physical substratum of the starlit night-sky. We know from other evidence, such as his passionate emphasis of the fourth day of creation, that this was an image of beauty which haunted Milton, particularly after the loss of his sight; but Milton does not tell us where and when he was exalted by looking up at the starry night: indeed there is no peculiar occasion which to him appears memorable: yet the effect of it is there in his verse, not as something described lovingly by itself but as something illustrating and fortifying an idea. It is experience issuing as metaphor.

This is the attitude characteristic of great poetry; behind the imagery, staring at us like a lion from a cage, is the poet's experience, a huge but dimly felt bulk of strength seen in reserve. The impact of the physical world, through great poetry, has a tendency to come not directly but as a component of larger forms whose total effects use it and make it subservient as imagery. Clearly then, to describe, as Wordsworth said, what he had felt and thought was something very different from the usual exercise of the imagination in the best poetry. It was, as I have suggested, a conscious reaching back to the material, normally left lying in the subconscious memory, from which poetry takes the basic and (one might say) primordial elements of its life; and the newness of Wordsworth's attempt lay in his determination to make of that itself a body of poetry, by which the past, with all its feeling as it then existed, was to be brought into sharp and vivid recollection. Now since the imagination is one faculty, and can hardly exercise itself in two disparate activities, Wordsworth was taking an unusual and considerable risk. 'I desire to press in my arms the loveliness which has not yet come into the world', wrote Stephen Dedalus. Creation normally concentrates its desire upon some future object still indistinct in its form, in the making of which countless fragments of unconsidered experience will be fused, the new whole having undistinguishable parts, whereas in what Wordsworth proposed creation was to take place at a more primitive level, with experiences being separated one from another and distinctly contemplated by a mind intent least of all on combining or embellishing or enriching them. Wordsworth was not perhaps aware when he began, though his boldness was to be justified, that his starting-point would have been a paradox for his great predecessors in poetry: he was to *imagine* his *recollections*. But imagination is a taking fire of the dead wood of ordinary thought and feeling, and whatever is described under that light, whether it is new or old, becomes new in the quality of vitality which informs it and allows it to enter and illuminate living minds. In most great poetry, in drama and epic, the poet imagines a series of actions in which he is not usually himself concerned, and the quality of his mind is known at second hand through the power of his statements and imagery; in *The Prelude* the personality of the poet is everything, and yet the imagination has roused itself, sometimes to the highest degree and in sustained stretches, over happenings and thoughts which in another poet might furnish the single metaphor of one line. There is little poetry that would conform to Wordsworth's definition of 'emotion recollected in tranquillity' taken in the strict sense he intended, but that was the phrase for his own practice, and it is of great interest to study this 'recollection' as a source of imaginative power, and so of poetry. What is important to discover is the relation of *The Prelude*'s theme to its manifesting of the imaginative power.

Wordsworth describes the main events of his life, as a child, at school, at Cambridge, in the Alps, in London, and in France, in considerable detail and with some reflection on them; the narrative is sometimes interrupted, but on the whole preserves its character as a personal history. Within this framework the central theme, as it emerges nakedly and purely from the events, is set forth with unmistakable clarity: the benign influence exerted by nature on the growing faculties of the whole man, the peculiar and perfect adaptation of nature to man, as of things made to interact, and the emergence of the complemental beauty of man's mind above but not severed from the beauty of nature. These aspects of the theme follow the course of the history. At the beginning, when the poet is a child, what is emphasized is the influence of natural forms in shaping his imagination and vision; at the end he has reached a point where the mind and character have developed a beauty in their own right, strengthened by human intercourse and sympathy but sustained still and always at the deeper wells of feeling in the presence of natural objects.

Such was the ultimate concern of the poet. Many events had to be related, however, and many sequences of thought followed out, for sincerity and completeness, which were certainly a part of his story but which tended to stultify his inspiration. These were usually scenes of human bustle and confusion, like the second-rate description of London streets in Book VII, and incursions into contemporary history and political and intellectual comment, as in Books IX–XI. For the first of these he was personally unsuited (as Lamb's letters amusingly remind us). His feelings were engaged by solitude and calm rather than by the hubbub of city crowds, and he was not able to write other than mechanically and dutifully about what he calls the 'perpetual whirl of trivial objects'. These things, not trivial in themselves, and indeed the centre of a huge mass of that very human life he was investigating, were trivial, disturbing, exasperating, and meaningless to Wordsworth; simplicity and the sense of order were wanting, and when they were absent he could not be at ease. Of the other less-than-successful part, dealing with 'residence in France', it is to be said that much of the material, reflections on theories and public events, was intractable, and behind the writing of the narrative part of these books we can often sense a deadening of impulse which seems to come from his knowledge that he is now to describe not advances and acquisitions but losses and retreats, the loss of his simple faith and a retreat from nature, and in such description he was cutting himself off from the two main sources of his strength. He had placed the books in a commanding position, and he gave the French matter very extended treatment, yet it appears in his life and can be used in the poem only as an incident which fortifies the deeper theme existing before it and victoriously returning after it. It had the great intellectual importance of being a testing-time

for that strength Wordsworth indicated himself as possessing, his lack
(as he says) of 'trepidation for the end of things', but feelings so
troubling to that strength were probably looked back on with positive
distaste and certainly without the necessary fire of mind. The inadequacy of such determined, laboured, and even pompous writing
as we often find in these books shows the main difficulty of the
recollectional method. The imagination works only sympathetically;
it is like the horse you take to the well but cannot force to drink; and
when it is used to describe things past, its enthusiasm will not spring
up unless what is being described has a lasting and present reality
to the poet's feelings. The result for the reader is boredom, when the
author, forgetting for a time that he must be communicatively lively
even when recollectionally serious, buries himself in his photograph
album and draws the dead leaves over his head. In prose, this boredom lurks in the most masterly and evocative reminiscential writers,
such as Proust and Gide; we cannot be surprised to find it in the
blank verse of a serious-minded poet. Wordsworth had felt and
thought deeply about the French Revolution, but this had sunk down
into his mind and had failed in the end to change the characteristics
which existed before it began, though it gave them perhaps a profounder meaning; and it is those permanent characteristics, as I must
now indicate, that Wordsworth had to learn how to tap and to use,
if his verse was to be raised above the merely discursive level.

In the first book we find him exploring his theme in a variety of
incidents, and indeed laying down the pattern he was to elaborate
again and again. There is simple description of the mere physical
delight of activity in the open air, in the skating episode, where pure
word-painting of scene and action in a self-contained form reaches
high art; there is description of an episode simple in itself but illustrative of the sense of mystery in nature which was important to
Wordsworth, in the night-piece where he speaks of snaring wood-
cocks in the hills and hearing the strange breathing and footsteps behind him; and there is the more detailed relation of an incident which
is a powerful incentive to description but had also a greater significance as showing the early workings of conscience and terror, in the
story of the stolen boat. This last example shows the beginnings of
what is going to be Wordsworth's method: he has some point of his
mental development to make clear, he wants to give it imaginative
utterance, he looks back not along the line of his thoughts but into
the actions he has been engaged in, he finds an incident where he

himself in conjunction with nature in some form was visited or refreshed by the idea in question, and then the scene he has chosen is described from the viewpoint of its significance, and becomes alive in the act of writing because this interlocking of scene and thought is his permanent possession. It is the recollection of emotion, but the emotion is unabstractable from circumstance; it is the poetry of time and place, the 'faces and places, with the self which, as it could, loved them' of *Little Gidding*. In this first book Wordsworth gives us his own version of what has just been said, as if in a careless summing-up of his art: he is speaking of composition itself, of the memorial process, and he praises

> those lovely forms
> And sweet sensations that throw back our life,
> And almost make remotest infancy
> A visible scene, on which the sun is shining.

With this should be compared some lines at the very end of the poem, where he says of the inception of his work:

> Anon I rose
> As if on wings, and saw beneath me stretched
> Vast prospect of the world which I had been
> And was; and hence this Song . . .

Nothing could be clearer than this identification, in which his childhood, and then his entire life, are seen as sunlit vistas of physical landscape. The one beauty on which his imagination fed was the beauty of nature, and whatever else he knew to be beautiful, whatever he had to lay before his imagination for working up into poetry, had to be related to natural objects and seen by the light that shone on them. His subject was the growth of his mind, an abstract and intangible one for any poet, yet for Wordsworth there was scarcely a difficulty in that problem which was not solved, apart from the few 'dead' patches already referred to, since at the most important stages of his progress he unerringly directed his imagination towards concrete and living scenes, and in the blaze of feeling which enwrapped his recollection of these he was instantly warmed to an appreciation of his subject adequate for poetry. So it is that for all purposes the inward theme emerges clearly as the influence of nature on human feelings, because for Wordsworth all feelings of worth go back to the early promptings of nature, and even those sympathies which are awakened with a new interest in men themselves are found to have come originally from his first association with such men as work continually close to nature.

(In this connection one is reminded of a strangely and improbably similar forerunner. It is curious to observe how Lucretius, grappling with the intangibles of the *De Rerum Natura*, turns his great and passionate mind towards the same poetic solutions. 'The nature of things' becomes 'things in nature'; an automaton is given breath; the atoms and their laws grow visible in earth and sky and sea. Compare, for method, *De Rerum Natura*, Book V, 1183ff., where he describes men's primitive superstitious fear in the face of snow and hail, comets and constellations, thunder and lightning, and strengthened by these physical references bursts out with the lyrical and majestic

O genus infelix humanum . . .!

with *The Prelude*, Book XII, 225ff., where Wordsworth describes the 'visionary dreariness' of the moor, the gibbet, the pool, and the solitary woman walking into the wind, and the full feeling again works itself up to the surface suddenly in his cry

Oh! mystery of man . . .!

In both, there is a rare lyricism of the abstract, reached through the living forms of nature.)

In the presentation of Wordsworth's theme, the more important steps may be noted.

First comes his dedication to poetry in Book IV. The recounting of this great moment of his life, which it was evidently his duty to make an occasion of excellent verse, is initiated with a characteristic care. Just before it, he reminds the reader of his method by evolving an elaborate simile describing how his recollectional activity 'incumbent o'er the surface of past time' has been like that of a gazer from a boat into the depths of the water he passes through; it is a fine example of the suggestive power of a concrete description exactly denoting events which take place at a different level, in this case within the creating mind. Then comes the story of the midnight dance, the journey back through the fields at dawn, and the poet's sense of his destiny and meaning on this earth. What is most remarkable in this passage is that scarcely any words are required to state the theme of it in intellectual terms: it is a triumph of symbolic natural description. After we leave the clamour and gaiety of the

dance behind and move on into the outstandingly evocative forms of
the breaking day, and feel the joy of it, and the sense of refreshment
and reawakening and preparation most aptly completed by the last
picture of the labourers going out into the fields to begin their work,
the reason for the whole description becomes so apparent that we
know it is Wordsworth himself who seems just such a labourer
meditating his work in such a dawn, and he needs only a few lines
more to confirm for us the knowledge, in more abstract terms, of his
dedication to the labour of verse.

My second example is from Book VI, at the point before the
travellers enter the Simplon Pass. Here, the subject is the tremendous
hunger of the imagination, unsatisfied except that it is itself a satisfaction to the soul, after that body of an invisible world which it
surmises from the glimpses and flashes it has seen through the glory
of natural objects:

> With hope it is, hope that can never die,
> Effort, and expectation, and desire,
> And something evermore about to be.

Again, the great passage is led up to and made immediate and actual
by natural description. The traveller, eagerly setting out after a rest
to conquer a new Alpine peak, has in fact taken the wrong path and
must now descend; the Alps have been crossed, and there is no
more climbing to be done; but his mind feeds on the imagined heights
he must leave, and is loath to accept the fact that its longing cannot
be satisfied, while at the same time recognizing that its desire is a
sign of its greatness, that 'the passions of men ... do immeasurably
transcend their objects' (*The Convention of Cintra*). The whole incident, written in simple narrative style, yet becomes a symbol of
considerable strength, because of this correspondence with the intellectual theme which is seen only after the reader has absorbed the
influence of nature.

At a third point, in Book VIII, Wordsworth is concerned to relate
some of the origins of his interest in his fellow-creatures and the
grandeur he feels them to possess. As always, he works from the
particular to the general, from one man to many; and from one
occupation of man, and from one moment of that man's occupation
when everything about it and him seemed to be significant. He
describes a shepherd as seen by him at three different times: on the
hills looming with his sheep through mist, walking in sudden sunset

light, and at a great distance standing at the edge of the horizon. From these appearances, where a man moved into the poet's consciousness clothed with something of nature rather than human rags, even though it was only illusions of light, his imagination was stimulated at an early age to see men as creatures of dignity and power and beauty, which later became an appreciation of the mind:

> hence [he says] the human form
> To me became an index of delight,
> Of grace and honour, power and worthiness.

The mist, and the sunset light, and the distance, are in fact the mysteriousness, the radiance, and the remotely-fetched greatness present in Wordsworth's own imagination as he looks on man.

Fourthly, I take the account of the death of Robespierre in Book X, and the release of some of Wordsworth's anxiousness and wretchedness over the failure of the Revolution to be what it set out to be. As before, the mental liberation, here related in the scant words 'Robespierre is dead!', is almost imperceptibly won out of the physical; it needed only those words to round off the joy that was already filling his heart from another source. This source, the natural scene of the river estuary, the sun, and the clouded mountain-tops, has a peculiar aptness in the manner of its description. Any such atmosphere, glorious in itself, might have been depicted to show something of a general happiness, but Wordsworth makes is significant by suggesting in the occasion the very thought he is to reveal. This thought is the glad announcement, from a band of travellers on the beach, of the death of the French tyrant; and in the preceding description, where the peaks and clouds are met

> In consistory, like a diadem
> Or crown of burning seraphs as they sit
> In the empyrean,

we see as it were the grand type of such an announcement, as if the consistory in the clouds had come together as the fountain and authorization of the news, as if those seraphs were speaking to the imagination what the human travellers were next to speak to the intelligence. The echo of the Satanic consistory at the beginning of *Paradise Regained*, from which Wordsworth's usage very possibly arose, strengthens the sense of an assembly of spirits met to give forth some important utterance.

For a fifth example, there is the passage at the end of Book XII dealing with the death of Wordsworth's father. What the poet wants to emphasize is the power past incidents have over the mind when they recombine with present thoughts, rising up like admonitions, not changed in substance from what they were but given poignance by the passage of experience; and what in fact this emphasis amounts to, though nowhere stated, is an account of the combining power of past and present feelings in the making of poetry. The point he has to set out is that natural incidents, events taking place fully in the outdoor world of nature or closely associated with that world, are impressed on the memory according to the human feeling of joy or fear or mystery surrounding them, and what seems at the time to be a power these scenes themselves possess is afterwards known to have been a reflection of the mind contemplating them by its 'auxiliar light'. Again he makes everything grow out of the concrete setting, and this time there are two stages of emergence from it. First he describes, in simple narrative with no comment, the desolate wild misty day on the crag where he is waiting impatiently for a sight of the horses that are to take him home. Then he tells how, after his father's death, that scene returned vividly to his mind, with all its imagery become symbols of bleakness, of loneliness, and of a more than physical cold. Lastly he recalls more recent visitations of that imagery, mingling suddenly with his ordinary thoughts for no reason apparent to the intelligence, but effecting in them a grave displacement and disturbance, various according as the emotion in which they first arose is agreeable or harsh to his present feeling. From these hints the reader must take what he can. Wordsworth is probing, in an almost Lucretian fashion, some of the seminal 'hiding-places of man's power':

> sic alid ex alio per te tute ipse videre
> talibus in rebus poteris caecasque latebras
> insinuare omnis et verum protrahere inde.

(I. 407–9)

A sixth and final point is taken from the last book, from the incident of the night on Snowdon. In the most awesome of all his pictures he builds up the vast prospect of mountain-tops, clouds, moon, and stars, seen like another sea stretching out from Snowdon into the Atlantic main, while from below he hears the roaring of torrents mounting up into the calm. Then with neither hedging nor pause, but rather with a full consciousness of adequacy, he plunges into the correspondence, one of the most audacious images in our poetry and perhaps the surest measure of his own mind. The mountain, with all the forms of clouds and waters surrounding and washing it, is his symbol of 'a majestic intellect' raised far above (but still a part of) the plain of ordinary feeling; the clouds and mists which stream out from its summit into the unbounded spaces above the Atlantic are the thoughts sent out by imagination over the bottomless depths of knowledge; and the sound of the torrents underneath is heard as the glad thoughts or poems of the thinker or imaginer issue from the profound unseen wells and springs of his nature. Just as the mountain appeared to lean up and out into space, so it becomes

> the emblem of a mind
> That feeds upon infinity.

And as the image here was particularly large and grand, so the verse which follows it is ample and sustained; and we have in fact not simply the majesty of the mountain, and from that the imagined majesty of the intellect, but finally an example of such majesty as that intellect in action can create. Thus we are first made to feel the power of the circumstantial situation; then we are introduced to the analogy describing the symbol; and in the end we have an application in poetry of the body of what has been said.

In all these examples we can watch Wordsworth coming to a realization of where and how his theme and his power were to be fused. He had to find out, from many kinds of description, from discursive reasoning, and from the analogies of tales and incidents, that anything he was to recreate through recollection must spring from the ground of the natural world, whether in itself a human emotion, an intellectual idea, or an article of faith; and he had to learn how to infuse into his natural descriptions that absolute suggestive correspondence which makes them reveal and underscore the theme itself. He had to overcome the abstractness of his subject not by writing of abstractions in thick concrete imagery, as Shakespeare did, but by giving clear brilliant pictures separated from the intellectual content while imaginatively evoking it as something about to be told, this being necessitated by the recollectional method contemplating actual incidents in singleness.

The resulting work, although it is a poem, is a poem of a very peculiar kind. It is rightly named 'The Prelude', because it is the prelude to an unwritten poem; but in the business of preparing for that poem it has drained off so much life from the imaginary work still gestating in Wordsworth's mind that we have another case of the child being father of the man – even a child unborn. *The Prelude* is not, therefore, completely unified in either intention or method. It is a record of the past; a creation of poetry out of the interaction of past and present; and a trial flight for imagined poetry of the future. Wordsworth's great victory came from his realization that these three processes had to find, and could find, a common meeting-ground.

Essays in Criticism, V, 4 (October 1955). Reprinted in *British Romantic Poets*, ed. S. K. Kumar, New York, 1966.

Wordsworth in 1970

> I doubt not that you will share with me an invincible confidence that my writings (and among them these little Poems) will co-operate with the benign tendencies in human nature and society, wherever found; and that they will, in their degree, be efficacious in making men wiser, better, and happier.

Thus Wordsworth in a letter to Lady Beaumont in 1807, at the end of his great period of writing and fully conscious of its force, but with nearly half a century of declining powers ahead of him. Two things are immediately striking: the 'invincible confidence', and the appeal to society in general and not to a clique of admirers or to the approval of fellow-writers or critics. How do we react to this, taking as fair test the two hundred years since he was born on 7 April 1770?

Although Keats objected to his 'egotistical sublime', and Byron snorted at that 'drowsy, frowzy poem, called the "Excursion",' Wordsworth has a bigness that allows a lot to be taken away without the collapse of a reputation. The question is what, and how much, we are willing to give up. It might be thought that Wordsworth is a poet of nature or he is nothing. Certainly the whole theme of his major poem, *The Prelude*, is the ceaseless, beneficent, admonitory flow of influences from the natural world into the mind of man and the mind's interaction with these influences. Certainly his heart leaps up when he sees a rainbow, or a jocund company of daffodils, or an 'evening of extraordinary splendour and beauty', or the stormy cloudscape in *The Excursion*:

> Oh, 'twas an unimaginable sight!
> Clouds, mists, streams, watery rocks and emerald turf,
> Clouds of all tincture, rocks and sapphire sky,
> Confused, commingled, mutually inflamed,
> Molten together, and composing thus,
> Each lost in each, that marvellous array
> Of temple, palace, citadel, and huge
> Fantastic pomp of structure without name . . .

And, as we know from 'Tintern Abbey', his feelings in the face of nature are not merely a range of sensations from the 'dizzy raptures' of adolescence to the grown man's 'sense sublime/ Of something far more deeply interfused' – these sensations are stored in a memory bank and are themselves not static but generative, and generative of his most mysterious claims:

> – that serene and blessed mood,
> In which the affections gently lead us on,
> Until, the breath of this corporeal frame,
> And even the motion of our human blood
> Almost suspended, we are laid asleep
> In body, and become a living soul.

This revelatory suspension out of the flux of living, like the ecstasy achieved by Donne's two lovers gazing into each other's eyes, or the vision of religious innocence shimmering through Thomas Traherne's recreated childhood, Wordsworth achieves through a recollection of woods, cliffs, and waters. Yet in that poem it is possible to be more moved by something quite different, by the

> wreaths of smoke
> Sent up, in silence, from among the trees!
> With some uncertain notice, as might seem,
> Of vagrant dwellers in the houseless woods.

The smoke of man, the tiny signal in the almost overpowering beauty of nature, the smudge in the landscape, silent and uncertain; and the man it signalizes is himself a mere smudge on time, a vagrant without a home. This, we find ourselves saying, is the real Wordsworth: unaccommodated man, the vagrant's smoke-signal. But would he have agreed?

Despite the poet's intense advocacy of a fruitful collusion between nature and man, despite the 'gravitation and the filial bond' that connect us with the physical world, despite the very stones on the highway to which he 'gave a moral life', despite the 'auxiliar light' that like an endless servomechanism between optic nerve and sunset kept a round of glory going in the act of perception – still it was true, and Wordsworth knew it was true, that the vagrant could not subsist without having the means of making his camp-fire, without having people to beg from, without having the odd shack or hut to lie up in when the need arose, without wearing clothes made by the labour of others. A labourer can look at a sunset, but if the 'auxiliar light' is

fitful, unfed by the conditions of life, what good does it do to say
that 'Nature never did betray/ The heart that loved her'? Whose heart?
What love?

> True is it, where oppression worse than death
> Salutes the being at its birth, where grace
> Of culture hath been utterly unknown,
> And poverty and labour in excess
> From day to day pre-occupy the ground
> Of the affections, and to Nature's self
> Oppose a deeper nature; there, indeed,
> Love cannot be . . .
> How we mislead each other; above all,
> How books mislead us, seeking their reward
> From judgments of the wealthy Few, who see
> By artificial lights; how they debase
> The Many for the pleasure of the Few.

The great honesty of Wordsworth keeps this black hard nugget
unassimilated to the exaltations and triumphs of his personal experience of nature. Even his own books, he knows, will mislead. Readers
will see 'figures in a landscape' where he wanted them to feel their
oneness with the wretched and the oppressed. In one of his letters
to Henry Crabb Robinson, Wordsworth implies he could agree with
those of his critics who maintain that he gives natural objects more
importance than they are entitled to, and accepts the same critics'
praise of him for

> in my treatment of the intellectual instincts affections and passions of
> mankind . . . having drawn out into notice the points in which they
> resemble each other, in preference to dwelling, as dramatic authors
> must do, upon those in which they differ. If my writings are to last
> it will, I myself believe, be mainly owing to this characteristic. They
> will please for the single cause, 'That we have all of us one human
> heart!'

This of course is what lies behind not only characters like Michael
and the Leech-gatherer but also the much-derided Simon Lee,
Goody Blake and Harry Gill, and Betty Foy and her idiot boy.
Without wanting to give up the idea that some poems are better
than others, one has to say that a good bad poem from Wordsworth's
Lyrical Ballads is at least as good as a bad good poem like Shelley's
'Epipsychidion' or Keats's 'Lamia'. I cannot agree with those who
think that *Lyrical Ballads* would be a poor book without 'Michael'

and 'Tintern Abbey'. After we have had our little laugh at the swelling ankles of old Simon Lee, or at Harry Gill with his teeth that chatter, chatter still, something remains, and it is this residue of something awkwardly haunting, clumsily but persistingly moving, something which comes from the story itself (even though, or perhaps because, the story is minimal in 'interest' or development), that is important to Wordsworth and was the cause of his fierce defence of some of these poems. When the poet tells how he helped the old huntsman to dig up the tree-root he would never have managed for himself, he is not doing this in order to retail his own feelings, although he cannot but indicate what they are: his aim is rather to bring us all into the diamond-like complex of an old man's tears – the shame of physical weakness, the joy of seeing a small necessary job completed, the thankfulness that would embarrass if it did not serve to show how men are linked in one chain:

> – I've heard of hearts unkind, kind deeds
> With coldness still returning.
> Alas! the gratitude of men
> Has oftener left me mourning.

In certain moods, one would trade quite a number of 'Hyperions', 'Bishop Blougrams', and 'Waste Lands' for the ability to write lines as directly piercing as these. This is not to say that Wordsworth is a better poet than Keats, Browning, and Eliot combined. But it is to say that he has a peculiar kind of dogged and perverse strength that is not always relatable to critically buttoned-up ideas of art. *The Prelude* can be taken almost as any other long and ambitious poem has to be taken, but *Lyrical Ballads* has a daring baldness and starkness about it that gives the same challenge we sometimes find in Tolstoy. It sticks in the throat of criticism, like Tolstoy's famous essay 'What is Art?' When Tolstoy rejects Wagner and Beethoven, Baudelaire and *King Lear*, Ibsen and Monet, and recommends *Uncle Tom's Cabin*, Dickens's *A Christmas Carol*, and Millet's *Man with the Hoe* instead, we 'know', as we say, that 'this will not do'. Yet in the course of reading that passionately felt and concerned essay we stub our toes on the central problem of art – who and what it is for – in a way that no other critic has ever forced on our attention so mercilessly. Perhaps Tolstoy's persuasiveness suffers as much from being non-Marxist as Wordsworth's does from being pre-Darwin. Both underestimate the sting and fillip of conflict. But

Wordsworth would have felt cheered that exactly a century after his *Lyrical Ballads*, ill received as they were in 1798, a writer as distinguished as Tolstoy should say:

> The task for art to accomplish is to make that feeling of brotherhood and love of one's neighbour, now attained only by the best members of society, the customary feeling and the instinct of all men.

It is not how he would have put it, but he is basically one who recognizes that task – 'having never read a word of German metaphysics, thank God!' Soon another century will have gone by since even Tolstoy wrote; that task recedes, has to struggle; others press. Ideology, far from shrinking, proliferates. Nature will soon be either National Parks or dumps, and Wordsworth would approve of neither. And it would be nice to hear what someone who hated workhouses thought of Eventide Homes, Whispering Glades and Loved Ones. Wordsworth was not a northcountryman for nothing. He stumbles through his readers still like a great blustery force, if they will let him, and not damn him with daffodils. Not that his daffodils are not very fine, but there is also that woman rocking dishevelled under the thorn-tree, whom he doesn't want us to forget:

> Cries coming from the mountain-head,
> Some plainly living voices were,
> And others, I've heard many swear,
> Were voices of the dead:
> I cannot think, whate'er they say,
> They had to do with Martha Ray.

Published as 'Don't Damn Him with Daffodils', *Glasgow Herald*, 4 April 1970.

The Poetry of Robert Louis Stevenson

STEVENSON is generally regarded as a very minor poet who never-theless produced a handful of poems which have been well known and well liked for quite a long time. Even this nucleus of famous poems would scarcely meet the most rigorous demands of the modern critic for a poetry that is really earning its keep from word to word, and Janet Adam Smith in her edition of the collected poems had to admit that: 'If we are looking for poetry that has mature passion and mystery, that explores sensibility, that drills down into the sub-conscious, we shall not come to Stevenson.' But she also said, in that edition, that she hoped her book would 'stimulate some real criticism, and encourage readers to take Stevenson's poetry seriously', and she seems to have felt that a due appreciation of Stevenson had in fact been blocked by the popularity of a few poems. That was twenty years ago, in 1950, and the situation has changed a little since then, but it could change a good deal more, in bringing a new range of Stevenson's poems to people's notice. When Douglas Young brought out his collection *Scottish Verse 1851–1951* in 1952, he was evidently hoping to follow up Janet Adam Smith's remarks, and included a fair number of poems which were less familiar; but they were not particularly well chosen to make the right kind of impact, and later anthologists have tended to revert to the tried favourites – 'In the Highlands', 'To S. R. Crockett', 'Requiem', 'The Spaewife', 'A Mile an' a Bittock', 'Ille Terrarum' – and of course there is no reason why they should not return to these poems if they are the best. But one anthologist who has been more adventurous, and who has given a genuinely fresh look at Stevenson which has to be taken into account, is George MacBeth in his *Penguin Book of Victorian Verse* (1969). In this collection he prints five poems, all of them worth reading, none of which are in any of the Scottish anthologies, and he also makes fairly large claims for Stevenson in his introductory note, saying that in some ways his verse is deeper, more personal, more piercing than his prose, and that he has quite a central importance in Scottish literature for his 'love of clandestine violence'. Mr MacBeth himself is not unknown for a love of clandestine violence, and you may want to discount something for that reason, but he is also Scottish and is pointing to a demonstrably Scottish preoccupation. These are subjects I shall return to; at the moment I want merely to indicate that there are aspects of Stevenson's poetry which have still to be illuminated and which are worth illuminating. It is extremely unlikely that any revaluation would make him more than a minor poet, but he can and should be shown to be a much more varied and interesting minor poet that his reputation suggests. Like his near-contemporaries James Thomson and John Davidson, he badly needs some proper critical attention, especially in Scotland.

Stevenson does not seem to have thought very highly of his own abilities as a poet – though one always has to be careful in evaluating comments of this kind. In one of his poems – 'To Dr Hake' – he talks about himself as trying to write poetry in the image of a sparrow feebly chirping in the wood before the better singers have roused themselves:

> Thus on my pipe I breathed a strain or two;
> It scarce was music, but 'twas all I knew.
> It was not music, for I lacked the art,
> Yet what but frozen music filled my heart?

This suggests that he thought he had the matter of poetry in him, but simply lacked the skill he knew was required to bring it out. In some other comments he shows a sort of exasperated puzzlement over the reaction of people to his poems, but seems largely to accept their verdict, as if he had little confidence in his own way of writing. The volume called *Ballads*, published in 1890, was badly received, and Stevenson gave a joky, uneasy half-defence of these poems in a letter to H. B. Baildon in 1891: 'They failed to entertain a coy public, at which I wondered; not that I set much account by my verses, which are the verses of Prosator; but I do know how to tell a yarn, and two of the yarns are great.' And in another letter to his friend Edmund Gosse about the same time he says: 'By the by, my Ballads seem to have been damn bad; all the crickets sing so in their crickety papers; and I have no ghost of an idea on the point myself: verse is always to me the unknowable.' Here he seems just to throw up his hands; both the public and the critics – or crickets – have rejected him, and yet he had thought that because he knew how to tell a great yarn he could hold them all enthralled in their seats. But the tone is humorous; there is no analysis of the shortcomings; he has other fish to fry. (These Ballads are not in fact good poems, with the exception of one short one called 'Christmas at Sea', and usually it's fairly clear why: he writes in a long rough lolloping rhyming couplet which quickly becomes tedious in a lengthy narrative poem.) In this instance, it is obvious that his wonderful command of narrative movement in prose fiction misled him into thinking that poetry presented no special problem if you wanted to tell a story in verse; but of course it does, as even a minor cricket could have told him. All this might suggest that Stevenson had never done much thinking about his art, but this is not true. He had quite a lot to say about the technical aspects of poetry, especially its sound-effects, which he discusses in his essay 'On Some Technical Elements of Style in Literature'; he experimented in a considerable range of verse forms from imitations of classical metres to the most up-to-date exercises in the free verse of Walt Whitman and Matthew Arnold; he gave some thought to his own native problem of language, whether, when, and how to use Scots instead of English; he wrote essays on a fair number of poets, both English-language and foreign, and was far from ignorant of the main movements of poetry in his time, even if these movements were not to him a matter of passionate concern. I would like to comment, in illustrative fashion, on two of these interests: the use of free verse, and the use of Scots.

To take Scots first of all. Stevenson, like Thomson and Davidson, may have been exiled from his native place, but he never regarded himself as anything but a Scotsman and a Scottish poet. Writing to J. M. Barrie from the South Seas, he gave this pen-portrait of himself:

> Exceedingly lean, rather ruddy, black eyes, crows-footed, beginning to be grizzled, general appearance of a blasted boy – or blighted youth . . . Past eccentric – obscure and oh we never mention it – present industrious, respectable and fatuously contented . . . Cigarettes without intermission, except when coughing or kissing. Hopelessly entangled in apron-strings. Drinks plenty. Curses some. Temper unstable . . . Has been an invalid for ten years, but can boldly claim you can't tell it on him. Given to explaining the Universe – Scotch, sir, Scotch.

One feels about that devastating portrait that it isn't only the last sentence which is Scotch, there is something Scotch in the whole approach, mocking and reductive, relentlessly truthful, down to the apron-strings which most authors would be ashamed to admit. In the subjects of his poems, then, it is hardly surprising that Scotland and Edinburgh should recur again and again, or that both should draw from him very strong reserves of feeling. The two great opposing, unresolved, often interlocking themes of his poetry are the desire for travel and the desire for home, and although in the end home in the physical sense became Vailima, mentally it was Scotland more deeply than ever because of time and distance, and the most popular poems of all are the ones that voice this feeling, such as 'To S. R. Crockett':

> Blows the wind today, and the sun and the rain are flying,
> Blows the wind on the moors today and now,
> Where about the graves of the martyrs the whaups are crying,
> My heart remembers how!
>
> Grey recumbent tombs of the dead in desert places,
> Standing-stones on the vacant wine-red moor,
> Hills of sheep, and the howes of the silent vanished races,
> And winds, austere and pure:
>
> Be it granted me to behold you again in dying,
> Hills of home! and to hear again the call;
> Hear about the graves of the martyrs the peewees crying,
> And hear no more at all.

The longing that is expressed there is of course not only a longing for a place but for a place with its history, even for a place as history. It wouldn't be a poem without the wind and the moors and the sheep and the whaups crying, but a steady look at it convinces you that its centre is not these things, its centre is blood, as its subject is death, the poet's own tiny nineteenth-century death merging into the blood of the martyrs of Scotland's hideous religious history and even that merging in turn into the far more distant prehistoric blood of the sacrifices at the standing-stones. It's Lewis Grassic Gibbon in twelve lines. And having said that, one is surely reminded of George Mac-Beth's point about the love of clandestine violence?

But 'To S. R. Crockett', although it is about Scotland, is not written in Scots, except for one Scots word in each of its three stanzas: whaups, howes, peewees. In a fair number of poems, though it is not a large percentage of his total output, Stevenson did use Scots, most of the Scots pieces being collected in one section of the volume *Underwoods* in 1887 with an important and interesting explanatory note. The main argument of this note is a defence of an eclectic use of Scots. He knows this eclecticism has to be argued because he is writing in one of the heydays of dialectology, when the examination and description of local dialects was having an influence which can be seen in several poets from Barnes and Hopkins to Doughty and Hardy. Dialect is not what Stevenson wants; he wants language; and if that language does not truly exist he must do what he can to give it a workable body. Here is what he says:

> I note again, that among our new dialecticians, the local habitat of every dialect is given to the square mile. I could not emulate this nicety if I desired; for I simply wrote my Scots as well as I was able, not caring if it hailed from Lauderdale or Angus, from the Mearns or Galloway; if I had ever heard a good word, I used it without shame; and when Scots was lacking, or the rhyme jibbed, I was glad (like my betters) to fall back on English. For all that, I own to a friendly feeling for the tongue of Fergusson and of Sir Walter, both Edinburgh men; and I confess that Burns has always sounded in my ear like something partly foreign . . . Let the precisians call my speech that of the Lothians. And if it be not pure, alas! what matters it? The day draws near when this illustrious and malleable tongue shall be quite forgotten: and Burns's Ayrshire, and Dr Macdonald's Aberdeen-awa', and Scott's brave, metropolitan utterance will be all equally the ghosts of speech. Till then I would love to have my hour as a native Maker, and be read by my own countryfolk in our own dying language: an ambition surely rather of the heart than of the head, so restricted as it is in prospect of endurance, so parochial in bounds of space.

What is rather striking about that passage is the way it seems to foreshadow the whole twentieth-century argument in Scotland about language and poetry. It looks forward to Hugh MacDiarmid in its determination to be eclectic, and yet it looks forward to Edwin Muir in the underlying pessimism with which it links the continued decline of Scots to that fatal separation of heart and head which was there in Allan Ramsay's day, to say nothing of Stevenson's. Stevenson could not foresee the revolution in poetry which was to take place after 1900 and which would be able, because of a new attitude to language, to induce or educe new attitudes to Scots; nor could he foresee how a new kind of political nationalism would help to conspire towards

the same result. In his time, he could only see his place at the end
of a long line, and although it is true that by going back behind the
nineteenth-century versifiers to Fergusson and Burns he was able to
refresh the tradition and at his best to write better Scots poetry than
most of his contemporaries, there was no real renewal of the existing
traditions in such a way as to broaden the intellectual basis of Scots
and to make it meet the demands of full expression. He wanted a
language, but all he had was a relatively thin medium which he used
with some skill and humour to produce late nineteenth-century
variations on earlier Scotch themes. It is interesting to see him
starting both with confidence and with a sense of inevitable limitations. In his poem 'The Maker to Posterity' he imagines some auld
professor in the future coming across his Scots poems and scratching
his head over them:

> *'What tongue does your auld bookie speak?'*
> He'll speir; an' I, his mou to steik:
> *'No bein' fit to write in Greek,*
>   *I wrote in Lallan,*
> *Dear to my heart as the peat reek,*
>   *Auld as Tantallon.*
>
> *Few spak it then, an' noo there's nane.*
> *My puir auld sangs lie a' their lane,*
> *Their sense, that aince was braw an' plain,*
>   *Tint a'thegether,*
> *Like runes upon a standin' stane*
>   *Amang the heather.*

'Dear to my heart as the peat reek.' This suggests that the kailyard
is not going to be very far away, and in fact superior kailyard is what
we find in a poem like 'Ille Terrarum' – literally kailyard in being
written in praise of the house and garden of Swanston cottage, but
literarily kailyard in its telltale vocabulary: the *auld housie weel
happit* in its garden trees, its chimneys smoking *couthy and bien*, and
when the poet thinks about its homely delights from the distractions
of the city he says *I mind me on yon bonny bield*. All these images of the
snug cosy homely place-to-return-to or place-to-dream-of are really
felt by Stevenson, and so the poem remains not a bad one, but its
vulnerable points are very near the surface, like the threadbare arms
of a chair that has been a bonny bield just too often. A much better
poem is 'The Spaewife', where, despite the use of an ancient ballad

dialogue form, something original and memorable has been produced, with its mysterious Yeatsian beggar figure giving her clas-
sically comfortless refrain-line at the end of each stanza:

> O, I wad like to ken – to the beggar-wife says I –
> Why chops are guid to brander and nane sae guid to fry.
> An' siller, that's sae braw to keep, is brawer still to gi'e.
> – *It's gey an' easy speirin'*, says the beggar-wife to me.

Equally successful, and again because it has managed to control its
romantic material in a classical way, is 'A Mile an' a Bittock', a
completely convincing hymn to youth and friendship, soaked in the
kind of nostalgia for the lost country of the young that goes so deep
in Stevenson and then miraculously dried out again through realism
and humour.

Many of the Scots poems, unfortunately, deal in a fairly conventional way with religious satire, owing a lot to 'Holy Willie's Prayer'
and ringing the changes on being anti-Calvinist, anti-clerical, and
anti-hypocritical. As might be expected by Stevenson's date, the
effects he obtains are often quite entertaining but hardly very subtle
or new. Stevenson has a favourite character, one of his 'masks', an
ex-elder of the kirk called Mr Thomson, and in the poem called
'The Scotsman's Return from Abroad', Mr Thomson comes back
from 'uncovenantit' foreign parts to see if his old church is still the
same: he has his doubts about some of the innovations, but these
are all dispelled once the minister launches into his sermon:

> O what a gale was on my speerit
> To hear the p'ints o' doctrine clearit,
> And a' the horrors o' damnation
> Set furth wi' faithfu' ministration!
> Nae shauchlin' testimony here –
> We were a' damned, an' that was clear.
> I owned, wi' gratitude an' wonder,
> He was a pleisure to sit under.

Stevenson's Scots poetry is always competent, and obviously written
with a good deal of enjoyment. Its limitations are not hard to define
and within these limitations it can give a lot of pleasure.

To turn now to Stevenson's use of free verse, where he was
moving out into much less charted territory, though it was also
being explored at the same time by his friend W. E. Henley. Even
today this side of his work is not represented in the anthologies

(including George MacBeth's), and I dare say some people are surprised when they discover that he did write free verse, and good free verse at that, long before the days of imagism and the modern movement. By free verse I mean poetry which has neither metre nor rhyme but which uses irregular effects of musical cadence and rhythm. It is essentially a twentieth-century phenomenon, but its forerunners are in the nineteenth century, and Stevenson was influenced by two of them, Matthew Arnold and (more importantly) Walt Whitman. Despite his uneasy and at times rather patronizing essay on Whitman in *Familiar Studies of Men and Books* (1882), Stevenson clearly fell under Whitman's spell, at least for a time, and in another essay, 'Books Which Have Influenced Me', he gives us some indication of what Whitman meant to him by including *Leaves of Grass*, between the New Testament and Herbert Spencer, as one of the seminal works in his reading experience. 'A book', he says, 'of singular service, a book which tumbled the world upside down for me, blew into space a thousand cobwebs of genteel and ethical illusion, and, having thus shaken my tabernacle of lies, set me back again upon a strong foundation of all the original and manly virtues.' So *Leaves of Grass* blew his mind, and at the same time blew his metric. In Stevenson's poetry, Whitman tends to show in his long lines, Arnold in the short. The two influences can be seen together in an attractive poem called 'Song at Dawn':

> I see the dawn creep round the world,
> Here damm'd a moment backward by great hills,
> There racing o'er the sea.
> Down at the round equator,
> It leaps forth straight and rapid,
> Driving with firm sharp edge the night before it.
> Here gradually it floods
> The wooded valleys and the weeds
> And the still smokeless cities.
> The cocks crow up at the farms;
> The sick man's spirit is glad;
> The watch treads brisker about the dew-wet deck;
> The light-keeper locks his desk,
> As the lenses turn,
> Faded and yellow.
>
> The girl with the embroidered shift
> Rises and leans on the sill,

And her full bosom heaves
Drinking deep of the silentness.
I too rise and watch
The healing fingers of dawn –
I too drink from its eyes
The unaccountable peace –
I too drink and am satisfied as with food.
Fain would I go
Down by the winding crossroad by the trees,
Where at the corner of wet wood
The blackbird in the early grey and stillness
Wakes his first song.
Peace, who can make verses clink,
Find ictus following surely after ictus,
At such an hour as this, the heart
Lies steeped and silent.
O dreaming, leaning girl,
Already are the sovereign hill-tops ruddy,
Already the grey passes, the white streak
Brightens above dark woodlands, Day begins.

There is real quality in that poem, and the freedom of the verse
seems to have helped Stevenson to bring romance and reality together, to have as a framework traditional images of sunrise but to
insert into the landscape a few details which can be very moving: the
figure of the lighthouse-keeper locking his desk when his huge lenses
grow faded and yellow as the natural light grows (this lighthouse-
keeper comes into other free-verse poems, and Stevenson is obviously
thinking of his father and of his difficult relationship with him), and
then the figure of the dreaming, leaning girl, unexplained, half-
symbolic yet very real, held like the poet by this moment of beauty
and calm before time starts up again and moves them away from the
scene, and also from youth.

I wanted, in quoting that poem, with its quiet, winding, subtle
movement, to emphasize the enormous difference of effect between
it and the banging satire of the passage previously quoted from 'The
Scotsman's Return from Abroad', with its cheery thoughts on universal damnation. Both poems work, but the distance between them
is one measure of what even a minor poet can do.

If we want to ask whether there is anything central, anything
between or among the various extremes in his work, anything at
least that can be defined, this is not easy to answer, since so much of

his effectiveness as a poet comes precisely from the thrill or pathos of oppositions – adventure versus the bonny bield, casting off versus landfall, present experience versus memory, sailor and hunter versus housebuilder and paterfamilias, the delicate and productive tensions of a prolonged immaturity of which he was well aware. Only in a few images, like that of the lighthouse-keeper, do the opposites seem to be temporarily resolved: the man in the lighthouse is both at sea and on land, he is both in great danger and unusually snug, he leads a solitary life but would not be employed if he was by nature un-balanced or morbid, and so he moves between loneliness and family, between the wild elements and the humdrum streets. Stevenson's father's occupation as a lighthouse-designer fascinated Stevenson, quite apart from the already close and tense relation that existed between them. George MacBeth is right in seeing this father-son relationship as being very important in Stevenson, and some good poems are concerned with it in one way or another. The boy's feelings towards his father were a mixture of guilt, envy, admiration, and love, but whatever the feelings were they were strong. When his father eventually became senile, a sick man, unable to recognize the members of his family, Stevenson wrote this short poem about him. It is called 'The Last Sight':

> Once more I saw him. In the lofty room,
> Where oft with lights and company his tongue
> Was trump to honest laughter, sate attired
> A something in his likeness. 'Look!' said one,
> Unkindly kind, 'look up, it is your boy!'
> And the dread changeling gazed on me in vain.

The remarkable power of that last line comes from the fact that the natural order of things *both* seems to be taking its course *and* seems to be turned upside down; the father has become helpless, like a child, in his senility, but unlike a child he has become an object of terror rather than pity to his son looking at him; he is a 'dread changeling' in whom something horrible has been planted from out-side. And there is the further irony that Stevenson himself might well have been called the changeling, in so far as he seemed doomed in his early years to disconcert his parents. The poem is curiously reminiscent of Hugh MacDiarmid's short poem about *his* dying father, 'The Watergaw', with its 'last wild look ye gied/ Afore ye dee'd!', and suggests a similar bond of family experience from which both poets drew some power.

Parents and children are therefore not an unexpected theme to find in Stevenson, and the poems in *A Child's Garden of Verses* (1885) fit very well into his preoccupations. They have been described as about rather than for children, though some children do like them. Reading them today, one can see them as looking straight forward to Ian Hamilton Finlay, who has many affinities with Stevenson's period and whose pre-concrete poems particularly have many of the same qualities as *A Child's Garden of Verses*. I am thinking especially of Stevenson's 'My Bed is a Boat', 'The Lamplighter', 'The Cow', 'Singing', and 'Rain', all of which have not only the sort of subjects Mr Finlay likes but also the same not-quite-innocent eye asking us humorously and gently to look at simple things.

> The rain is raining all around,
> It falls on field and tree,
> It rains on the umbrellas here,
> And on the ships at sea.

Opinions have varied about this part of Stevenson's work, especially as he also wrote a mass of self-confessedly light verse for which no poetic claims were to be made. The *Child's Garden* poems seem to me to have great charm, and not to be light verse in a pejorative sense. The note of his light verse, perky and devil-may-care, is quite different, as in this example from his 'Rhymes to Henley' (VIII):

> We dwell in these melodious days
> When every author trolls his lays;
> And all, except myself and you,
> Must up and print the nonsense, too.
> Why then, if this be so indeed,
> If adamantine walls recede
> And old Apollo's gardens gape
> For Arry and the grinder's ape;
> I too may enter in perchance
> Where paralytic graces dance,
> And cheering on each tottering set
> Blow my falsetto flageolet.

Well, Stevenson did blow his falsetto flageolet quite a lot, and it is no great thing, though even here 'paralytic graces' is good. But the poems in *A Child's Garden* are different, and of better calibre. Are they all, however, boats and rain and cows and lamplighters? Is everything in this garden lovely? There are a surprising number of soldiers and guns and battles around. 'Now, with my little gun, I crawl/ All in the dark along the wall' . . . What is Stevenson doing with his little gun? In another poem, called 'The Dumb Soldier', he tells a very fey tale of how he buried one of his lead soldiers underground in the lawn, and means some day to dig him up again to ask him what it was like lying alone in the dark of the earth. And when, in another poem, he looks for pictures in the fire, what does Stevenson's child see? Armies and burning cities.

> Armies march by tower and spire
> Of cities blazing, in the fire;
> Till as I gaze with staring eyes,
> The armies fade, the lustre dies.
>
> Then once again the glow returns;
> Again the phantom city burns;
> And down the red-hot valley, lo!
> The phantom armies marching go!
>
> Blinking embers, tell me true
> Where are those armies marching to,
> And what the burning city is
> That crumbles in your furnaces!

Every boy, perhaps, plays with soldiers and sees armies in the fire. But there does seem something particular, something underlined, in these poems of Stevenson's – notably the one where he buries the unresisting soldier in the lawn. It was not for nothing that A. E. Housman found himself so strongly attracted to Stevenson, and looking at it from a wider angle one can think back to George MacBeth's remark about the 'love of clandestine violence'. The fact is that there is an aspect of Stevenson to which violence appeals, and in this he is linked to a number of his contemporaries, including Housman, Henley, Kipling, and Davidson. A full picture of Stevenson must therefore take this into account. Under the velvet jacket, the arm is covered with thick black hair. In his essay on Edgar Allan Poe, Stevenson says of his story 'Berenice': 'Horrible as it is, [it] touches a chord in one's own breast, though perhaps it is a chord that had better be left alone.' In his prose, as we know, he could not leave it alone, and so we have *Dr. Jekyll and Mr. Hyde*, *Markheim*, *Thrawn Janet*, and many other intimations of a dark sub-world which was extremely real to him and of which he gives a powerful account. But in the poetry too, the violent world now and again looks out at us and makes us wonder about the sources of Stevenson's art. In one of the poems included by George MacBeth in his *Penguin Book of Victorian Verse*, a poem called 'To S. C.' (that is, Sidney Colvin) Stevenson writes his friend a verse letter, a verse meditation, from the South Seas, looking back from a night scene of throbbing sea and flailing palm-trees to the calm London streets near the British Museum. But the familiar exile's poem is given a strange twist: what he asks Colvin to do, the next time he goes to the British Museum, is to stop and gaze at the huge Easter Island statues at the entrance – they too are exiles, though exiles of a different kind:

> One moment glance, where by the pillared wall
> Far-voyaging island gods, begrimed with smoke,
> Sit now unworshipped, the rude monument
> Of faiths forgot and races undivined:
> Sit now disconsolate, remembering well
> The priest, the victim, and the songful crowd,
> The blaze of the blue noon, and that huge voice,
> Incessant, of the breakers on the shore.
> As far as these from their ancestral shrine,
> So far, so foreign, your divided friends
> Wander, estranged in body, not in mind.

It is a firmly controlled and striking passage where Stevenson, in the South Seas, identifies himself with the displaced Easter Island gods, and what he associates these blank mysterious gods with is human sacrifice, 'the priest, the victim, and the songful crowd'. Like the graves of the martyrs on the Scottish moors, and the Standing Stones behind that, the Easter Island monoliths move and disturb him in a way that he does not want to analyse.

But although he does not analyse it, he lets the evidence appear again and again. In one of the longer poems in his posthumous volume *Songs of Travel* (1896) he lets us into a larger area of this experience. This poem, 'The Woodman', takes as its subject the clearing of jungle overgrowth in Vailima when he was building his house there. It was very hard and difficult work, and he felt increasingly, as he hacked away at the lianas, that nature was not indifferent but hostile to man, and had a frightening life of its own which could never be understood but could only be combated, to the death if necessary. He ends up in a position that might be described as exactly the opposite of Wordsworth's, bearing out rather neatly the argument that 'Wordsworth in the tropics' would be a very different man. Of course Stevenson is writing after Darwin, and Darwin is in the poem too. But mainly it is the reflection of personal experience, and the reader gets the impression that Stevenson, by the time he reaches the last section of the poem, has almost frightened himself with the discovery of his own ruthlessness and ruthless enjoyment of the struggle. The battle here is only against vegetable nature, yet he senses, unmistakably, that his feelings reverberate outward into the whole human struggle, into human society both at peace and in war. Here is how the poem ends:

> The common lot we scarce perceive.
> Crowds perish, we nor mark nor grieve:
> The bugle calls – we mourn a few!
> What corporal's guard at Waterloo?
> What scanty hundreds more or less
> In the man-devouring Wilderness?
> What handful bled on Delhi ridge?
> – See, rather, London, on thy bridge
> The pale battalions trample by,
> Resolved to slay, resigned to die.
> Count, rather, all the maimed and dead
> In the unbrotherly war of bread . . .
> Why prate of peace? when, warriors all,
> We clank in harness into hall,
> And ever bare upon the board
> Lies the necessary sword.
> In the green field or quiet street,
> Besieged we sleep, beleaguered eat;
> Labour by day and wake o' nights,
> In war with rival appetites.
> The rose on roses feeds; the lark
> On larks. The sedentary clerk
> All morning with a diligent pen
> Murders the babes of other men;
> And like the beasts of wood and park,
> Protects his whelps, defends his den.
>
> Unshamed the narrow aim I hold;
> I feed my sheep, patrol my fold;
> Breathe war on wolves and rival flocks,
> A pious outlaw on the rocks

> Of God and morning; and when time
> Shall bow, or rivals break me, climb
> Where no undubbed civilian dares,
> In my war harness, the loud stairs
> Of honour; and my conqueror
> Hail me a warrior fallen in war.

A pious outlaw on the rocks/ Of God and morning'. This is a very different Stevenson from the rather precious and namby-pamby figure we sometimes, though wrongly, persuade ourselves we are beginning to see in him; it is different even from the self-portrait quoted earlier; the constant imagery of war and warriors is partly the invalid's quite natural desire for action and adventure, it is partly the husband's equally natural protective gesture over his property and environment, and yet again it is something more, and 'the love of clandestine violence' is a phrase that although loaded is not entirely off the mark. As Housman loves the soldiers he kills in his verse, so Stevenson seems to be attracted by what he calls 'the man-devouring Wilderness', and by that 'handful' that 'bled on Delhi ridge'.

I have tried to show that Stevenson's poetry is not all of the surface, though even the surface has more variety than is commonly supposed. He has his depths, his surprises, his shocks for the unwary reader. He was writing at a time when it was difficult for poetry to be good, and one must not fall too hard on shortcomings which he often shares with his contemporaries. When one compares him with Gerard Manley Hopkins, who lived at the same time and also died in his mid-forties, then of course it is impossible not to see the difference between a man who was a poet to his finger-tips and one who like Stevenson was an occasional poet whose main work lay elsewhere, in prose. But Hopkins is dazzling and it is important to give Stevenson his due. His verse is a genuine part of the tradition of Scottish poetry, which it extends in more than one direction, and in addition to that it holds out a range of poetic effects and pleasures which is, I believe, a good deal wider than we have been accustomed to assume. The hunter may be home from the hill, but at least he brought something back.

Edinburgh Stevenson Lecture, 1970.

Part Three

Part Three

Registering the Reality of Scotland

I SWITCH on the telly; a fierce, black, wild-haired, utterly un-Caucasian face fills the screen; an American Black Panther is being interviewed about his aim to establish a separate black state in America; then he speaks – and when I hear the familiar flat American drawl it is almost as if he was being dubbed, there is such disparity between the man and his language. And I can't help saying to myself, No, it won't work: no black language, no black state; make your speech in Yoruba, man, then I'll believe you. That the black Americans have lost their original languages beyond recovery goes without saying. Or does it? If I was a Black Panther I would be thinking about the problem. But that may be only because as a Scot I have an age-old language problem in my own country and am extrapolating irrelevancies from it. There is undeniably something very attractive about the idea of a language expressing and preserving the 'soul' of a people. The Russians have always felt this particularly strongly, but they are far from being the only ones. Language riots, whether in Canada, Belgium, or India, continue to testify that the global village is in no mood yet to plug itself in to a universal circuit. On this untidy planet, linguistic and national boundaries will often refuse to coincide, and yet, as the history of a small, much-conquered, much-oppressed country like Hungary shows clearly, the language of the people can be the strongest and in the end most potent national binding-force and inspiration. It is where history has dropped its stitches all over the place that an apparently insoluble problem will go on rankling and grumbling for centuries, until sheer time and change, rather than literary will or political action, simply cut the knot, and 'what is left' is 'the solution'. When one lives in one of the linguistically untidy places, the consciousness of this attritional process is what stabs the heart. Everyone knows that languages, like moas and dinosaurs, do die. What stories did the Etruscans tell their children? Or the Easter Islanders? Their dumb scripts fill us with rage and pity.

Scotland is one of the untidy places, and Scottish speech is both extremely varied and extremely unstable. Gaelic, no doubt slowly declining but giving out notably vigorous kicks in the process from poets like Sorley Maclean and Iain Crichton Smith, has less place in the national life than Welsh has in Wales, largely because it is not the only alternative to English, and Scottish patriotism and nationalism have tended to gravitate to the more accessible alternative, Lowland Scots (or 'Lallans', or simply 'Scots'). Lowland Scots today may be only the shreds of a language, but they are remarkably tenacious and expressive threads which show no signs of disappearing. The answer to the question, What do people speak in Scotland? cannot be given directly, since it depends to an unusual extent on social relations and social habits, and the instability, the mixture of Scots and English forms, which one can hear every day, is so thinly reflected in literature and journalism that the realities of the linguistic situation either seem to be poorly recognized, or are felt to be unproductive. On the whole, people seem not to *want* to recognize them. Newspapers, for example, reporting interviews with working-class citizens, never report what such speakers actually say – it is all tidied up and normalized into English, and yet quotation marks are used, even though no local reader of the newspaper, if he thought about it, would believe it was a direct quotation. Recently, a BBC (Scotland) news announcer with a marked Glasgow accent was removed, after letters of protest had been received from outraged sensibilities. Yet the non-English, almost like a non-conscious underground movement, persists. There's a good comment on the whole problem in Gordon M. Williams's novel *From Scenes Like These* (1968). The young hero, a boy of fifteen from the tenements of an Ayrshire industrial town who is working on a near-by farm, is trying to puzzle out the shifts and stances of the 'languages' he hears in the different environmental situations he is involved in:

> It was very strange how the old man [i.e. the farmer] changed accents. Sometimes he spoke to you in broad Scots, sometimes in what the schoolteachers called proper English. They were very hot on proper English at the school. Once he'd got a right showing-up in the class for accidentally pronouncing butter 'bu'er'. Miss Fitzgerald had gone on (him having to stand in front of the class) about the glottal stop being dead common and very low-class, something that would damn you if

you wanted a decent job. A decent job – like a bank! His mother spoke proper English, but then she was hellish keen on proving they were respectable. His father spoke common Kilcaddie, which he knew his mother didn't like. When the Craigs spoke broad it wasn't quite the same as common Kilcaddie – some of their expressions sounded as though they came straight out of Rabbie Burns! Telfer had a Kilcaddie accent, but he pronounced all his words properly, no doubt from seeing too many pictures. McCann spoke very coarse and broad, but there was something false about him, as though he put it on deliberately.

He still spoke the school's idea of proper English, he knew that all right because every time he opened his mouth he could hear himself sounding like a real wee pan-loaf toff . . . It would be a lot healthier if folk spoke one way. Sometimes you heard them say 'eight' and sometimes 'eicht', sometimes 'farm' and sometimes 'ferm'. Sometimes 'ye' and sometimes 'youse' and sometimes 'yese' and sometimes 'you'. Sometimes 'half' and sometimes 'hauf'. Was it your faither or your father? Your mither or your mother? . . . Why teach kids that Burns was the great national poet and then tell you his old Scots words were dead common? What sounds better – 'gie your face a dicht wi' a clootie' or 'give your face a wipe with a cloth'? One was Scottish and natural and the other was a lot of toffee-nosed English shite.

What emerges from this interesting passage – and it is very true to life – is that the complexities and ambiguities of the language situation in Scotland mirror the uncertainties, antagonisms, and ambitions of social life, not only in what is usually regarded as the most obvious difference between Scots/vulgar/slovenly and English/educated/articulate (i.e. the class-conscious sense that bank clerks and glo'al stops just don't go), but also in the marked town/country difference between the less broad Ayrshire Scots of the boy's towns-man father and the much thicker Scots of the farming Craigs, and then again in personal differences like that between the cinema-influenced Telfer and the deliberately earthy McCann. And of course running through these differences, to remind us how unstable they really are, is the latent bilingualism in which accents and vocabularies can be quickly trip-switched to meet matters and encounters as they arise. My cleaner will regale me with a racy account of a man so mean that 'ach, he widny gie a blin hen a wurrm!' – and the next moment she will be answering the telephone in a pretty fair imitation of standard English. To the boy in Gordon Williams's story, it would be 'a lot healthier if folk spoke one way'. It would, if we equate a sort of linguistic schizophrenia with the whole social and national uncertainty of what 'being a Scotsman' is, and it is tempting to make this equation. On the other hand, national feeling exists, and can override the weird geological faults we carry about with us in our speech-systems. Clearly, an independent Scotland would have to think about the national tongue, make decisions and recommendations, and perhaps try to raise the status of spoken and written Scots by easy stages, though at the same time it would be haunted, given the political realities of the modern world, by the burdensome spectre of bilingualism (Scots and English) or even trilingualism (Scots, English, and Gaelic). But until that situation comes about, I would certainly feel that heavily entrenched positions regarding language in Scotland are not very profitable. I would rather see the mixed state that exists being explored and exploited, more truthfully and spontaneously and hence more seriously than at present, by writers, and by playwrights and novelists in particular. It may be that we have a blessing in disguise. But if we want to uncover it we shall have to use our ears more and our grammar-books less. Archie Hind has a good but at times rather sticky novel about working-class Glasgow called *The Dear Green Place* (1966). There is also a taped interview with him in *Scottish International* 11 (September 1970). If he could inject into his fiction a stream of the free, vigorously tumbling immediacies of that spoken interview – then we would be getting somewhere.

It is no doubt from the accumulation of small specifics, quite as much as from any overbearing and indefinable sense of a huge hinterland of national qualities or 'soul', that we can still find something meaningful in the phrase 'the Scots tongue'. Nor would there necessarily be Gaelic opposition to such a concept, though the Gaelic poet in his cups might be the first to make merry with the excesses of the modern Lallans poets. It was encouraging to find the highly gifted and articulate Gaelic poet Sorley Maclean, at a conference on Scottish culture held in Aberdeen in 1970, making this comment on Scots:

> Here is Scots, you have a language which is a Teutonic language like English, so near to English, and yet in many ways so different. It raises questions about what poetry is at any rate, or what communication in any kind of language is: you can just put the same thing, put the thing with a fair intellectual certainty very close intellectually, you see, and yet it is so completely different . . . Even when it's fairly English, you see. 'You're not Mary Morison.' . . . Eh? That raises questions

about this business of the consciousness as far as the consciousness can be expressed in language!

(from transcript of recorded discussion, published in
Scottish International 10, May 1970)

Sorley Maclean was absolutely right: to a Scottish ear, the apparently minute difference between an anglified 'You're not Mary Morison' and what Burns in his song actually wrote – 'Ye are na Mary Morison' – is a significant and unforgettable difference. But how much licence do such minimal distinguishing marks confer? To that question, no one yet finds an easy answer; the main thing is to keep searching for it.

Planet, 4 (February–March 1971).

The Resources of Scotland

AN OLD pot seething with dissatisfaction which fortunately can be relied on never to come to the boil might be the English politician's view of Scotland. Something of the same irritability, allied to a similar short-circuiting of full power, has often been felt in the past to characterize the Scottish literary scene. The egg cracks, and out steps Vociferous Fissiparous, son of Antisyzygy. The Pictish succession is assured. But there are signs of change, signs of a dissolving of this stereotype, which have been emerging gradually in the past three or four years.

No one could say that a spirit of sweet cooperation has descended on Scotland, but there is evidence that the old polarities do not command the devotion they did. Many writers (and educators and others) have clearly decided that some approach to a concerted effort is both possible and opportune, not only as a rescue operation for Scottish writing of the past (including the recent past) which is neglected or out of print but also as a positive encouragement of contemporary writing through information and discussion. The Association for Scottish Literary Studies, the Lallans Society, Comunn na Cànain Albannaich (the Scottish Language Society), and Club Leabhar (the Highland Book Club) are all recently formed organizations which may have a diversity of aim but which taken together are beginning to plot out, show, recommend and develop the whole literary culture of Scotland.

'Literary culture of Scotland' is a desperately plastic phrase for what people actually feel, write, read, speak, sing, and act, and obviously the literature of any place will remain to some extent as unamenable to encouragement as to polemic or apathy. You can't help Sholokhov; you can't hinder Solzhenitsyn. Yet the bristly, defensive divisiveness of so much Scottish culture, however well-rooted it has been in real differences and real difficulties, has had a long innings and not always a very productive one, and we might well give its opposite a chance.

The feeling that accompanies these remarks – and I know that others share it – is rather like the end of Philip Larkin's 'The Whitsun Weddings', a sense of disparate things coming together and (because they are brought together) being released towards a destination. Those who share the feeling would not always agree as to whether the destination is the recovery of a national self-respect (a *natural* self-respect – a national self-*credibility*, for God's sake!) or something that in the end can only be political, whether devolution or independence. Political in the widest sense it already is, if anything that earnestly concerns the cultural health of a nation is political – and Tom Scott's long, gritty social meditation 'Auld Sanct-Aundraeans: Brand Soliloquises' is neither more nor less so concerned than Ian Hamilton Finlay's 'The Olsen Excerpts' with its punning double tribute to the Scottish fishing industry and to Charles Olson and the genius loci. Between two such extremes of literary expression (and Tom Scott would no doubt deny that 'The Olsen Excerpts' is even literary) there is scant hobnobbing, yet someone like Ezra Pound would understand both, and how both can be related to the needs of a time and a place.

But the pressure towards something that would be political in the narrower sense is also undeniably present in the general movement I have been outlining. There is not only a very widespread feeling that some sort of devolution is necessary, but there is also, now, the awareness that the constitutional changes which must take place in Ireland, and even in the United Kingdom itself as a result of entry into the Common Market, give the first opportunity for hundreds of years of rethinking the whole constitutional situation. It is significant that when *Lines Review* 37 (June 1971) was given over completely to an anti-nationalist essay, 'The Knitted Claymore', by the poet Alan Jackson, this proved to be rather a damp squib. Those who were attacked replied; but there was no great debate, as there would have been ten years ago. This is not to say that the essay was not useful in launching a few sprightly darts at the uglier, knuckle-rapping, xenophobic side of nationalism (which of course is not peculiar to Scotland), but Alan Jackson pushed his case too far until it began to topple over, and it was indeed virtually contradicted by some of his own passing parentheses (since he is an honest man). The main effect revealed by the essay, however, was that writers as a whole were no longer eager to join in the false fray of a flyting since flyting is an art form and not a true agent of change, for all its appearance of violent involvement.

So although it would obviously be untrue to say that 'we are all nationalists now', there is nevertheless something approaching a consensus among Scottish writers that what is being produced here – forgetting all the older and perhaps threadbare definitions of 'Scottish' – has some value and is worth encouraging, especially by writers being willing to stay and work in their own country. But what guarantee have we got that what we are doing is distinctive and could not have been produced anywhere else?

The mature answer would be that there is no such guarantee and that it does not matter: Scottish writers must simply write as well as they can, and leave it to others to decide whether their provenance stands out, and what value it infuses into their work. Unfortunately Scotland is not in a mature state, and that mature answer would still be something of a luxury. So long as the political situation remains unhappy, the economic situation unhappier, and the language situation as complex and confused as it is, a Scottish writer will tend to be tugged, kicking against the pricks as hard as he likes, into at least the but if not the ben of involvement with the whole north-of-the-border ethos problem. Here, bad vibrations abound for many. What – do your own thing, in Scotland?

> inner attractional
> somebody says death
> and they all come rushing
> home to agree and look stern and solemn:
> enter fourteen editors with analysis kits.

(Tom McGrath, 'Nicotine Withdrawal' Psychotic Rage Poem)

And how to relate yourself to traditions that may seem more like locks than keys?

> let us exorcise
> the old god of Scotland
> with his knotted brain and jellyfish eyes
> who has tormented his children
> from generation into generation

(Tom Buchan, 'Exorcism')

And history? What use is history? Is history not the opium of the imagination?

> (Eastward
> Culloden

where the sun shone
on the feeding raven.
Let it be forgotten!)

(Iain Crichton Smith, 'The White Air of March')

These quotations may suggest that the contemporary Scottish writer often finds himself saying: Redefine my task; redefine my field of operations; redefine my country.

To a Highlander like Iain Crichton Smith, bilingual in Gaelic and English, and prolific in poetry, novels, short stories, plays, essays and reviews, the problem of definition must always be particularly acute because the national aspirations of (mainly) Lowland Scotland can scarcely be his, because his 'country' is not only Oban and Lewis but a country of the mind that stretches from Robert Lowell to Kafka and Dostoevsky, and because his first language, Gaelic, is so obviously in a state of decline that to attempt to extend and modernize its expressive potential (as he has done – and been blamed for it by conservative Gaels) can only seem a paradoxical activity. In one of his Gaelic poems he speaks of himself in the image of a court jester, dressed in motley – 'Beurl' is Gàidhlig, dubh is dearg' (English and Gaelic, black and red) – and fears that in the rainstorms of his anxiety the two colours will run into one and become indistinct and muddy. Yet, although his Gaelic is freely peppered with English words, both in order to produce special effects and also (as he admits) for experiment's sake, he is clear in his mind that such things have to be done and tried, whatever hope or lack of hope there may be for the future of the tongue. As he points out, Gaelic and English are in entirely dissimilar situations, each of which offers its special challenge to a creative writer: 'So much has *not* been done in Gaelic that confronted by such a huge uncharted waste one is tempted to spread one's energies, and to try new things. So much in English has already been done that the situation is different.'

Gaelic poetry, then, not only survives but survives strongly, in the work of Iain Crichton Smith, Derick Thomson, George Campbell Hay, Donald MacAulay, and above all, Sorley Maclean. But as Colm Brogan has remarked, 'It is no good trying to be the Proust of the Hebrides.' The Gaels have never taken to the novel as a literary form and there are few serious examples of it. Nor is there any Gaelic professional theatre, though many plays have been written for the amateur stage, and Gaelic drama has been produced on television, played somewhat stiltedly by amateur actors. Poetry and song can be trusted to survive under the most adverse conditions, and it is the meagre development of the other forms that shows the relative weakness of the Gaelic cultural position on any over-all view.

Gaelic writers themselves are not given to making optimistic pronouncements about the future of the language, and the prospect of its ever becoming the national tongue of Scotland is even more remote than that of its sister-languages in Ireland and Wales. Comunn na Cànain Albannaich, founded in 1969, is devoted precisely to the implementation of that remote end, and this organization has the brave slogan 'Tìr gun chànain, tìr gun anam' (The country without a language is a country without a soul). But what is Scotland's language? Most people would regard the Society's title, Scottish Language Society, as a somewhat high-handed appropriation, since Gaelic looms less large in the Scottish consciousness than Welsh does in Wales. The 'Scottish Language', for most Scots who think about the matter, is primarily Lowland Scots, or Scots, or Lallans – it is best called Scots. The Lallans Society, established in 1972, would have called itself the Scots Language Society but for the naughty pre-emption of Comunn na Cànain Albannaich. There is obviously a place for both groups, however, and they could even draw together in a growing climate of opinion that favours de-Londonization as a general aim.

One of the chief objects of the Lallans Society is 'to foster and promote the emergence of Lallans as a language'. This'll no gang faur furrit till mair an mair fowk – educatit fowk anaa – kin be persuadit tae *yaise* the leid an no fin it lauchable tae dae sae. Gin ye're lauchin owre whit's prentit here thenoo, I'se tak ye tae the Race Relations Board, ma mannie, an nae boather. The trouble is that 'Scots' is itself a far from monolithic term, ranging in applicability from the Scotch English that is mainly a matter of accent plus the occasional 'scunner' or 'outwith', to the varieties of urban and rural Scots which at their raciest (Glasgow, say, or Aberdeenshire) depend on quite a thick complex of non-English speech-habits.

All of these are available to, though underexploited by, the Scottish writer, for both verse and prose. The Scottish writer's dilemma today is that while he might want to keep helping a general literary Scots to develop, whether in the eclectic or 'Synthetic Scots' tradition of Hugh MacDiarmid or in some other way, he is on the other hand strongly urged, by the movement towards not only a spoken poetry (if he happens to be a poet or perhaps a playwright) but also a 'sincerity' theory of artistic expression (whether in verse or prose), to write on a basis of the actual language of men. On the whole, the second alternative is in the ascendant among younger poets using Scots (e.g., Donald Campbell and Duncan Glen) or more specifically an urban dialect (Stephen Mulrine, Tom Leonard). Novelists, possibly frustrated by their London publishers who are afraid that glo'al stopes, or even bus-stopes, might reduce sales, are disappointingly smooth and untruthful in their dialogue these days, with very few exceptions; it is high time they reasserted the ear and the tongue. The Glasgow speech in short stories by Alan Spence shows a nice awareness of what is wanted.

There is also a great deadlock to be broken in the theatre, where directors and managements seem to be hypnotized rigid by the polarity of Received Standard versus Costume Scots – neither of which any Scotsman actually speaks. Only rarely do Scottish theatre audiences hear that modest and unforced reflection of their own living speech-habits which an English or American audience takes for granted. Revivals of Bridie; C. P. Taylor's *Bread and Butter*; Stewart Conn's *I Didn't Always Live Here*; Bill Bryden's *Willie Rough*; recent plays by Joan Ure and Alasdair Gray; and that's about the list. The small and still struggling Stage Company (Scotland) has been formed to encourage the writing and performing of such plays, and this is a hopeful sign, though it remains to be seen what real impact the company will make. Naturalism is no panacea, and in any case television to some extent takes care of it, but it would be good to have at least one theatre which was devoted to exhibiting and exploring the actual state of life in Scotland. At the same time, an honest observer has to admit that such an alien and unScottish theatre as the Glasgow Citizens' has become under Giles Havergal also has a useful function, a function recognized by its enthusiastic and often young audience, despite unrelenting rifle-fire from Scottish critics. What could be more incongruous than a company who eschew Scottish plays and Scottish actors developing a stunningly physical, spectacular, antiverbocentric, and markedly transvestite theatre on an island of the crumbling half-demolished Gorbals? Stuffy old uptight heterosexual Scotland may not take kindly yet to the gestures of a male Cleopatra, riggish as they come, but disguise and trans- formation and the use of the body are what theatre is about, and the Scots have been apt to forget this, in their strongly literalized and often literal-minded ways of thinking. The very incongruity of the Citizens' is dialectically productive – and highly suited to Glasgow, that incongruous place.

But suppose we strip away the props, the local speech, the language societies, the desideria. What minimum exists that would make us say, This is a Scottish, and not an English or 'British' writer? Subject-matter or thematic interest would give us an answer in many cases: George Mackay Brown's Orkney, though stylized, is still Orkney; the Edinburgh of Sydney Goodsir Smith and Robert Garioch, and the Aberdeen of Alexander Scott, come through strongly as places, even if satirized or fantasticated; the Glasgow of Archie Hind or of Cliff Hanley has not been imagined or got up; the brooding intensity with which 'the matter of Scotland' is treated in Fionn MacColla could only come from a ruthless identification with one place, one country. But is Norman MacCaig's 'Culag Pier' really about Culag Pier? Is the sharp-clawed creator of Miss Jean Brodie, a writer quoted as claiming that she must remain an ex-patriate Scot since she 'could not hope to be understood' in Edinburgh, a Scottish novelist? Is Sheila MacLeod (ex-Stornoway) or Campbell Black (ex-Glasgow) a Scottish novelist? The strict answer to these questions can only be an unsatisfactory 'yes and no', since life and the pursuit of literature are not tidy and docketable.

But it is a matter of contexts. Within Scotland at the present time, with the desire to gather together rather than to disperse, and with the consciousness of a common effort being at last not utterly inconceivable, the inclusiveness of 'yes' – whatever the risk of accusations of chauvinism – would be preferred to the pedantry of 'no'. The ongoing bibliography of current Scottish writing published in the extremely useful and (one is ashamed to say it) pioneering *Scottish Literary News* (the newsletter of the Association for Scottish Literary Studies) makes no apology for including all items emanating from Scottish hands, so that Chaim Bermant and Flashman rub shoulders with Helen Cruickshank's *Collected Poems* and Sorley Maclean's *Poems to Eimhir*.

And this is as it should be, it is impossible not to add. There comes a time when out of respect for itself a country must collect its resources, and look at its assets and shortcomings with an eye that is both sharp and warm: see what is there, what is not there, what could be there. Perilously, without any political underpinning yet, Scotland is now consciously at that stage, and that is mainly what I as both observer and participator have wanted to write about here, rather than draw out a painful and familiar filigree of the 'Scottish qualities' of X's novel or Y's poem or Z's play. We can hope that, having taken certain almost tacit decisions within Scotland, we are now getting on with the job.

The Times Literary Supplement, 28 July 1972.

The Beatnik in the Kailyaird

A FEW years ago I was walking through Kelvingrove Park in Glasgow, on a fine summer afternoon, when two little girls came running up to me. They looked rather frightened. The older one, who would be about eight or nine, said: 'Oh mister, wid ye take us oot the park?' I asked what was wrong, and apparently a man had been following them, and had spoken to them. 'I didny like the looks of him.' And the final sinister touch: 'He spoke kinna English.'

No doubt a philologist would maintain that the girl too was speaking a 'kind of English', but the point of the story is that she had instantly reacted to the stranger's suave Suddron accent, with its wellbred consonants and unforthright diphthongs, as to a thing that was alien and suspicious in itself. And this may serve to illustrate something wider: although Englishmen do not have to worry about their relation or attitude to Scotland, the Scots have, and have long had, to worry about their relation and attitude to England, or to the English-speaking world. No country which has once been independent, and is then overshadowed in union with a more powerful partner, can develop naturally and happily. Its political history is officially closed, but emotionally it remains unfinished. Its cultural traditions soon begin to show a lack of integration, and though this does not preclude fine work in a variety of styles it does mean that the steady maturing and enriching of traditions which is characteristic of the greatest cultures is constantly frustrated, either by a sentimental native conservatism or by desperate attempts to imitate the modes of the dominating neighbour culture.

For a century after the Union of 1707, it seemed as if Scotland might escape these dangers. The patriotic desire to rediscover and make creative use of Scottish traditions and history, which we associate with Ramsay, Fergusson, Burns, Scott, Galt, and the ballad-collectors, was balanced by creative intellectual activity in philosophy, science, and technology which placed men like Adam Smith, Hume, Watt, and Telford squarely within the European frame. When we add to this a resurgence of Gaelic poetry in Alexander MacDonald, Duncan Ban MacIntyre, and Rob Donn, and the astonishing impact of James Macpherson's Ossianic rifacimentos, it might seem that Allan Ramsay was being unduly pessimistic when he complained in 1719:

> The chiels of London, Cam, and Ox,
> Ha'e rais'd up great Poetick Stocks
> Of Rapes, of Buckets, Sarks and Locks,
> > While we neglect
> To shaw their betters. This provokes
> > Me to reflect
>
> On the lear'd days of Gawn Dunkell,
> Our Country then a Tale cou'd tell,
> Europe had nane mair snack and snell
> > At Verse or Prose;
> Our Kings were Poets too themsell,
> > Bauld and Jocose.

Yet within these lines one can see something of the reasons why the eighteenth-century brilliance was shortlived, why after the death of Scott in 1832 (to take a convenient date) Scottish writing declined rapidly in sharpness, depth, and international interest, although it retained and increased its local popularity. Ramsay is keenly aware of English literature, of the new vigorous sophisticated neoclassical tradition centring on Pope; with his Scotch pride he wants to 'shaw their betters'; but all that his mind offers him is a wistful reflection on how fine things were in the good old days of Gavin Douglas and the Makars. Back to Douglas, or forward with Pope? Later poets may say, Back to Dunbar, or forward with Yeats (or Eliot, or William Carlos Williams) – but the problem is the same, and this particular dilemma has dogged Scottish writers like the ghost of their country's history.

The real challenge of the nineteenth century was not met, because our authors still hankered after an increasingly simplified, blunted, and vulgarized vision of the native tradition (the 'world of Scotch drink, Scotch religion, and Scotch manners' that Matthew Arnold spoke of), a tradition which could no longer serve a living literature without drastic reconstruction to meet the drastic social and economic changes that had taken place in Scotland since 1750. Writers found an easy popularity within certain overworked but never-failing stereotypes (indicated by the titles of some poems in the mid-Victorian *Whistle-Binkie* anthologies: 'The Harp and the Haggis', 'Brandy versus Beauty', 'Friends around the Table Set', 'My Granny's Fireside': an unfortunate, exaggerated reinforcement, by general Victorian sentimentality, of the genuinely popular themes already made dangerously legendary by Burns. One misses the robustness of the eighteenth century – the robustness of the chapbooks, and of the chief chapbook poet and storyteller Dougal Graham, the wandering pedlar and later 'skellat bellman' of Glasgow whose work in verse and prose earned the praise of Sir Walter Scott ('coarse but excessively meritorious pieces of popular humour') and who was described by a contemporary as being 'an unco glib body at the pen, and could screed aff a bit penny history in less than nae time. A' his warks took weel – they were level to the meanest capacity.' The racy Scottish dialogue and earthy authenticity of Graham - some of his crude, hastily-sketched genre pictures read like a sort of proleptic rebuttal of 'The Cotter's Saturday Night', to say nothing of 'My Granny's Fireside' – belong no doubt to a degenerate 'minstrel' tradition of recited or sung and half-dramatized literature which could scarcely survive the establishment of newspapers and popular magazines; but although this can be recognized as a tradition in decay, these chapbooks are in some ways much closer to the life of their period than the more moralistic Victorian equivalents are to theirs. As William Harvey wrote many years ago: 'The distinctive chapbook ... affords a faithful reflex of life as it really was. Graham was an early 'kailyairder', who reared his plants from a stronger and more strictly Scottish soil than Barrie or Maclaren or Crockett.' (*Scottish Chapbook Literature*, 1903)

Intellectuals and reformers, of course, must guard against lashing themselves into a fury over the Kailyaird. Not only is there an important place for sentiment and pathos in any literature, but the whole history of nineteenth-century culture in Scotland, and the reasons for the continued appeal of some form of Kailyaird right down to the present time, still remain to be properly investigated. No one would blame the modern Scottish Renascence writers for their violent reaction against the Kailyaird, but such a reaction was liable to depreciate certain central qualities, as if a man should refuse bread because he finds he can eat oysters. (What may be legitimately criticized, for example, in some of Hugh MacDiarmid's writing, is simply a lack of warmth, a failure or a banishing of ordinary human sympathy. When other powers and virtues are gained, this may not seem a severe price to pay; yet it is necessary to remember that it is a price.) Scottish critics have remained surprisingly incurious (apart from George Blake in his useful survey *Barrie and the Kailyard School*) about a tradition which so hugely embraces – to throw good, bad, and mediocre together – Burns and Galt, D. M. Moir and S. R. Crockett, J. J. Bell and Annie S. Swan, Barrie and Joe Corrie, William Soutar and Harry Lauder, the *Sunday Post* and the *One O'Clock Gang*. A revaluation of Kailyard will come, if only because some deep-rooted human feelings are involved in the phenomenon, and it may then be possible to study what it has to offer, while continuing to reject its falsifications.

A typical Kailyard theme of the Maclaren-Crockett school at the end of the nineteenth century might show the 'lad o' pairts' in some country village who is carefully nurtured by the local dominie and minister, goes to university in a city like Glasgow, and quickly dies of consumption, perhaps with a ray of light from the setting sun falling neatly on his calm white face as he expires. What is wrong with these stories is not that they bear no relation to the realities of Scottish life – there were plenty of promising students who came to Glasgow and died young from tuberculosis in the appalling lodgings they had to live in – but that these incidents are being used by the author for sentimental purposes, for a luxurious wallowing in a supposedly uplifting grief. The Kailyard writer was not concerned with tracing the social conditions that led to such happenings, or with the altering or removal of these conditions. He would not accept that the death of the lad o' pairts was an ugly and shocking thing, instead of a mere occasion for beautiful sentiment and religious consolation. In this the Kailyairders were far behind enlightened opinion in Scotland, but they could still appeal – perhaps all the more strongly – to that large body of both middle-class and working-class readers which disliked (and still dislikes) having to readjust its ideas in the pages of a work of fiction. This does not mean that they were not dealing with situations where a strong and genuine pathos was waiting, like the sword in the stone, to be liberated by a master hand. There could have been a Dickens, a Gogol, or a Chekhov, who would deal with narrow, provincial, Kailyard material but would transform it into art by his anger or satire or hope. The alternative to Kailyard was not necessarily John Davidson and his Nietzschean 'cohabitation with eternity', or John Davidson's admirer Hugh MacDiarmid. In fact it was not poets Scotland needed so much as good novelists, and one of the most disappointing features of modern Scottish literature has been our failure to develop the novel, or even to take the novel seriously as a dominant literary form. There are plenty of Scottish novels, many of them highly entertaining; but how many are there that we can even begin to study seriously as works of art – comparing them with the best examples from England, America, or Russia? The one thing a novelist, however imaginative, must be able to do, is to look at life honestly and use human experience on a basis of observation. But in Scotland the step from a more or less documentary realism to a developed novelistic realism has proved particularly hard to take, partly because Scottish documentary writers – in reminiscences, autobiographies, diaries, etc. – have been so excellent as to make fiction seem an indulgence and a delusion. There is really no English equivalent of John Galt's *Annals of the Parish*, a work of such accepted truthfulness in its portrayal of a changing society that it is quoted by historians; yet when Galt came to write novels which were based less closely and continuously on social documentation, novels which were in the real sense 'fiction', some of his art deserted him, and the *Annals* remains his finest book, even though pigeonholers are doubtful whether to call it a novel or not. It seems to me, therefore, no accident that a work like the geologist Hugh Miller's *My Schools and Schoolmasters*, packed with interesting fact and circumstance, has a greater value than most of the mid-Victorian Scottish novels contemporary with it; or that Neil Munro's 'chronicle' *The Brave Days* is more rewarding in the end than most of his stories of Highland life; or that George Blake should have been able to wield a livelier, more convincing pen as a commentator and historian of his times than as a novelist. The deep, thrilling imaginative realism of the novel, which is found sporadically in Scott and Stevenson, and flared up grandly but isolatedly in Lewis Grassic Gibbon, has never established a lasting tradition in Scotland; interrupted now by sentimentality (the Kailyairders), now by facetiousness (Eric Linklater and Compton Mackenzie), now by a return to the ground-swell of semi-documentary (from *The Cottagers of Glenburnie* in 1808 to *My Friends the Miss Boyds* in 1959). The short story, too, has had most of its successes pretty safely within the documentary belt, though one must except the formidable and underrated Cunninghame Graham, and a few remarkable stories of more recent date (remarkable for Scotland in that they are genuinely imaginative yet written without Scottish rhetoric) by Dorothy K. Haynes.

It would be as well to include at this point a note on William McGonagall, who is also in his way a documentary writer. I don't know of any parallel to the portent of McGonagall, where the fame and popularity of such a bad writer have lasted so long and the writing has been so widely imitated. He clearly supplies some need in the Scottish soul, and we must ask what that need is. Apart from the obvious fact that his verse is funny, unintentionally funny, I think he lasts because he gives us a kind of inverted Kailyaird; he writes in such a way as to make us laugh at some of the things the real Kailyairders would want us to drop a tear over. He upholds all the institutions from Queen Victoria downwards, but he does it in such a ridiculous way that the institutions seem to be being mocked. He gives us an outlet, quite unconsciously, to all those irreverent feelings which were held in check by the writers of 'My Granny's Fireside' and its co-tranquillizers. He also presents a running commentary on his time – 'The Tay Bridge Disaster', 'The Newport Railway', 'The Famous Tay Whale', 'Grace Darling', 'The Horrors of Majuba', 'The Battle of Tel-el-Kebir' – and he has that Victorian eye for detail, for fact, which sometimes keeps a thing interesting longer than more grandiose but vague and general descriptions. When we laugh at McGonagall, we are to some extent laughing at the Fool who though a scapegoat is capable of showing us the shortcomings of his contemporaries. McGonagall unhesitatingly wrote about the world he saw around him, and when he describes a new railway being opened he has no difficulty in praising the event. And it is not only a matter of aesthetics –

> The train is most beautiful to be seen,
> With its long, white curling cloud of steam

– but also of economics, since the Newport Railway

> . . . will clear all expenses in a very short time;
> Because the thrifty housewives of Newport
> To Dundee will often resort,
> Which will be to them profit and sport,
> By bringing cheap tea, bread, and jam,
> And also some of Lipton's ham . . .

Where were the *real* writers, when Scotland was being industrialized? I have always thought it was a nicely symbolic accident when Burns tried to visit the Carron Ironworks and was refused admittance. Certainly the rapid industrializing process presented unusual problems in Scotland, whether to poet or to novelist. A crucial imbalance developed with the intellectual decline of Edinburgh and the enormous growth of Glasgow, and the swing of work and population to the Clyde area. This imbalance may have been felt, but its full implications – in terms of cultural centrality and continuity – were not faced. Minor writers who tried to express, in the absence of criticism, in the absence of leadership, something of the specifically new experience of the nineteenth century – the alcoholic autodidact James Macfarlan, Janet Hamilton the 'poor man's Mrs Browning', Alexander Smith with his powerful stanzas on industrial Glasgow, the interesting Whitmanian James Y. Geddes rediscovered by Douglas Young – these, like the later James Thomson and John Davidson, take their place as symbolic figures in the struggle of the 'modern' to break out of the trammels of the time. James Macfarlan will serve as their clumsy but moving spokesman:

> Mighty furnaces are flaring like a demon's breath of fire.
> Forges like great burning cities break in many a crimson spire . . .
> Toiling there the poor Boy-poet grimes within a dismal den,
> Piles the fire and wields the hammer, jostled on by savage men.
> Burns his life to mournful ashes, on a thankless hearth of gloom,
> For a paltry pittance digging life from out an early tomb:
> And the soul is dwarfed within him that was cast in Titan mould,
> And the wealth of Heaven he loses for the lack of human gold.

> (from 'The Wanderer of the West')

When the Scottish Renascence movement began in the 1920s, in an atmosphere pungent with ideas of Scottish nationalism, it looked back with no love at the nineteenth century, and set itself a double aim, the two parts of which have been hard to keep compatible. Hugh MacDiarmid, as its leader, wanted the movement to be *modern*, in the sense that it would risk dealing with contemporary subjects and would experiment with new forms, but he also wanted it to be unmistakably *Scottish*, if possible by a revival and extension of the Scots vocabulary. MacDiarmid's own poetry is a good enough guarantee that this double aim can be realized; but looking at the movement as a whole, I think it is clear that the language problem, the problem of Scottishness, has proved something of an incubus, and the fact that it is a real and unavoidable incubus (shake it off, and you leave scars and puncture marks) makes it all the more difficult for the Scottish writer to develop integrally. In Hugh MacDiarmid there is a large freedom from anxiety which allows him to use Scots of English, or a mixture of the two, as he will; but it is possible that when an exclusive choice is made, as with Sydney Goodsir Smith (Scots) or Norman MacCaig (English), there may be some psychological loss to offset the gain of verbal concentration: not a loss that prevents vivid and interesting creative work, but one that brings the constant hazard of a narrowing of outlook, since Scottish speech itself is still very fluid in the range from broad Scots to standard English, even among individual speakers. There is no reason now to suppose that a Scottish poet cannot write good poetry in English, as Edwin Muir, Norman MacCaig, W. S. Graham, and Hugh MacDiarmid himself have done. There is equally no point in questioning the achievement in Scots of *Under the Eildon Tree* or *Sangschaw* or Soutar's bairnsangs and whigmaleeries. It would seem sensible to preserve an unanguished flexibility in this matter of language, suiting your diction to your subject, or to the occasion and the audience.

After Norman MacCaig's anthology of recent Scottish verse, *Honour'd Shade*, appeared in 1959, there was much argument in the correspondence columns of the *Scotsman* about the existence of a 'Rose Street Group', centred in Edinburgh and (it was suggested) biased towards Lallans. When the correspondence had smouldered out, after many weeks of inflammatory toing and froing, a group of seven non-Rose-Street non-contributors to the anthology put together a tape-recording of readings of their own poems and called it *Dishonour'd Shade*. These were all users of English, and it is true that they might well have been represented in the anthology – particularly Shaun Fitzsimon, W. Price Turner, and Ian H. Finlay, whose work has often as Scottish a 'flavour', though written in English, as a 'Scotch-at-all-costs'-er could ask for. However, I could not help feeling that this 'great argument', for all that it was lively and fascinating and distinctly engagé, was not really such an indication of a healthy Scottish literary life as it might seem. One of the *Scotsman* letters, from Tom Scott, touched on more desperate issues than people are yet willing to take up in Scotland, though it is essential that they should begin to do so. Tom Scott wrote:

> It would have been more to the point if your reviewer had compared the work shown in this anthology with the great work of our Scottish past. Such a comparison is sobering and chastening. The sense of com-

munity, of abundant, vigorous social life has almost completely gone. There is wealth of talent . . . but something vital has gone, or almost gone. That something is Scotland.

Without feeling that either in the diagnosis or in the cure of this situation would I agree with Tom Scott, I am sure that the situation is rightly indicated, and that it applies to fiction and drama just as much as to poetry. In its excitement at having established a new literature – *A Drunk Man Looks at the Thistle*, *A Scots Quair*, *Under the Eildon Tree*, *Carotid Cornucopius*, *In Memoriam James Joyce* – the Scottish Renascence has begun to loosen its hold on life. It has allowed life, both in Scotland and elsewhere, to move on rapidly and ceaselessly in directions it chooses not to penetrate, and the result in 1960 is a gap between the literary and the public experience which is surprising and indeed shocking in a country as small as Scotland. Despite the efforts of Hugh MacDiarmid to deal with the nameably real in contemporary experience, this aspect of his work has been least taken up and developed by others. Too many heads are attracted by the sand. There is a new provincialism – in a move-men which, in MacDiarmid at least, stretched out internationally and fought the philistines. Almost no interest has been taken by established writers in Scotland in the important postwar literary developments in America and on the continent. Ignorance is not apologized for. The Beat writers are dismissed as a throwback to the 1920s. The Italian poet Quasimodo visits Edinburgh and Glasgow and is greeted with something like indifference – though his ideas on the future of poetry, to say nothing of his creative work, are highly relevant at the present time. Lovers of the past fight tooth and nail to delay the development of a twentieth-century architecture in our cities. When I saw Sydney Goodsir Smith's play, *The Wallace*, at the 1960 Edinburgh Festival, I found it hard to believe that such a talented and sensitive man could write, theatrically and stylistically, as if the whole of twentieth-century drama had passed him by – Brecht for presentation, Miller or Williams for language, even Shaw for argument.

There is no virtue in mere fashion: I am not asking for that. *The Wallace* has a success on its own level, as a festival chronicle play. But I am certain that Scottish literature is being held back, and young writers are slow to appear, not only because of publishing difficulties but also because of a prevailing intellectual mood of indifferentism and conservatism, a desperate unwillingness to move out into the world with which every child now at school is becoming familiar – the world of television and sputniks, automation and LPs, electronic music and multi-story flats, rebuilt city centres and new towns, coffee bars and bookable cinemas, air travel and transistor radios, colour photography and open-plan houses, paperbacks and water-skiing, early marriage and larger families: a world that will be more fast, more clean, more 'cool' than the one it leaves behind. How ridiculous to list distinguishing features of contemporary culture – material ones at that! Yet material differences in society imply spiritual, moral, and aesthetic differences, and although writers can struggle along for a time on language, on myth, on nature, on 'eternal emotions', there comes a day of reckoning when they realize that they are not speaking the same terms as their audience. What-ever reservations anyone has about the quality of John Osborne as a serious dramatist, there are thousands of young people who will vouch for the fact that he 'spoke their language' as no previous play-wright had done. Postwar Scotland has not produced its John Osborne, or any other compelling young writer. There has been much work of interest: the novels of Robin Jenkins, the short stories of Dorothy K. Haynes, the poetry of Iain Crichton Smith and Ian Hamilton Finlay, to take a choice among many talented names. Robin Jenkins has an intense feeling for the life and world of the schoolboy in the west of Scotland (*Happy for the Child*, *The Change-ling*); Dorothy Haynes ranges from the humorous to the macabre, and uses both modern and historical settings; Iain Smith gives sharpness to universal feelings and situations, expecially those of loneliness, old age, and ambition, against a present-day Highland background; Ian Finlay shows that the word Beat is not merely a journalistic gimmick. Yet they represent only a partial breakthrough. Too much of the experience of living in Scotland – still in many ways different from living in England – is not being reflected by novelists and playwrights. Life in a 'new town' like East Kilbride – in some of the huge suburban housing estates – on a hydro-electric construction scheme – at Dounreay or Hunterston – in a recipient town for Glasgow 'overspill': there is so much experience that seems to cry out for literary embodiment, for the eye of a sharp but sympathetic observer to be turned upon it. And I make no apology, in the present context, for emphasizing the contemporary aspect of things. 'Scot-land's heritage' is hung about our necks like a taxonomical placard. Conform or depart! Well, there is a time for gathering up one's history and traditions, and there is a time for showing the face of the present and looking forward. The second of these is what we need now. To tell the new Scottish generation that crow-stepped gables, Auld-Nick diablerie, and the art of piobaireachd should be Scotland's 'living traditions' would be to invite the rebuff the young Peter Grimes – looking about him – gave his father: '"This is the Life itself," the Boy replied.' Nature still abhors a vacuum. The 'vacuum' or 'hiatus' or 'blank' which so many intellectual commentators – both Edwin Muir and Hugh MacDiarmid agreeing on this – have deplored at the centre of Scottish life, based on the absence for several centuries of a capital city or a separate culture (for which the Scots have mainly themselves to blame), is really a sort of figment torn from the heart of the frustrated, an understandable and (as I myself believe) sometimes necessary distortion of the facts. It is not a vacuum, though it may be a ragbag. Writers may dislike what the popular fancy fills it with, but to refuse to see that it *is* filled is futile, since this merely prolongs the unnatural isolation of the critic and the intellectual from the life they could help to transform. The weakening in literature of a 'sense of community, of abundant, vigorous social life' which Tom Scott deprecated is a deep flaw in the relations between writer and community, and for this flaw it is the writers rather than the public who must shoulder the greater responsibility, though the public has its responsibility too. There *are* patterns and meaning is modern Scottish life, but writers who are most conscious of their Scottishness are often afraid to look for them in case the vivid image of the truth should overturn their notions of what 'Scottish' ought to mean. If we see a beatnik in the kailyaird, he is as well being studied as shot down.

Better still, if he will come forward and tell us his story.

New Saltire, 3 (Spring 1962).

Scottish Poetry in the 1960s

THE difficulty is to write naturally. The Scottish air tends to be thick with advice and assertion, much of it hectoring, strident, unconsidered. Vehemence, and various sorts of fierceness, we have; but reason and thought and justice, and the stillness out of which a personality can grow to its full stretch without spikiness and shoulder-chips – these are harder come by, and much to be desired. The bad old days of Scottish education, so nicely summed up by Alexander Scott in his two-line poem on that subject –

> I tellt ye
> I tellt ye

– may be going, but they have left their mark, and now that we are struggling out from under, and looking at the world, and flexing our muscles, and whistling a bit, and even doing our own thing, there is all the confusion of release coupled with the delight of escape. The spate of recent anthologies of Scottish poetry has shown that we can claim a fairly vigorous and varied scene as we look back through the last decade, yet more than one reviewer has pointed out that vigour and variety don't guarantee a direction or consolidate an achievement. Perhaps these are worries we can leave to the youngest, or the next, generation. It seems more important at the moment to be ourselves and to let the grids catch us if they can. As Tom McGrath wrote in *Glasgow University Magazine* (editorial, June 1971):

> Recognise the life you have: recognise your flesh, recognise that this absurd conglomeration of backgrounds and social norms that are pressing in on you all the time, be they Catholic Protestant Conservative Labour or Hip, recognise that you can discard them right now, this very moment, just by seeing them in your mind, all those inhibitions and present attitudes . . . and you can see how they have no substance, they have no basis, they have no justification – you can see that and step free of it, just by deciding to – you have, after all, only this life, don't

let inhibitions unlive it for you – you can say goodbye to it all and step into freedom.

But the step into freedom may be for the Scottish writer the hardest step. A residue of moral nervousness, a shying before images of joy or strangeness or abandon, can still cripple him with bonds that easily seem virtues. Obligations bark at him on all sides as he goes down the path to the gate. There is so much that he is asked to, or may legitimately want to, relate himself to. He is aware of native traditions that are distinct from English traditions – Dunbar, Lyndsay, Burns, MacDiarmid, the Gaelic poets, the Kailyard – and even when he turns aside to Olson and Ginsberg (Tom McGrath) or Jung and Camus (Alan Jackson) the subterranean Scottish notochord may still be tingling, and carrying messages even from a disowned past. The over-emphasis on Scottish tradition which is so tempting to the more beleaguered-feeling, nationalist-minded poet, is in the end stultifying when it is allowed to inhibit the naturalness of voice and heart in whose absence anyone aiming to address his contemporaries might as well stay in bed plucking the coverlet. Yet the shifting complexity of the situation is such that to say this is not to deny that (for example) Scots language or dialect is still perfectly viable in the right hands at the right moment. It is perhaps not so surprising to find that viability evident in the 1960s, since unashamedly non-metropolitan poetry has willingly used the accents of Newcastle and Liverpool, to say nothing of Gloucester, Mass. Poetry in Scots persists on a knife-edge: rejoicing in its expressive lexical potential, but afraid to nail its colours to the mast of real local speech-patterns. The MacDiarmid 'renascence' of a general synthetic Scots fifty years ago can still be felt, and learned from, but the move should now be towards the honesty of actual speech, and in the decade which has been a decade of spoken and recorded poetry and the poetry-reading explosion, this is indeed what has been happening. The Edinburgh poet Robert Garioch shows that the natural vividness associated with speech is by no means incompatible with formal poetic patterns. Some of his 'Edinburgh Sonnets', of which 'Heard in the Cougate' is an example, are virtuoso pieces in this respect, though with none of the coldness virtuosity can bring:

'Whu's aw thae fflag-poles ffur in Princes Street?
Chwoich! Ptt! Hechyuch! Ab-boannie cairry-on.
Seez-owre the wa'er. Whu' the deevil's thon
inaidie, heh?' 'The Queen's t'meet

The King o Norway wi his royal suite.'
'His royal wh'?' 'The hale jing-bang. It's aw in
the papur. Whaur's ma speck-sh? Aye they're gaun
t' day-cor-ate the toun. It's a fair treat,

somethin ye dinnae see jist ivry day,
foun'uns in the Gairdens, muckle spates
dancin t' music, an thir's t' be nae

chairge t'gi'in, it aw comes aff the Rates.'
'Ah ddae-ken whu' the pplace is comin tae
wi aw thae, hechyuch! fforeign po'entates.'

Garioch's approach may be compared with that of a young poet
from Glasgow, Tom Leonard. In his pamphlet *Six Glasgow Poems*
(1969) the uncompromising spelling, which in no way exaggerates
natural Glasgow dialect, serves as a useful reminder of how inade-
quate southern standard English is when it tries to extend its shaky
empire into the big cities of the north. 'The Good Thief', with
admirable economy, unites the two Glasgow preoccupations of football and religion, and non-Scottish readers should not be put off by
its apparent strangeness:

> heh jimmy
> yawright ih
> stull wayiz urryi
> ih
>
> heh jimmy
> ma right insane yirra pape
> ma right insane yirwanny uz jimmy
> see it nyir eyes
> wanny uz
>
> heh
>
> heh jimmy
> lookslik wirgonny miss thi gemm
> gonny miss thi GEMM jimmy
> nearly three a cloke thinoo
>
> dork init
> good jobe theyve gote thi lights

Worries about language, like worries about 'national identity', can be unhelpful to writers and tiresome to readers, but one feature of the 1960s has been the persistence of Gaelic poetry, as well as poetry in English and Scots, even while the native-speaking strength of the language seems to be draining steadily into the machair, and while bilingual Gaelic/English poets utter their cries about its disappearance. Iain Crichton Smith's remarkable poem 'Am Faigh a' Ghàidhlig Bàs?', translated by himself as 'Shall Gaelic Die?', does not seem like an elegy despite its sharp sense of the imminent loss of one more of the world's languages (give it a century perhaps?), and the Celtic-Twilight tushery with which the theme would once have been larded has now been pared away to the bleak but glittering frame of a philosophical meditation on the 'world' that a language uniquely embodies. And the fact that the Gaelic here is sown with English words – 'neon', 'orange', 'mauve', 'furniture', 'barometer', 'melodeon', 'skeleton', 'maze', 'dictionary', 'spectrum' – doesn't have the effect of linguistic contamination and decline but rather the opposite: a necessary injection of new life, hazarded against the objections of Gaelic purists and traditionalists. Here is Section 5:

> He who loses his language
> loses his world.
> The Highlander who loses his language
> loses his world.
>
> The space ship that goes astray among planets
> loses the world.
>
> In an orange world how would you know orange?
> In a world without evil how would you know good?
>
> Wittgenstein is in the middle of his world.
> He is like a spider.
> The flies come to him.
> 'Cuan' and 'coille' rising.*
>
> When Wittgenstein dies,
> his world dies.
>
> The thistle bends to the earth.
>
> The earth is tired of it.

* 'sea' and 'wood'.

Wittgenstein prowls round Oban Bay. A spaceship lands on Lewis. An orange world, having been imagined, exists. A Gaelic poet becomes a 'Gaelic' 'poet' and looks at himself from behind the mirror. The very title-question of the poem flickers on and off like a neon sign as if to mock the too plodding enquirer. This is living poetry, and its flashing, jumping, discrete quality says no to Highland mists. Iain Crichton Smith's English poetry has also advanced and matured during the sixties, shedding some of the decorative devices of his early work and moving into more direct confrontations with society. Both in long poem-sequences and in some very striking short poems he has emerged as a poet of great potential for Scotland: sensitive and concerned, but too intelligent to fall for easy slogans. In his sequence 'The White Air of March' (1969) he wrote: 'It is bitter / to dip a pen in continuous water / to write poems of exile / in a verse without honour or style.' And this theme of being an 'exile in one's own land', a theme that is driven about with some satire and irony as well as through occasional straight bitterness, is linked to the idea of 'excellence' and its rarity and the search for it, among the rocks if need be. 'The Cuillins tower high in the air – Excellence.' But the man who says this should have read his Wittgenstein, his Kafka, his Dostoevsky; innocence is as culpable as fanaticism; Ossian is bones.

> In the white air of March
> a new mind.

Norman MacCaig, who draws much imagery and sustenance from the Highlands, and who published half a dozen collections during the sixties, would doubtless appreciate these ideas of Iain Crichton Smith, though his own poetry is more delicately surefooted, and less troubled and passionate, than Smith's. An extraordinary gift in observation and comparison is used by MacCaig as a lever to flype reality with, and after this metaphysical process the new reality is tried on for size, paraded a bit (but without name-dropping), and eventually returned to nature in its original shape, but touched by human hand. Short on alienation, but surprising, accurate, and well-turned, his poetry offers many pleasures. Its urbanity is by no means unable to get under the skin, though he himself has complained (in 'A Sort of Blues'): ' – My luck to live in a time / when to be happy / is to have no neighbours.' A characteristic report on experience, which manages to be convincingly realistic while remaining sardonic and sly, is 'Basking Shark':

To stub an oar on a rock where none should be,
To have it rise with a slounge out of the sea
Is a thing that happened once (too often) to me.

But not too often – though enough. I count as gain
That once I met, on a sea tin-tacked with rain,
That roomsized monster with a matchbox brain.

He displaced more than water. He shoggled me
Centuries back– this decadent townee
Shook on a wrong branch of his family tree.

Swish up the dirt and, when it settles, a spring
Is all the clearer. I saw me, in one fling,
Emerging from the slime of everything.

So who's the monster? The thought made me grow pale
For twenty seconds while, sail after sail,
The tall fin slid away and then the tail.

'So who's the monster?' MacCaig's question has many echoes in
the liberated and often forceful Scottish poetry of the last ten years.
Iain Crichton Smith in his *From Bourgeois Land* (1969) makes a
Janus-monster of Calvin and Hitler, watches 'gauleiters pace by
curtained windows' in tidy Scottish towns, while 'distant Belsen
smokes in the calm air'. Sorley Maclean, master Gaelic poet of this
century, finds something similar but perhaps worse, because mindless and anarchic, in the monsters of Glasgow:

> The broken bottle and the razor
> are in the fist and face of the boy
> in spite of Auschwitz and Belsen
> and the gallows in Stirling
> and the other one in Glasgow
> and the funeral of (John) MacLean . . .

> ('Am Botal Briste', trans. by author)

George Mackay Brown, writing lovingly of the ancient simplicities
and sanctified rituals of life in Orkney, sees his disruptive twin monsters as Protestantism and Progress. 'The Rackwick croft ruins are
strewn with syrup tins, medicine bottles, bicycle frames, tattered
novels, rubber boots, portraits of Queen Victoria.' And so

The poor and the good fires are all quenched.
Now, cold angel, keep the valley
From the bedlam and cinders of A Black Pentecost.

('Dead Fires')

Alan Jackson, who like George Mackay Brown has emerged strongly
in the sixties, has many monsters, beasts, and dragons in his anthro-
pological, antropological ('the study of the anteriors') verse; they
have to be fought in psychology as well as in history, and 'the worstest
beast' of all is man himself at his present stage of responsibility and
power –

he's the worstest beast because he's won
it's a master race and it's almost run

('The Worstest Beast')

D. M. Black filters through verse of clipped, staccato resourcefulness
a half-surreal brood of monstrous judges, dwarfs, hangmen, sperm
donors, ants as big as motor-bikes, 'monsters at large on / every cliff:
they / gather and peer down / into a sea stiff with reptiles' – but these
seem props and try-outs, establishing tone, mask, stance, on the way
to a more lucid and experiential poetry. Really experiential monsters,
on the other hand, torn lavishly and deliberately from the historical superficies of our time, are pinned squirming on the pages of
Tom Buchan, from Heydrich to Nixon, and Scotland the Brave
becomes an American staging-post with its once holy lochs patrolled
by 'obsolescent new submarines':

Bohannan held onto a birch branch
by yon bonny banks and looked down
through several strata of liquid
– there is someone somewhere
aiming a missile at me (he thought)

('The Low Road')

And glacial monsters underpeer the quiet, lean, scalpelled verse of
Robin Fulton, deceptive waters washing between statement and
incantation. A prolific but conscientious and precise poet, he has
talents that can be seen deepening during the decade as he himself
moves more closely into committed involvement with the subject. His
sequence 'Hung Red' (in *The Man with the Surbahar*, 1971) is one of
the striking poems of the end of this decade in Scotland – an eye,
which is also a TV eye, staring and flickering out at recent history and

horrors, caught between the desire to be effaced in the white glare of ideal ends and the necessity of being 'hung – red' on the rack of our terrible means. Fulton, outward-looking but not unaware of native traditions, mingles in this sequence a central image drawn from Hugh MacDiarmid's 'The Glass of Pure Water' with others that may have been suggested by Beckett and Bacon. Here is Section 3:

> *hold a glass of pure water to the eye of the sun*
> the sun will score your retina like a merciless razor
>
> hold up a glass of the Mekong or the Jordan
> the eye of the sun will be safe now only a glimmer
> in the cloudy element our substitute for daylight
>
> the cloud preys on itself yet the cloud survives
> always at the infinite cost of those who do not survive
>
> (this is the non-miracle, repeated daily and exactly,
> the putrid water struck from *the rock of capitalism*)
>
> the water of the Ganges is also cloudy: what kind
> of cleanliness justifies the wet pilgrims?
> there's a scum of filth on the naked eye, don't trust the eye

Other single longish poems which in different ways are able to show, it seems to me, the sort of seriousness or awareness that Scottish poetry has been jolted into (as opposed to certain stereotypes of 'entertainment' and 'character' which have always been available) are Alan Bold's 'A Memory of Death' (an elegy on his father, warm, imperfect, moving), Pete Morgan's 'The Meat Work Saga' (a poem for performance, and one of the best examples of that genre), and Roderick Watson's 'Fugue for Parker' (montage technique to relate the agony and achievement of an individual musician to the world of 1939). And if these are all poems with monsters – death, alcoholism, war, heroin, the atom – it must be remembered that Scotland in the sixties has also produced the tranquil, ordered, playful, and above all anti-monstrous little world ('a little world made cunningly', indeed) of Ian Hamilton Finlay. Beginning with an attractively whimsical lyrical verse in traditional form (*The Dancers Inherit the Party*, 1960) and moving out into concrete poetry, poster-poems, postcard-poems, poem-objects, and environmental or landscape poems, Finlay has proceeded impressively step by step in the search for a new lyricism which would still be basically verbal but would take into account the changes in our sensibility induced by developments in the plastic arts, design, typography, and (especially) constructivist aesthetic theory and practice. Concentration on a narrow range of familiar images, particularly those drawn from the sea – fishing-boats and nets, stars and sailors – has enabled him to explore a small field (and he claims no more) in depth and with great originality, producing a series of metaphors from one area of human experience with have been made into concrete objects for contemplation and use. Beauty – dirty word or not – is what those objects have, but it is not a wet beauty. The effects have point, often wit, usually clarity. Contrasted with (say) the hard muscular Scots of Alexander Scott's long poem on Aberdeen ('Heart of Stone'), Finlay's poetic language may seem frail, and out of phase with the supposed perfervidness of the Scottish genius. Yet the world of little things, when it is also a world of art, can stand confidently among the larger social commentaries. If Scotland seems traditionally cast as Kokoschka-country, there is surely reason to welcome a touch of Mondrian.

This essay has not attempted anything like an exhaustive survey, but has aimed merely to offer a series of pointers across and through the scene. For a fuller picture, reference may be made to the following anthologies:

The Scottish Literary Revival, ed. George Bruce (Collier-Macmillan, 1968)
The Akros Anthology of Scottish Poetry 1965-70, ed. Duncan Glen (Akros, Preston, 1970)
Contemporary Scottish Verse 1959-1969, ed. Norman MacCaig and Alexander Scott (Calder & Boyars, 1970)
Four Points of a Saltire (Reprographia, Edinburgh, 1970)
The Ring of Words, ed. Alan MacGillivray and James Rankin (Oliver & Boyd, Edinburgh, 1970)
Twelve Modern Scottish Poets, ed. Charles King (University of London Press, 1971)
Voices of Our Kind (Saltire Society, Edinburgh, 1971)
Scottish Poetry 1-6, ed. George Bruce, Maurice Lindsay, and Edwin Morgan (Edinburgh University Press, 1966-71)

From *British Poetry since 1960*, ed. M. Schmidt and G. Lindop, Carcanet, 1972.

Edwin Muir

It is a world, perhaps; but there's another.

IT is always interesting, and often valuable, to examine the work of a poet who is out of the main stream of his contemporaries' verse. Edwin Muir was little interested in the technical innovation and linguistic experiment that characterized the literature of his period, and his poetry failed to make much impact until, towards the end of his life, the fading of the 'modern movement' allowed his plainer virtues (like those also of Robert Graves) to come into some prominence. Muir himself came late to poetry, and owing to his scrappy education had many initial difficulties to surmount, some of them difficulties a younger man might have taken in his stride in the natural excitement of discovering, following, and discarding poetic models. As he says in his *Autobiography*: 'I had no training; I was too old to submit myself to contemporary influences ... Though my imagination had begun to work I had no technique by which I could give expression to it.' It may fairly be said, I think, that he never did develop an entirely sure-footed technique; even his last poems are liable to be flawed by some awkward rhythm, some clumsy inversion, some flatness of vocabulary: yet by going his own way he establishes the point that what is awkward or flat is not necessarily more fatal to poetry than what is tediously admirable in accomplishment. Without wanting to praise slackness over slickness, a reader can find himself admitting that a thought-provoking piece remains a thought-provoking piece, even when its critical viability is well under proof. Muir of course has many drab, dull poems which don't come to life at all, and that is another matter. But the best of them have a quiet, persistent, winning quality which overcomes the occasional stammering of the voice.

Although in his reliance on traditional verse-forms and avoidance of startling or broken imagery Muir was out of step with his time, his search for a usable mythology links him to his contemporaries.

In this very recalcitrant problem his solution is no more successful than that of Yeats, Pound, or Eliot. Instead of casting a wide net like these poets, he practised economy and restraint, relying on a narrow range of recurrent images – road and journey, labyrinth and stronghold, living and heraldic animals – and a handful of unrecondite myths in which the chief figures are Hector and Achilles, Odysseus and Penelope, Oedipus and Prometheus, Adam and Abraham. It is through such legendary and often heroic figures (supplemented now and again by such later historical characters as Knox and Calvin) and such Kafkaesque imagery (drawn frequently from his own dreams, which were at various periods of his life obsessionally powerful) that Muir projects his experience and vision of the world of time against the imagined world of eternity. But with what success?

> My childhood all a myth
> Enacted in a distant isle . . .

As P. H. Butter points out in his very useful introduction to Muir's work,* Muir was the last born of a fairly large family on an Orkney farm and so grew up in a seemingly solid, secure, timelessly established environment: a glowing self-sufficient world that too readily lent itself to the myth of an Eden, once its charm had been shattered by the luckless family migration to Glasgow. The idea of Eden, a Fall, and a search for reconstituted unity and harmony, is central to Muir's poetry. As an idea it is overworked, and often brought in unconvincingly, but clearly the poet was haunted all his days by the contrast between his protected Orkney boyhood and the harsh realities of industrial Glasgow he was plunged into as a youth, and a philosophy so rooted in early personal experience needs careful watching if a poet is to persuade others of its value. Muir took to myth too eagerly. His poetry would have been strengthened by a greater realism and materiality. Powerful material which he is able to make use of in his prose (e.g. his memorable description of the Fairport bone-factory in his *Autobiography*) he cannot allow into the world of his poetry. Perhaps by a natural modesty or diffidence, he seldom presents his experience directly – despite his admiration for Wordsworth – and this sometimes results in muted or shadowy effects where we feel an unexpressed resonance beating vainly back from

* *Edwin Muir*, Writers & Critics Series, Oliver & Boyd, Edinburgh and London 1962.

the poem towards the past instead of outwards towards us. Professor Butter assumes, for example, that in the early 'Ballad of Hector in Hades', which is based on a childhood recollection of being rather frighteningly chased home from school by another boy, the mythologizing of the experience into the hunting of Hector by Achilles 'has enabled him to objectify his personal experience, to universalize it and make it into a work of art'. But I feel on the contrary that this very Wordsworthian incident would have taught Muir more as a poet if he had tried to say more directly and sharply what it meant or seemed to mean to him. To translate it into the terms of classical mythology is, in a poetic sense, too easy, even if the resulting poem is not a bad one.

It is only fair to add that to Muir himself the 'fable' accompanied and brooded over the 'story' at almost every moment of life: not only, as most obviously, in Orkney, where as he tells us 'there was no great distinction between the ordinary and the fabulous; the lives of living men turned into legend', but later as he motored through the desolate *paysage moralisé* of the slag-hills round Glasgow –

> dwarf-like and sinister, suggesting an immeasurably shrivelled and debased second-childhood . . . I saw young men wandering in groups among these toy ranges, and the sight suddenly recalled to me the wood-cuts in *The Pilgrim's Progress* which I had read as a boy; perhaps because this scene really seemed to be more like an allegorical landscape with abstract figures than a real landscape with human beings.
>
> (*Scottish Journey*)

We must grant him the reality of this feeling, and yet we can be disappointed that he moves so quickly into the abstract, allegorical landscapes. He confesses in the *Autobiography* that 'dreams go without a hitch into the fable, and waking life does not.' This means in practice that his poetry does not always fully 'earn' the mythology it presents. And conversely, when Muir does want to comment on contemporary life he may be rather at a loss, wanting to mythologize but being too timid to euhemerize. Muir's chief weakness, indeed, is that he came to use Good and Evil as flags of convenience. The poem 'The Good Town', for instance, leaves a melodramatic impression because one knows very well what the poet is talking about but one simply doesn't accept the 'universalizing' black-and-white opposition between the Danny Kaye 'streets of friendly neighbours' where lock and key were 'quaint antiquities fit for museums' while

ivy trailed 'across the prison door' and their later metamorphosis
into a place where

> If you see a man
> Who smiles good-day or waves a lordly greeting
> Be sure he's a policeman or a spy.

In his *Essays on Literature and Society* Muir attacked Alexander
Blok for being too responsive to historical change, but Blok could
with some justice have blamed Muir for deliberately muffling his own
very real responsiveness to change and for persuading himself –
against all the evidence, not least the evidence of his own Christian
faith – that 'Nothing can come of history but history.'

What Muir felt most deeply and expressed most movingly was
the sense of aftermath – the slow passage of time after some great or
terrible event, the endurance or patience or suffering of survivors,
the crumbling of wasted cities: Eden after the Fall, Troy after it was
sacked, Penelope remembering Odysseus and Telemachos remembering Penelope, Oedipus old and blind, Prometheus on the rock
and later in his grave, Abraham the wanderer, Scotland with its
long annals of 'wasted bravery idle as a song', the world after an
atomic war. Muir's acute sense of time in its relation to action is
seen in the fine 'Telemachos Remembers' –

> The weary loom, the weary loom,
> The task grown sick from morn to night,
> From year to year. The treadle's boom
> Made a low thunder in the room.
> The woven phantoms mazed her sight.
>
> If she had pushed it to the end,
> Followed the shuttle's cunning song
> So far she had no thought to rend
> In time the web from end to end,
> She would have worked a matchless wrong.
>
> Instead, that jumble of heads and spears,
> Forlorn scraps of her treasure trove.
> I wet them with my childish tears
> Not knowing she wove into her fears
> Pride and fidelity and love.

– and in a larger, geological context in his remarkable poem 'The
Grave of Prometheus':

> Yet there you still may see a tongue of stone,
> Shaped like a calloused hand where no hand should be,
> Extended from the sward as if for alms,
> Its palm all licked and blackened as with fire.
> A mineral change made cool his fiery bed,
> And made his burning body a quiet mound,
> And his great face a vacant ring of daisies.

In the poem 'Troy', the aftermath of calamity is chosen, not the moment of destruction itself, and this gives a peculiar horror to the situation: an old Trojan warrior, gone mad, is living in the sewers under the city, fighting hordes of rats; he is discovered by a band of robbers and dragged to the surface; he sees the city like a graveyard

> With tumbled walls for tombs, the smooth sward wrinkled
> As Time's last wave had long since passed that way,
> The sky, the sea, Mount Ida and the islands,
> No sail from edge to edge, the Greeks clean gone.
> They stretched him on a rock and wrenched his limbs,
> Asking: 'Where is the treasure?' till he died.

Muir's emphasis on the pointlessness of history was not always as cruel as this, but it is a theme that was never very far from his mind. Connected in part with his consciousness of a lost Eden, it also owes something to his dreams and nightmares with their fears of 'eternal recurrence', and to his own lack of sympathy with contemporary history, which he saw as a series of defeats, disappointments and growing threats. There is a strand of pessimism in his reflections on human destiny which his religious hope was never quite robust enough to dismiss, and he outgrew such early belief as he had in economic and political solutions. This does not mean that the pessimism is not shot through with hope and longing, often a stoic hope and a metaphysical longing. The nightmarish poem 'The Combat', based on dream material, describes an endlessly recurring fight between a powerful and an apparently defenceless animal in which the 'soft brown beast' is mauled and savaged but always manages to escape and live to fight again; neither animal 'loses', but

> The killing beast that cannot kill
> Swells and swells in his fury till
> You'd almost think it was despair.

One might say that if this is an image of life, of man's fate, life would would hardly be worth living on such terms. Yet on second thoughts one can see history through the eyes of the poem, and man not unlike the 'undefeatable' animal in the fable, whether the huge opponent has been monstrous beasts, natural calamities, oppressive rulers, or even some less visible enemy. The least visible, of course, may be the worst of all, and Muir's poetry shows, for all his 'gentleness' which critics have perhaps stressed too much, great awareness of the latent cruelties and inexplicable attacks that life – and man, and Muir himself – seem to guard as sources of pride and assurance. One short poem gives forcible expression to this.

The Face

See me with all the terrors on my roads,
The crusted shipwrecks rotting in my seas,
And the untroubled oval of my face
That alters idly with the moonlike modes
And is unfathomably framed to please
And deck the angular bone with passing grace.

I should have worn a terror-mask, should be
A sight to frighten hope and faith away,
Half charnel field, half battle and rutting ground.
Instead I am a smiling summer sea
That sleeps while underneath from bound to bound
The sun- and star-shaped killers gorge and play.

'A sight to frighten hope and faith away.' Muir had undoubtedly felt such presences, and his later poetry, some of it on themes of atomic war, is much concerned with it, but he persisted obstinately on his journey ('The heart in its stations/ Has need of patience') and was rewarded with those lyrical gleams of quiet meditative joy or hopefulness which are among his most personal utterances – poems like 'The Bird' (a beautiful Bridges-like counter-poem to 'The Face'), 'The Question', 'A Birthday', 'In Love for Long', 'The Debtor', 'The Poet' and 'I have been taught by dreams and fantasies'. The particular sweetness of Muir's lyrical style when it is successful is like the sudden scent of some wild flower which a freer inspiration has allowed to break through the rather abstract and heraldic character of his verse.

I never felt so much
Since I have felt at all
The tingling smell and touch
Of dogrose and sweet briar,

> Nettles against the wall,
> All sours and sweets that grow
> Together or apart
> In hedge or marsh or ditch.
> I gather to my heart
> Beast, insect, flower, earth, water, fire,
> In absolute desire,
> As fifty years ago.

('A Birthday')

The group of brooding prophetic reflections on future war and destruction which he wrote in the 1950s – 'The Horses', 'After a Hypothetical War', 'The Last War', 'Petrol Shortage', 'The Day before the Last Day' – is a powerful though imperfect last attempt by Muir to speak more directly than through myth and symbol on issues that haunted and distressed him. Perhaps because he is looking forward – however doubtfully – instead of back, perhaps because in these poems the air of science-fiction lends paradoxically a greater reality and urgency than is usual with Muir, this group of poems leaves a strong impression (a much stronger impression, for example, than the poems on specifically Christian themes which he was also developing in the 1950s).

> 'The sun rises above the sea, and they look and think:
> "We shall not watch its setting." And all get up
> And stare at the sun. But they hear no great voice crying:
> "There shall be no more time, nor death, nor change,
> Nor fear, nor hope, nor longing, nor offence,
> Nor need, nor shame." But all are silent, thinking:
> "Choose! Choose again, you who have chosen this!
> Too late! Too late!"
> And then: "Where and by whom shall we be remembered?" '

('The Day before the Last Day')

These poems form, as he says, an 'imaginary picture of a stationary fear', the fear that a possible atomic devastation would destroy not only what is physical but human values as well ('No place at all for bravery in that war'). Yet by a curious closing of the circle he brings this fear round to his own intimations of hope, by suggesting in 'The Horses' and 'Petrol Shortage' that a post-devastational return to primitive pastoral life might restore man to the protection of the earth he had become increasingly estranged from. Men who have no tractors begin to tame wild horses: 'Our life is changed; their coming our beginning.' Butter describes this as 'a vision of a more hopeful kind' and also quotes John Holloway's statement that though in Muir's vision 'the powers of evil were great, ultimately the powers of good and goodness were greater; and they were greater because they were also humbler, more primaeval, nearer to life in its archaic simplicity'. Well, one man's hope is perhaps another man's despair. Muir's primitivism, returning all post-atomic mankind to an Orkney farm, not without a certain austere satisfaction, seems to me to be more insulting than comforting to man's restless spirit and aspiring brain. Let your survivors tame the horses of the Moon, the dragons of Mars: I would call that hope. But Muir was in search of a simplicity which the future was unlikely to reveal unless by a return to the past, and even the simplicity of the past is more myth than reality. So weakness mingles with strength in his search: the weakness of an underlying evasion and escape, the strength of a sincere and moving desire for good. Muir retreats from the wonderful challenge which the apparent menace of the scientific and political future has thrown down to us in mid-century, but he expresses the menace in unforgettable images.

> I see the image of a naked man,
> He stoops and picks a smooth stone from the ground,
> Turns round and in a wide arc flings it backward
> Towards the beginning. What will catch it,
> Hand, or paw, or gullet of sea-monster?
> He stoops again, turns round and flings a stone
> Straight on before him. I listen for its fall,
> And hear a ringing on some hidden place
> As if against the wall of an iron tower.

The Review, (5 February 1963).

MacDiarmid Embattled

To write literature of any value one must somehow write about life. This may be done very directly (Defoe's *Journal of the Plague Year*) or very indirectly (Blake's Prophetic Books), but the pressure of life upon the work must be communicated, and the pressure the work seeks to exert upon life must also be communicated. Where such pressure wears thin, as in some of the writing of Yeats, Henry James, and Wallace Stevens, literature is endangered, and endangered in an insidious way because of the high art with which the retreat from life covers its tracks.

Here a second proposition is relevant: To write *about* literature, one must somehow write about life. This is certainly no truism to the modern critic, any more than my opening proposition has been a truism to the modern writer. A good example is Susanne Langer, who in her book *Feeling and Form* insists on the insulated quality of literary statement: the critic can talk about what the writer *thought* he was writing about, and relate that to life, but cannot talk about what the work really says, and relate this to life. Such a relation, on her view, either does not exist or if it does exist is deleterious to literary art. Poetry, she says, is only 'a creation of illusory events, even when it looks like a statement of opinions philosophical or political or aesthetic'. *Paradise Lost* may reveal to us an interesting pattern of the tensions in Milton's thought, but we are not legitimately to take it as telling us anything about the destiny and aspirations of mankind. Mrs Langer only represents in extreme form the modern critic's gloved and suspicious approach to the *human content* of any work of art – whether it is Byron's *Don Juan*, or Victorian anecdotal painting, or Shostakovich's '1905' Symphony. Every branch of the New Criticism has found it hard to say anything profitable about such poets as Chaucer, Burns, Byron, Whitman, and even Wordsworth, where the human content is so inescapable and the formal interest is so soon exhausted. There are signs, in Donald Davie, D. J. Enright, Christopher Logue and others, that this situation is about to be changed. Life, cap in hand perhaps, can be seen coming up in the distance by those who watch from the door of art. If this strange and uncouth figure should return and again be received among us, there will be some change of emphasis in discussions of the contemporary literary scene, and writers who might expect to have their work taken more seriously would certainly include Hugh MacDiarmid.

Where MacDiarmid differs from most other modern poets is in his desire to touch modern life at as many points as possible. His method, being more inclusive than selective, and being fully tolerant towards facts, names, things, persons, and statistics, tends to baffle those who find in his respect for *fact* a sort of sin against the divinity of the *word*, which should somehow always be 'expressing' more than it 'says'. As the sardonic Enright puts it in his poem 'The Interpreters':

> . . . Whore, you may be sure,
> refers to some mysterious metaphysical temptation;
> hunger was his image for a broken dream; bread
> an old religious symbol; his typhoons the wind of God.
>
> Good lord, if a poet really meant what he said,
> we should all be out of a job – why on earth
> would he sing of the merely real?

'The merely real' commands those who do sing of it to forget for a moment the ease with which as imaginative men they can find universals lurking behind every particular. They are invited to stop at the particulars, and see what happens. Is such a poetry, in the result, non-poetry or anti-poetry? Well, is Guillaume Apollinaire without pathos? Is Bertolt Brecht without depth? Is Christopher Logue without song? Call this writing, and the later writing of Hugh MacDiarmid, an 'anti-poetry' if you will, but it is only an anti-poetry in the dialectical sense that it opposes one conception of poetry which it believes to be unequal to a task history is more and more clearly placing before it; if it can shoulder the burden of this task, and retain readers and convince critics, it will then become the 'poetry' of the next epoch. Having had a good laugh once at Wordsworth's *Lyrical Ballads*, Britain is not likely to prove a forerunner in the appreciation of any stark and unrosy theory of poetry. Even Robert Conquest, in the Introduction to his recent anthology of European dissidence *Back to Life*, seems hardly aware that he is dealing (in poets like

Adam Ważyk) with a new kind of poetry, the poem which does not have to be apologized for in translation, what Ważyk himself calls the 'naked poem', the 'poem for adults'. But Britain certainly has its forerunners in the attempt to *write* such a poetry, and it is against the whole European background of movement towards 'the merely real' that Hugh MacDiarmid must be set. The fact of his Scottishness may predispose him, as it predisposed Burns and Lyndsay, in the general direction of realism (though historical as well as national characteristics have to be taken into account in these matters), but the links with the world outside Scotland are important, and help to make his aims and experiments seem less purely wilful. W. A. Gatherer has written (*Lines Review* 14) in general terms of MacDiarmid's relation to the Scots politico-religious flyting tradition; Burns Singer has made a good introductory defence of the non-lyrical poems (*Encounter*, March 1957); what I want to do here is to offer some remarks centring on the recently published long poem *The Battle Continues* (Castle Wynd Printers).

The Battle Continues will not, I think, be regarded as one of MacDiarmid's best works, but it is very instructive for all that, and it poses in acute form some of the problems that attach to the 'anti-poetry' I have been describing. It is a poem of some four thousand lines, and was written twenty years ago in answer to Roy Campbell's *Flowering Rifle*. Campbell had celebrated Franco's victory in the Spanish Civil War; MacDiarmid's aim was to blast Campbell and his views off the face of literature. *Flowering Rifle* is written in rigid rhyming couplets, in a swashbuckling rhetorical style with plenty of lurid imagery; *The Battle Continues* is in a conversational free verse interrupted by rhyming and stanzaic passages and by quotations in prose and verse. Both poems are too long, lack organization, and repeat themselves, but the monotonous form of Campbell's poem makes it less readable than MacDiarmid's diversified presentation. Campbell stands on a platform with a machine-gun in his hand and rants; MacDiarmid prowls about his study, ruminates at the window, bangs a book on the table, kicks the sofa, turns on the wireless, and has a constant stream of surprised visitors arriving and departing as he talks. Although the occasion of both poems was the war in Spain, they range over a much wider area than that. Campbell's pet hates include – quite apart from Spanish republicanism – Marx, Freud, Jung, Einstein, Charlie Chaplin, Aldous Huxley, Herbert Read, André Gide, Marie Stopes, 'MacSpaunday', Bloomsbury, the Church of England, and 'the creeping wowsers'. He has kind words for Dryden, Camõens, Franco, Claudel, and Wyndham Lewis. It is significant that although both poems are vituperative, Campbell is much more negative and sterile. MacDiarmid, while expressing hatred for Campbell and even (ironically enough) for some of the things Campbell himself attacks (e.g. Bloomsbury, MacSpaunday, and England in general), enlists a great roll of positive coadjutors on his side, and these – ruthlessly packed bedfellows though they are: Lenin and Jeremiah, Burns and Buber, Thales and Milton, Vanzetti and St Cadoc! – give his tirades the foil of a body of civilized reference not to be found in Campbell.

The Battle Continues is clearly in the Scotch flyting tradition, but that tradition seems to have two branches. The kind that has become most familiar – e.g. the *Flyting of Dunbar and Kennedy* – is a sophisticated exercise in literary virtuosity, its devastating railleries not necessarily springing from any rancour against either a person or a society, but growing out of a desire to produce savage and stunning comedy. Such a poem is not meaningless, since real personal and social references are made use of (the Lowlander/Celt controversy in Dunbar's flyting), but the prime interest appears to have been bardic, formal, and comedic. The *Flyting betwixt Montgomerie and Polwart* (*c*.1582) is careful to warn the reader:

> No cankring envy, malice, nor despite,
> Stirred up these men so eagerly to flyte;
> But generous emulation . . .
> Anger t'asswage, make melancholy lesse,
> This flyting first was wrote – now tholes the presse.

'Anger t'asswage', however, was by no means the aim of Montgomerie's contemporary, Robert Sempill. This rough and furious sniper at episcopacy shares with Hugh MacDiarmid a different view of the flyter's function:

> Gif ony be that will Judge me
> To speik bot in dispyte,
> Gar mend the mis committit is,
> And I na mair sall flyte.

(Maddeis Proclamatioun)

'Get what is amiss put right' – the reader is being addressed seriously and purposefully, and the flyting poem becomes more hortatory and less fantastic; it still has to be entertaining enough to sell and be read, but amusement is subservient to political zeal.

MacDiarmid in *The Battle Continues* takes this a stage further. Here, the comic moments are few and far between. The anger is too real, too impatient, to risk an assuaging wash of laughter. Sporadic puns occur, infiltrations of irony, a deal of the customary scatological play, and the odd passage of downright verbal fun:

> The general admission of the Rebel leaders
> That but for this bogus Byron, this great Reichs-Marksman,
> Moscow had won!
> Single-handed almost,
> This second Cid, this Robert Coates of the Theatre of War,
> This Gun-Smoke McGonigall, this vest-
> Pocket edition of the *Decline of the Wild West*, etc. . . .

Even this is a laboured humour, a concession to the form of the flyting: compare it with Byron or Swift, and its lower level of efficacy is obvious. Efficacy, however, for what? Unlike the author of *The Vision of Judgment*, MacDiarmid places little trust in satire, except as entertainment or light relief. This is partly because he himself lacks the sophistication of mind required for continuously sparkling satire, but (more importantly) because he feels that his theme, and the times he is writing in, must be served by a more direct treatment. If he only says, 'See how absurd and ridiculous Roy Campbell is!' – will people ever get to a vehement hatred of the ideas Campbell stands for? When Wyndham Lewis was writing his Introduction to the semi-jubilee edition (1955) of his satire *The Apes of God*, he remarked:

> In rereading the pages of *The Apes of God*, it is their light-heartedness which, more than anything else, impresses one. If I were to write satire today there would be no doubt about its justifying its name – it would be satire pure and simple, there would be absolutely no laughter in it.

This is a conclusion MacDiarmid seems to have reached before Wyndham Lewis.

Real hatred can undoubtedly motivate real literature, and our own period has seen some remarkable examples of it: the boisterous and mindless anti-progressivism of Campbell, the more pathological, sadistic power-fantasies of Lewis, the great hammering insolent disgusts of Pound – and MacDiarmid, blue-eyed in the howdah of his disinterested juggernaut, the twenty-first century. Ezra Pound –

give him his due – has written in his 'Hell' Cantos (XIV-XV) a poetry of hatred that has no equal for expressiveness: the wells of revulsion and horror overflow, and yet the revulsion is art and the horror is truth, and the poet says something to which, though we may shudder, we assent.

> . . . dead maggots begetting live maggots,
>   slum owners,
> usurers squeezing crab-lice, panders to authority,
> pets-de-loup, sitting on piles of stone books,
> obscuring the texts with philology,
>   hiding them under their persons,
> the air without refuge of silence,
>   the drift of lice, teething,
> and above it the mouthing of orators . . .

The success of the 'Hell' Cantos is a success of craftsmanship – choice and placing of words, attention to rhythm, cinematic 'cutting' of syntax – and to MacDiarmid this would be too artful as a method, in dealing with these great issues. *The Battle Continues* depends more on statement than on imagery, more on fact than on suggestion, and this is a harder poetry to write because of our ingrained fear of the prosaic. MacDiarmid risks the prosaic for the sake of being clearly understood, and of showing that poetry (as Wordsworth said in his famous Preface) 'can boast of no celestial ichor that distinguishes her vital juices from those of prose; the same human blood circulates through the veins of them both'. At times he relies simply on the statement, hoping that it will either convince, or arouse a dialectical disagreement which will at least force the reader to consider its truth:

> Poetry is a progressive art. No true poet today
> Can worship superstition and defend false beliefs,
> Or celebrate revenge and war,
> As the primaeval poets did.

At other times he permits himself a spare Brechtian image which is brilliantly successful:

> Anywhere you go in Britain today
> You can hear the people
> Economising consciousness,
> Struggling to think and feel as little as possible
> Just as you can hear a countryside in winter
> Crepitating in the grip of an increasing frost.

And of course there are a few fairly elaborate analogies (his trade-mark in the long poem), like the comparison of Britain to a termitary:

> . . . Though stone-blind they manage to communicate,
> Both by touch and by some sort of wireless,
> And if they have no arts they are
> Like the British people
> Exceedingly versatile and accomplished craftsmen . . .

The function of the frequent quotations and translations is an extension of the principle of analogy; they are deliberately *not* worked into the texture of the poem, because in their jutting, unassimilated state they make more of an intellectual appeal – their edges are not melted off by being forcibly fused into some pattern either of verse or of 'poetry'. The finest example of this is the 'Parable of Chamberlain', which uses a translation of Count Alexei Tolstoy's grotesque poem on the court chamberlain Delarue, who keeps smiling when the assassin tries again and again to stab him, in the specific application of the appeasement of Fascism in the 1930s; and then to this comment on appeasement a further comment is added – a long and extremely interesting footnote quoting the philosopher Vladimir Soloviëv's interpretation (*Three Conversations*, 1900) of the poem, and of the whole moral and political problem of 'benevolence' in the sharp social contexts of the modern world. It is in passages like these that MacDiarmid warms to the heart of his subject, which is philosophical as well as political. His own position is not in doubt: he accepts Marxist distrust of the 'worthy people who would fain offer their good-will as a substitute for the proletarian class struggle'. But while opposing an undirectional goodwill, whether Laodicean or Samaritan, and while rejecting neutrality and non-resistance as politically naïve, MacDiarmid returns again and again to the opposite point of view, which he knows many of his readers will hold, and tries to win them away from it by various arguments lucidly and pithily expressed. The war in Spain, he says, concerned an opposition of ideas and beliefs as clearcut and inescapable as we are likely to find; non-intervention may have been humanitarian in aim but was pro-Fascist in effect and was therefore not in humanity's best interests. The doomed struggle of the Republicans and the International Brigade shines like a good deed in a naughty world, and although they failed in a material sense they will only have failed in a spiritual sense if we refuse to take up their challenge. The battle,

in fact, must continue, and this battle reflects MacDiarmid's intense
and often ruthless reading of the doctrine of evolution:

> It is no use saying to me
>   That what we need
> Is an imagination reaching out
> To embrace the great reality
> Which unites the combatants.
> The other monkeys had their points
> But man evolved from a particular kind . . .
>
> – I am not interested in a plea to 'live and let live'
> When it means to abandon the right to pick and choose
> Between the poison and the antidote
> On the ground that they naturally grow alongside each other
> And are both manifestations of life.

– Now this is of course an orthodox Marxist defence. Tolerance of
diversity can come only within an already socialized world, and by
that time diversity will not be so hysterically praised as it is at present,
and so will not present a problem. Only revisionists dare suggest that
this black-and-white view of the world is too inflexible for 1958
(when like Mao Tse-tung you shell your enemy on alternate days of
the week, with due warning, or like Gomulka make a pact with
your most insidious foe, the Roman Catholic Church), but when
MacDiarmid rejoined the Communist Party in 1957 after signing a
joint letter to the *Daily Worker* (published in the *New Statesman*
1 December 1956) condemning Soviet action in Hungary, I don't think
he, so much as life itself, was being inconsistent. As he wrote later
in *Encounter* (May 1957), he 'never had any intention of throwing
out the Marxist baby with the humanitarian bath-water'. This is no
doubt true, but at the same time it shows how alarmingly surprising
history is, especially to those who need immediate explanations.

There are three great animating passions: the passion for justice,
the passion for truth, and the passion for unity or harmony. Hatred
attaches itself most to the first – hatred of injustice; love, to the last.
A poet is peculiarly susceptible to the passion for unity. A new work
of art is more literally a labour of love than anything except a new
human being. The uses of hatred and anger in art are strictly limited,
both by the lower necessity to give pleasure and by the higher
compulsion to record a positive vision. The Marxist, like other
human creatures, has his benedictive vision; his difficulty is the

appalling one of accommodating the sure and blessed future to the snarl of trends in the present: a far harder task than that of the Christian, whose 'future' is trans-temporal and so needs no rational accommodation to the world. (It is the recognition of this that makes Dante and Milton such major poets – social realists as they are!) The Marxist poet has therefore a double battle on his hands: the battle with the dying but lively forces of history, and the battle with art. To any serious poet, Marxist or non-Marxist, consciously or unconsciously, these battles are always being engaged, and must continue. John Singer's couplet comes to mind:

> Where I was born near Stepney Green
> Some read Lenin, but none Racine.

Fair enough! – though the would-be *poet* in Stepney Green had better have a look at both.

If *The Battle Continues*, in spite of its vigour and sincerity and intellectual attack, fails to satisfy as the poetry in the *Three Hymns to Lenin* and *Stony Limits* volumes satisfies, this is due rather to its being a 'song of hate' unmitigated than to its being concerned so much with 'the merely real', with the dirt and error and suffering of a specific time and place. The merely real will not ruin poetry, and indeed this poem bears out, with its faults as well as its successes, one of the most relevant statements of the matter I have come across.

> It has been easy to say in recent times that everything tends to become real, or, rather, that everything moves in the direction of reality, that is to say, in the direction of fact. We leave fact and come back to it, come back to what we wanted fact to be, not to what it was, not to what it has too often remained. The poetry of a work of the imagination constantly illustrates the fundamental and endless struggle with fact.

It should mollify both MacDiarmid and his opponents to note that the unlikely author of that passage was Wallace Stevens.*

Lines Review, 15 (Summer 1959).

* In a comment on his poem 'Examination of the Hero in a Time of War'.

Poetry and Knowledge in MacDiarmid's Later Work

IN the Preface to the *Lyrical Ballads*, Wordsworth makes some striking comments on poetry and science which are quite often quoted but very seldom believed. After claiming that poetry is the 'impassioned expression which is in the countenance of all Science' (a phrase referred to approvingly by Hugh MacDiarmid), he goes on in no less confident vein:

> If the labours of Men of science should ever create any material revolution, direct or indirect, in our condition, and in the impressions which we habitually receive, the Poet will sleep then no more than at present; he will be ready to follow the steps of the Man of science, not only in those general indirect effects, but he will be at his side, carrying sensation into the midst of the objects of the science itself. The remotest discoveries of the Chemist, the Botanist, or Mineralogist, will be as proper objects of the Poet's art as any upon which it can be employed, if the time should ever come when these things shall be familiar to us, and the relations under which they are contemplated by the followers of these respective sciences shall be manifestly and palpably material to us as enjoying and suffering beings.

Wordsworth envisages not simply the acceptance by poetry of facts or things or attitudes which science may unavoidably set within man's future environment (once they have become an intimate part of that environment), but also a more positive co-operation by which poets will be 'carrying sensation into the midst of the objects of the science itself' – in other words, helping to further the process of assimilation instead of passively hoping that schools, television programmes, 'popular science', and the passage of time will float the new material some day into the trembling ambit of the sensitive but unknowledgeable muse.

A good deal of MacDiarmid's poetry, from the *Stony Limits* volume of 1934 onwards through *A Kist of Whistles* (1947), *In*

Memoriam James Joyce (1955), and *The Kind of Poetry I Want* (1961),
has been a practical exploration of both aspects of Wordsworth's
ideal. His search, as he says in *In Memoriam James Joyce*, is for

> The point where science and art can meet,
> For there are two kinds of knowledge,
> Knowing about things and knowing things,
> Scientific data and aesthetic realization,
> And I seek their perfect fusion in my work.

Some would deny that there is any such meeting-point, or argue
that there may have been once but could not be today, or fall back
on the belief that to press for such a fusion would be inevitably to
dilute both science and art. One does not have to evoke the theory of
'two cultures' to feel that there is something unduly inhibiting about
such views. A poetry of knowledge may be difficult to produce, but
its challenge is present in our time, and its absence ought to tantalize
and stimulate. It should not be necessary to apologize for such
attempts as are being made within the arts to show man inhabiting
a world of which science and technology are a formidable part. It
should not be necessary, but it seems to be; because we are apt to
forget how unhelpfully and unhealthily anti-scientific the dominant
literary atmosphere has been. This is where the later work of Hugh
MacDiarmid would have value even if only the value of a corrective
to the onesidedness of (for example) Yeats and Lawrence. Such a
corrective is surely to be welcomed, and studied carefully and without
prejudice. Only those to whom 'a poem is a poem and I am not
interested in anything else' can turn unconcerned from the spectacle
of a man writing with the quixotic aim of seeing poetry, or one kind
of poetry, accepted as

> A protest, invaluable to science itself,
> Against the exclusion of value
> From the essence of matter of fact.

MacDiarmid himself would readily admit that success in writing
such poetry, and success in recommending it to others, can only be
achieved gradually, and to some extent luckily. The 'lucky poet' is
here the poet who chances his reputation by courting heavy odds.
When a hard thing is beginning to be done, failures have to be
accepted, but one moves ahead. The appeal to the future, either as
a period when better poetry of the same kind will be written or as a

period more likely to understand the value of the first stumbling efforts, is sometimes made in these poems of MacDiarmid's, and although it is not in itself the strongest of arguments it is an essential part of the evolutionary credo implicit in the poetry. *In Memoriam James Joyce*, as I have described elsewhere,* is concerned with the fragmentation of human cultures and the desirability of bringing together (as the 'imaginary museum' of modern photographic repro-duction has done for painting and sculpture) the knowledge, achieve-ment, and beauty left isolated and sterile in unfamiliar languages and literatures. The interests and faculties required to assimilate this material will grow, though slowly, until the ideal situation heaves in sight with 'Omnilateral aristology obligatory on everybody'. Appeal to the future, however, does not banish the haunting problem communication, even for MacDiarmid, as is clear from a passage like the following, where he says he has

> spent many of my happiest busman's holidays
> In books like Leonard Bloomfield's *Language*,
> Happy as most men are with mountains and forests
> Among phonemes, tagmemes, taxemes,
> Relation-axis constructions,
> The phrasal sandhi-type and zero-anaphora.
> (What? Complaint that I should sing
> Of philological, literary and musical matters
> Rather than of daffodils and nightingales,
> Mountains, seas, stars and like properties . . .)

That comment shows him still on the defensive, which is hardly surprising when we consider the inaptness of the word 'sing' as applied to the preceding lines. This does not mean, however, that it is impossible to write poetry about phonemes and taxemes; only that in order to do so, one must replace a bare catalogue of terms by a more persuasive, sophisticated proof that these things can be related to us all as (in Wordsworth's phrase) 'enjoying and suffering beings'. In relying so much as he does on the catalogue, on mere mention of the thing itself, MacDiarmid is doing no more than initial spadework; he sacrifices 'poetry' for the sake of an advance in the art of poetry which he believes to be feasible, though others may carry it further than he can. The kind of poetry he wants is 'a learned poetry', and also 'a poetry which fully understands/ That the era of technology is

* 'Jujitsu for the Educated', *Twentieth Century*, September 1956.

a necessary fact'. He is willing to accept the extremer implications of this, as in the short poem 'The Changeful World':

> Earth has gone through many changes.
> Why should it now cease changing?
> Would a world all machines be as strange as
> That in which the saurians went ranging?

But this science-fiction mood is not so typical as his concentration on present knowledge (and theory) and his attempts to relate this to human experience and to his own aesthetics. In all his 'poems of knowledge', therefore, the method of analogy is widely used, sometimes with carefully worked out parallels, sometimes with an oblique hint thrown off to the agile reader. Although this method, which has become MacDiarmid's trademark, can quickly be ridiculed or parodied, it has at its best produced a very remarkable blending of fact and imagination. In *In Memoriam James Joyce* itself, there is the fine passage on the importance to the work of art of what is *not* present, led up to by the introduction of the haemolytic streptococcus which is 'in the sore throat preceding rheumatic fever' but at the height of the fever is gone, like the mysterious 'silence supervening at poetry's height' or an awesome pause in music. In many of the shorter poems there are striking illustrations of the same mastery of unexpected anaology: in *Stony Limits*, the elegy on Charles Doughty, where the growth of the poem that he wishes he could write to praise Doughty is described in terms of crystal growth in rocks and then, by a daring shift of perspective, in terms of the great rayed craters of the moon; in 'Dytiscus', with the mocking comparison between the water-beetle and man striving to breathe a 'diviner' air than that of his muddy environment; in 'Cornish Heroic Song for Valda Trevlyn', the buccal cavity of the white whale with its 'heavy oily blood-rich tongue which is the killer [whale]'s especial delight', and the analogy drawn between the Celtic genius and the 'hideous khaki Empire' of the English; the parturient, self-flyping guinea worm of 'To a Friend and Fellow-Poet' [Ruth Pitter], with its extraordinary description of a desperate yet delicate fecundity applied to the process of poetic creation; the extraction of mercury from cinnabar in 'Crystals Like Blood', where iron piledrivers are crumbling the ore and a conveyor draws it up into a huge grey-white kiln –

> So I remember how mercury is got
> When I contrast my living memory of you

> And your dear body rotting here in the clay
> – And feel once again released in me
> The bright torrents of felicity, naturalness, and faith
> My treadmill memory draws from you yet.

Surely the main thing to be said about this poetry is not 'the details are not always accurate' or 'the process has not always been fully understood by the poet' or 'in any case these are only analogies or extended similes which are being used by the poet for normal aesthetic purposes'. To an expert in some particular discipline (e.g. linguistics in *In Memoriam James Joyce*,* geology in *Stony Limits*†) MacDiarmid is bound to reveal some inadequacies which betray the lack of an intimate familiarity with the subject. Such inadequacies seem, however, fewer or less damaging than one might suppose. Further investigation of the scientific background of these poems may qualify this statement, but it looks at present as if Wordsworth was right in assuming that the poet could still use his natural insight and mental tact in penetrating regions of knowledge as well as the more obvious regions of feeling. As for the objection that these analogies are no more than a refurbishing of heroic simile, it must be remembered that something more than illustration is at stake. The poem 'To a Friend and Fellow-Poet' is equally 'about' the guinea worm and the poetic process; if it shows the poetic process in a new light, it also throws poetic light on an extremely interesting bit of zoology.

The Kind of Poetry I Want affords the best vantage-point for considering the whole problem. A fair amount of technical material is scattered throughout, but very often in reference to easily assimilable activities and pursuits – fishing, piping, dance, film, music – and

---

* The poem speaks about 'Vogule,/ The smallest of the Baltic-Finnish language group,/ Spoken by only 5,000 people'; but there is no 'Baltic-Finnish language group', and even if there was, Vogul (which is wrongly spelt) could hardly belong to it, since it is spoken in Siberia, thousands of miles from the Baltic area; it is spoken by more than 5,000 people, and even if it was spoken by only 5,000 it would not be the smallest of the group MacDiarmid is referring to (under the wrong name). Vogul is a Ugrian (or Finno-Ugrian) tongue, belonging to the Uralian linguistic stock, and there are at least two smaller languages, Livonian and Vodian, in the group.

† To a geologist, 'crossing shear planes' are not 'extruded' as the poem says they are; and 'ultra-basic xenoliths that make men look like midges' (presuming that this refers to size rather than durability) would be exceedingly unlikely since most xenoliths are even smaller than man-size.

the originality consists mainly in the precision with which things like 'a 3-inch anti-kink minnow, brown and gold' are mentioned. Most of these references are analogical: the activities described are models, in their richly ordered complexity and grace, for the sort of poetry MacDiarmid would like to see. At the same time – and this is what is distinctive – the analogies are intended to be themselves examples (not always successful, naturally) of such a poetry in its early stages of development. I say 'early stages of development' because it is more a 'poem of knowledge' than a 'poem of science': it opens out into various sciences, but is concerned to present the reader with thresholds and vistas rather than with entry and possession. It distinguishes its own aim, nevertheless, pointing clearly in a direction taken by few:

> The poetry of one who practises his art
> Not like a man who works that he may live
> But as one who is bent on doing nothing but work,
> Confident that he who lives does not work,
> That one must die to life in order to be
> Utterly a creator – refusing to sanction
> The irresponsible lyricism in which sense impressions
> Are employed to substitute ecstasy for information . . .

What in fact happens in *The Kind of Poetry I Want* – and it is a measure of the poem's great interest – is that a balance is struck between 'sense impressions' and 'information' which makes it possible for much of the information to be seen not in a textbook context but in a life context, and this, though not the poem's primary intention, helps the reader to edge his way in towards the more intellectual passion at the centre. The kind of poetry MacDiarmid wants to see is glimpsed through glasses of varying fineness and power. It is likened to the dancing of Fred Astaire (complex but apparently easy); to bagpipe music (involving skilled improvisation); to fishing (observation, choice, grace of action); to bending a piece of wire back and forward to breaking-point (an experiment with an aim – finding out how words, like atoms, behave); to the mixture of races in Spain and the mixture of cultures in India (a wide range and fusion of individual enriching factors); to the eleven-year cycle supposed by some to govern sunspots, Nile flood levels, wheat prices, tree-rings, measles epidemics, Bank of England discount rates, and many other phenomena (a Jamesian 'figure in the carpet', perhaps, though the analogy is not made syntactically clear); to living flesh suddenly touched in a mineral world (shock of the unexpected); to a busy, sparkling operating theatre 'in which the poet exists only as a nurse during an operation' (devotion of contributing to a larger, complex whole – no doubt the 'operation' of apathectomy on all mankind); to a documentary film about sheep-dogs in which physical setting and elementary natural movement are more important than the story being told (information better than ecstasy – though the information itself is a sort of ecstasy); to the ironic baa of a wild goat chased by man on to crags where he can't be followed (posing questions rather than giving easy answers); and to hedge-laying (craftsmanlike but abstruse).

From these analogies, two main and apparently contradictory models for poetry emerge. On the one hand MacDiarmid wants a poetry of great complexity, coupled with great order, 'organized to the last degree', a product of the 'crystallizing will', subtle yet proportioned, 'masterpieces of intricate lucidity' on the highest level, and on the lowest at least 'artful tessellations'. Where this conception is leading is seen in the admiring reference to Coleridge's 'coaduna-tion' and 'multeity in unity', and in the autobiographical passage describing the changes in a man's life – and in all life – from less to more organic. Like the humble but exemplary lancelet which almost crossed the gulf from invertebrate to vertebrate and pointed the way as a prototype for others –

> If I have evolved myself out of something
> Like an amphioxus, it is clear
> I have become *better* by the change,
> I have risen in the organic scale,
> I have become more organic.

The poem as organism, as a complex structure ordered with such finesse that the code has swallowed the key, is of course a familiar model in recent aesthetic theory, but it would be surprising if Mac-Diarmid accepted it as it has usually been propounded, since he does not himself write, or apparently very much enjoy, poetry conceived on such principles. He does not, however, go the whole way with organism, despite his praise of 'the more organic'. The important difference is that he demands lucidity (whereas in organismic theory ambiguity is welcome), and tries to ensure it by his insistence on reference to 'fact and science' rather than to (say) myth and myth-making: that is, poetry should emulate the expository power of a

T. H. Huxley or a J. P. Joule in making the abstruse stand out 'in cut-gem clearness'.

But as a far greater qualification of this model of poetry, other analogies lead MacDiarmid away from 'organizing', though not necessarily from 'the organic'. We have his belief in poetry that is 'never afraid to leap', poetry improvising like expert pipe-music, poetry going up like fireworks, poetry with unforeseen Beethovenian modulations into remote keys, poetry that is 'wilder than a heifer/ You have to milk into a gourd', the 'poetry of one like a wild goat on a rock'. We have the notable passage where he asks for a poetry

> With something about it that is plasmic,
> Resilient, and in a way alarming – to make cry
> 'I touched something – and it was *alive*.'
> There is no such shock in touching what
> Has never lived; the mineral world is vast.
> It is mighty, rigid, and brittle. But the hand
> That touches vital matter – though the man were blind –
> Infallibly recognizes the feel of life, and recoils in excitement.

Yet this, and in the same sentence, is the poetry he describes as 'full of *cynghanedd*, and hair-trigger relationships'. Of a marriage between Wallace Stevens and Allen Ginsberg one might well say: No go. There is indeed a contradiction here, and it reflects a central contradiction in MacDiarmid's nature which shows elsewhere in the 'metaphysical materialism' of his philosophy. But although Mac-Diarmid makes it difficult for the reader to envisage in the abstract a poetry which is 'organized to the last degree' and yet 'the poetry of one like a wild goat on a rock', it is important to see that this is not a complete contradiction; nor is *The Kind of Poetry I Want* devoid of hints as to how we must bring the ideas together. Just as some extremely intricate Celtic interlace may gain, not lose, by being slightly asymmetrical; or as film-makers have found (or re-learned, after the great painters), how a carefully played scene will gain, not lose, power by having in the background something irrelevant which shows ordinary 'non-art' life going about its business: so, in poetry, Virgil writes a short line, Shakespeare sketches Parolles, Milton 'by occasion foretels the ruine of our corrupted Clergy'. And so too, although *The Kind of Poetry I Want* like most of MacDiarmid's long poems is loosely rather than closely organized, it shows in some passages how improvisation can still help to prove theme, and how 'irrelevance' can become relevant. The wild goat, following its instincts in jumping from crag to crag, may be tracing patterns which science cannot yet describe. Is the passage on Mary Webb a 'digression'?

> A poetry abstruse as hedge-laying
> And full as the countryside in which
> I have watched the practice of that great old art,
> – Full of the stumbling boom of bees,
> Cuckoos contradicting nightingales all through a summer day,
> Twilight deepening with a savage orange light,
> Pheasants travelling on fast, dark wings,
> – Or like a village garden I know well
> Where the pear-trees bloom with a bravery of buds,
> The cydonia blossoms gloriously against its wall,
> And roses abound through April, May, and June,
> – And always with a surprising self-sufficiency
> Like that of almost any descriptive passage of Mary Webb's
> – The fact that she was not wholly herself in all she wrote
> Creating a sort of finality and completeness
> In each part of any given whole,
> The integrity of her experience revealing itself in many ways,
> In the fulfilment of rare powers of observation,
> In the kind of inward perception which recognized
> 'The story of any flower' is 'not one of stillness,
> But of faint gradations of movement that we cannot see',
> The outer magic and the inward mystery imaginatively reconciled,
> Her deep kinship, her intuitive sympathy with leaf and flower
> Extending without a break into the human kingdom,
> And flowering there in an exquisite appreciation
> Of the humours of single characters,
> And a rare power to make them live and speak
> In their own right and idiom.

Now Mary Webb's novels are not abstruse; but consider the modulations of the lead-in, if it is a lead-in. The abstruse art of hedge-laying quickly passes into the thick, complicated, rich-looking texture of the hedge itself, the rich living world and natural habitat of the hedgerow, the richness being a link between the 'abstruse' art and the 'full' countryside which is the next comparison; poetry should be full, as fouthy in its language as the English countryside is in sounds and colours or a village garden in flowers. Then comes the oblique move to 'a surprising self-sufficiency', a phrase which, added to the abstruseness and fullness, reminds us of the 'intricate lucidity' mentioned earlier in the poem but which hardly prepares us for the sudden illustration from 'almost any descriptive passage of Mary Webb's'. She has floated in, perhaps, on the wings of the pheasants, but very soon we become absorbed in what the poet says about her art, and probably we forget any analogy to poetry. If we stop at this point, we may ask ourselves whether the passage is not simply a pleasant interpolated tribute to someone who was a personal friend of the author's. When we read on, we see that it is, and it isn't. The quoted passage is followed by another thirty-odd lines which meditate generalizingly on the value of such a writer, who with her 'practical working knowledge' can 'capture the elusive spirit of a countryside' –

> literary graces concealing
> No poverty of context, lack of virility, emptiness of thought,
> But, held in perfect control,
> Contributing the substance of poetry
> To subjects 'with quietness on them like a veil',
> A manifold of fast-vanishing speech,
> Customs and delights.

The only thing that links Mary Webb and MacDiarmid's aims for poetry is the idea of a rare, intimate knowledge being used for artistic purposes. Our first reaction when we see her name is that few writers could be more different, and we wonder how MacDiarmid could possibly enlist her among his Zouave acrobats and *cynghanedd*. She is brought upon the scene without premeditation, but having been brought, she justifies the suddenness, and we find ourselves looking at the main ideas of the poem from a new angle.

What MacDiarmid seems to be adumbrating in *The Kind of Poetry I Want* – it is nowhere made sharp and definite – is a poetry which is highly organized in parts, but not prescriptively with regard to the whole. It is not so much an organism as a colony, a living and in one sense formless association of organisms which share a common experience. Shape and architectonics are not so important as the quick movements of the thought – the feelers in the water, moved partly by the surrounding currents and partly by their own volition and partly in response to the movement of neighbour tentacles – while a succession of images, illustrations, and analogies is presented to it. As zoologists may argue whether a colony is an organism, critics may hesitate to say that the kind of *poetry* MacDiarmid wants is a kind of *poem*. A movement towards a more 'open' conception of

the poem than has prevailed in the modern period is however
gaining ground, and I see no reason why we should deny ourselves,
for love of architectonics, the ingredient and emergent pleasures of
a poetry in evolution.

> The ingredients resemble the things
> For which a woman with child longs.
> Like the juice of the oyster,
> The aroma of the wild strawberry,
> The most subtle and diversified elements
> Are here intermingled to form
> A higher organism.

The longings are perhaps not 'sensible', perhaps not 'compatible';
and yet they are a part of the great process of creation, they take
their place in the effort to bring something new into the world. That
is the value of Hugh MacDiarmid's later poetry.

From *Hugh MacDiarmid: A Festschrift*, ed. K. D. Duval and S. G.
Smith, 1962.

MacDiarmid at Seventy-five

THE great temptation, in talking about Hugh MacDiarmid's poetry, is to try to sum up its quality and value by picking out the best pieces and rejecting the rest fairly firmly. At its most extreme, this method produces the view of some, that MacDiarmid has only six good poems, all very short and all written before 1926. No one wants to say that the best of the early lyrics are not among the best things he's ever done; but it isn't necessary to depress the early poems in order to stake out claims for the later work. What is troublesome and difficult is to show the relation of both earlier and later work to any enduring or overriding conception of what poetry is. The poems in *Sangschaw* and *Penny Wheep* are concentrated and laconic, they use regular metrical forms, they are clearcut completed objects, and they have a great originality – partly of viewpoint and perspective but also simply of verbal juxtaposition. The late poems like *In Memoriam James Joyce* and *The Kind of Poetry I Want* are long and discursive, they're in free verse, they're not complete but only the top parts of a still larger, submerged, unpublished poem, and although they're original in their total appearance they're made up to a great extent as a patchwork of facts and quotations. It's maybe not surprising that he himself has spoken of this change as a 'violent break', a 'crisis', a 'new departure'. Yet something continues and remains, from the first work to the last, and the present occasion seems a good one to throw a few pointers towards defining what it is.

It's worth remembering that his first book is not *Sangschaw* but *Annals of the Five Senses* which came out in 1923. This strange collection of prose and verse is both hard to read and hard to describe, but what one can say about it is that a good deal of the later Mac-Diarmid is already there in essence – so much so, in fact, that one might think it was *Sangschaw* which provided the interruption, rather than the later work which drove him off the rails. This is a book of – what? Autobiographical sketches in the third person? Studies in morbid psychology? Experiments in a convoluted prose style?

Reflections on the recent war, on sex, on God, on clothes, on eternity and destiny? It's all these and more, it has the omnivorous and encyclopedic quality of the later MacDiarmid, the same lack of concern for the reader's comfort, the same interweaving of quotations and references – Swinburne and Chesterton, Donne and Hopkins, Conrad and Galsworthy, Bacon and Edward Carpenter, Browning and Wordsworth, Henry James and William James, the Bible and the *Saturday Westminster Gazette*: all is swept in, all is ransacked, indiscriminately, as a habit of mind already. He calls it a book of 'mosaics' – a word that would apply later to *A Drunk Man Looks at the Thistle* and *The Kind of Poetry I Want* – and he uses in his introduction two similes to indicate his line of defence in such a literary method or anti-method:

> As fish are seen through an aquarium so these perhaps strange fish of mine are discernible almost entirely through a 'strong solution of books' – and not only of books but of magazines and newspaper articles and even of speeches. What I have done is similar to what is done when a green light on a railway replaces a red light, or *vice versa*, in a given lamp.

Annals of the Five Senses is a pretty indigestible book taken as a whole, but it has some remarkable passages, and it establishes at once some of his leading characteristics: his simultaneous fondness for grand themes and catalogues of minute particulars, his uncritical amassing of material from every source, his belief that the evolution of life does not and cannot stop at social betterment. There is something engaging about this super-Autolycus, this lover of loose ends, but he's not so magpie-minded, even in this early book, as to be unaware of the difficulties such a person faced if he wanted to commit himself to a cause. He describes how he 'used to plunge into the full current of the most inconsistent movements, seeking – always in vain, until he was utterly exhausted, not having failed, however, to enrich every one of them – to find ground upon which he might stand foursquare'. When he came later to write his 'Second Hymn to Lenin', part of his friendly argument with Lenin centres on just this point, that the politician can be ruthlessly singleminded, but the poet can't:

> For a poet maun see in a' thing,
> Ev'n what looks trumpery or horrid,
> A subject equal to ony
> – A star for the forehead!

. . . . . .

> He daurna turn awa' frae ocht
> For a single act o' neglect
> And straucht he may fa' frae grace
> And be void o' effect.

Why, one may ask, should the poet 'fall from grace' if he neglects what looks like a 'trumpery or horrid' subject? The answer to this would seem a superstition to a Marxist critic but it is deeply true to MacDiarmid's nature. In *Annals of the Five Senses* he defends his all-inclusiveness by saying that he recognizes 'in that prodigiousness of the universe a safeguarding excellence, since it must hold infinite resources and he might allow it some credit without accusing himself of improvidence'.

To regard the prodigiousness of the universe as being excellent is merely a Shakespearian view, but to add that this is a *safeguarding* excellence is much more striking and provocative. What, after all, is being safeguarded? Multiplicity is being safeguarded from classification, mystery is being safeguarded from reason, vision is being safeguarded from theory. Can we add that nature is being safeguarded from art? It's certainly being protected from any art that goes too quickly for design and order without having accepted the aleatory discipline. MacDiarmid's view could lead to a completely aleatory conception of art, and this is in fact borne out by the interchangeability of large parts of his later poetry, by mosaic or anti-organicist methods of composition as in *A Drunk Man Looks at the Thistle*, by the widespread use of long, direct, and often unacknowledged quotation which although it is an act of choice on the poet's part increases the element of chance in the total product. All this is no doubt largely untheorized and undeliberate on the part of MacDiarmid, who hardly sees himself as a forerunner of Burroughs and McLuhan. But what he has done, all through his life, is to insist on the importance of the multiplex, as against simplistic solutions, and this involves paying tribute to chance. His fondness for dictionaries and word-lists, for instance, shows this. There are quite a number of passages in his poetry which are bristling with uncommon words beginning with the same letter or with letters from the same part of the alphabet, and it's clear that these passages make use of lists of words which have been collected by the poet for their richness and curiosity value. Many of the words will have no apparent semantic connection with the theme that's being dealt with, but they're given relevance by the ingenious way they're worked in – often by a brilliantly unexpected use of metaphor. So a purely chance connection of rare words is transformed into an apparently and of course temporarily ordered and meaningful connection. There's a passage in 'Cornish Heroic Song for Valda Trevlyn' where in the space of fourteen lines we get the words *resipiscence, reptant, raphe*, (un)-*rabbetable, réseau, retitelarian, rempli*, and *rhabdite*; and the last few lines of 'On a Raised Beach' give us *ébrillade, enchorial, encrinite, entrochal*, and *epanadiplosis*. All these words are, by virtuosity, built into their respective contexts.

It's this longing for fullness, this fear that values may escape by being buried in dictionaries, which to a large extent lay behind his attempt to develop Scots. The national, patriotic aim was secondary to his discovery of the sheer expressive richness of the Scottish language, with its surprisingly large vocabulary of words that unfortunately were often obsolete or obsolescent. As he wrote in *Scottish Chapbook* in 1923:

> The Scots Vernacular is a vast storehouse of just the very peculiar and subtle effects which modern European literature in general is assiduously seeking . . . It is an inchoate Marcel Proust – a Dostoevskian débris of ideas – an inexhaustible quarry of subtle and significant sound.

These are high terms for something that in practice wasn't so easy to carry out. The storehouse of effects and the quarry of sound are admirably rifled in his onomatopoeic tribute to James Joyce, 'Water Music', or in the strong, swinging, shaggy stanzas of 'Tarras'; but antiquarian enthusiasm tends to overrun a poem like 'Scots Unbound', with its subtitle 'Divertissement Philologique'. The possibilities and the limitations could only be found by trial and error, and it will always surely be in MacDiarmid's favour that he took these enormous risks with vocabulary, whether in English or in Scots.

These are the risks of plenitude, the heady pleasures of excess. Much of MacDiarmid's work, where this extraordinary plenitude is to be found, will never please those who want a pared-down muscular poetry, or a watertight poetry, or a non-referential poetry. But it has its own particular surprises for anyone who's eager to write it off as boring, and these surprises couldn't be sprung by any other means. The means are wasteful, but one must simply add What is wrong with that? – Consider, in the following passage from *The Kind of*

Poetry I Want, how the fish seem to keep slipping off the hooks and yet there they are laid out before us at the end:

>As it was in the beginning
>So it is again at the end of life.
>Think of the decrepit old human being,
>Bent over, head bowed,
>Seated in a weary, curled-up position
>Exactly similar to the unborn babe's.
>The cycle of life begins and ends
>In the same design. Only the proportion,
>Size, and shape of the human being
>Change as he passes through the stages
>Of babyhood, youth, maturity, and old age,
>The eternal oval, the egg itself.
>A poetry therefore to approach with two instruments
>– Which, being mutually destructive,
>Like fire and water, one can use
>Only one at a time
>– Even as one may attempt to describe
>The relative positions of the Imperial Palace,
>Hagia Sophia, and the Circus, in Constantinople.
>On the one side the Palace was connected,
>By open arcades and paradoxical gardens,
>With the Golden Egg of Hagia Sophia;
>On the other side an intestinal system
>Of passages and winding stairs
>Led to the Circus. But as regards
>Byzantium in especial, these things are merely
>The elements which combine to form
>A stupendous life pregnant with symbolism.
>Because the theme of that life
>Was the world-embracing mystery
>Of God and man
>It stands supreme
>Above its ingredients.
>The ingredients resemble the things
>For which a woman with child longs.
>Like the juice of the oyster,
>The aroma of the wild strawberry,
>The most subtle and diversified elements
>Are here intermingled to form
>A higher organism.

Opposites are always meeting in MacDiarmid. Although he has this passion for inclusiveness and multiplicity of ingredients, he's been equally attracted by emptiness, silence, space, the alien and the inhuman, and some of his finest poetry is a confrontation of these things. This also runs all through his work, from the bare worlds like mammoths' bones in *Sangschaw*, through the powerful geological meditation of 'On a Raised Beach', and the elegies on Rilke and Charles Doughty, to the elemental rock and water of 'Direadh III' and 'The North Face of Liathach'. But what is the nature of the attraction? What draws the poet, in these poems and others, to the mountain-top, the Arabian desert, the Shetland island, the glaciers of Greenland, the craters of the moon? A man may want to go to Mars or Venus because there is the possibility of finding new forms of life there. On the other hand, a man may want to go to the moon because the possibility of life can almost be ruled out. Most people I suppose would grudgingly admit that they can understand the former, but when they think about the latter they tend to encounter a blank. Yet the rock, the desert is a challenge not only to man's physical exploration and endurance but also in a curious way to his intelligence. Looking round the subhuman forms of life, we can make something of a monkey, a dog, a frog, even an oak-tree or a sunflower; but what about a stone? We think of Martin Buber staring into his cat's eyes, of Edwin Muir and his Orkney horses; but where does MacDiarmid on the raised beach get us? Like Robbe-Grillet, he is determined to emphasize the alienness, the non-humanness of so-called inanimate nature, and he's searching for its value in its very expressionlessness, its silence and incommunicability: these, he says, are to remind man of the importance of a permanent and awe-inspiring openness to experience, to time and weather and chance and change. As one line puts it: 'There are plenty of ruined buildings in the world but no ruined stones'. So our only bond with the geological earth is that it reminds us, shatteringly, how far we have gone from it, and therefore how far our remote descendants, to whom we shall be no better than stones, will one day be from us.

The figure of Doughty in the Arabian desert exerted a strong appeal for MacDiarmid. Doughty was explorer, geologist, word-collector, epic poet, man of independent mind – everything that MacDiarmid admired – but he was also a man who exposed himself to the elemental things, to the most ancient and unassimilable part of the human environment. The end of MacDiarmid's elegy on Doughty, *Stony Limits*, puts this with great persuasiveness:

I know how on turning to noble hills
And stark deserts happily still preserved
For men whom no gregariousness fills
With the loneliness for which they are nerved
– The lonely at-one-ment with all worthwhile –
I can feel as if the landscape and I
Became each other and see my smile
In the corners of the vastest contours lie
And share the gladness and peace you knew,
– The supreme human serenity that was you!

I have seen Silence lift his head
And Song, like his double, lift yours,
And know, while nearly all that seems living is dead,
You were always consubstantial with all that endures.
Would it were on Earth! Not since Ezekiel has that faw sun ringed
A worthier head; red as Adam you stood
In the desert, the horizon with vultures black-winged,
And sang and died in this still greater solitude
Where I sit by your skull whose emptiness is worth
The sum of almost all the heads now on Earth
– By your roomy skull where most men might well spend
Longer than you did in Arabia, friend!

Between the poems of emptiness on the one hand, and the poems of plenitude on the other, there's an enormous gap of ordinary human experience which MacDiarmid's poetry scarcely represents at all. Hardly ever, in any poem, do you get a sense of a man who is committed emotionally to something other than ideas, words, or landscapes. The beautiful and terrible bonds that are not geological but between individual persons, bonds of love or friendship, of desire, misery, doubt, or forgiveness – these are strikingly absent. This is the greatest lack in MacDiarmid's poetry – though he would hardly agree. He must be the most unexistential poet ever to have written. The deficiency would cripple any writer who had less to fall back on, in himself and in books, than MacDiarmid has always had. I said he wouldn't agree with me, because this deficiency goes hand in hand with a polemic. He would regard it as an essential part of his historical mission as a Scottish poet to undo the over-reliance on human feelings and human situations in Burns and his Victorian successors. As he remarks disgustedly in the Foreword to *The Kind of Poetry I Want*: 'Almost all modern Scottish poetry gives off a great sense of warmth and offering, like a dog when it loves you.' Well, this is fair enough in the sense that we don't want a wet poetry. But a poetry of human feeling is not necessarily wet, and one would suspect that an inadequacy as well as a polemic lay behind this rejection of warmth.

The compensations however are extraordinary enough: a poetry which gives itself the liberty to turn without notice from Sacco and Vanzetti to God's Recording Angel, or to use the reproductive self-eviscerations of the Guinea worm as an unforgettable analogy for poetic creation, or to attack A. E. Housman for praising an army of mercenaries (and how seldom is an angry poem successful): in other words, a poetry that has managed to bring together science, religion, politics, aesthetics, and certainly polemics, and to devise its own Pisa-like tower of simile and allusion, cemented with the loosest syntax known to Christendom, and yet to stand, as impressively in the end as any twentieth-century verse. Eccentric and often maddening genius he may be, but MacDiarmid has produced many works which, in the only test possible, go on haunting the mind and the memory and casting Coleridgean seeds of insight and surprise. He has shown once more, and against much twentieth-century doctrine, that the *anima poetae* is what matters.

Broadcast on the BBC Third Programme 10 and 11 August 1967. Reprinted in a shortened version in the *Listener*, 10 August 1967.

The Raging and the Grace: Some Notes on the Poetry of Iain Crichton Smith

THE NOTE of joy is conspicuously absent from Iain Crichton Smith's poetry, but this absence helps to define the values that are present. Joy goes with release and affirmation. Lacking the experience of release and affirmation, a poet will probe and even nourish his natural tensions, or deal with the tensions in the world to which he is most sensitive. This does not necessarily result in a more profound poetry (though the twentieth century has tended to assume so), but it does ensure that the reader who comes in looking in vain for something visionary will go out differently pleased, stirred to consider solution-less problems: of change, of pain, of loneliness, of old age, of failure and success, of death. In a BBC talk on his own poetry (Scottish Life and Letters, October 1963) Iain Crichton Smith said: 'I have always believed in a poetry which contains fighting tensions and not in a poetry of statement.' He also mentioned some of the tensions relevant to his own case (that of a Lewisman who has lived most of his life in the Highlands): between mind and body, between legalism and open-ness, between the old Highlands and the new. And the sort of poetry which comes out of such tensions will generally not state, affirm, recommend, or preach so much as hold within itself 'a precarious balance between opposing elements'. How does his poetry appear in relation to these ideas?

Perhaps basic, as a ground of such tensions and balance, is the sense of place, of the Western Highlands, of Lewis and Oban: the sense of this as the inescapable source of his personal experience, yet simultaneously as a stubborn, anomalous, but not unchanging bastion of the past thrust into twentieth-century international and metro-politan values and influences. To the poet this place offers everything -- except its encouragement and comprehension! Without these he is on a treadmill within his own mind, a treadmill he will find it hard to escape from, since it turns, after all, the wheels of his art. In the fine 'Poem of Lewis' he makes this problem explicit.

> Here they have no time for the fine graces
> of poetry, unless it freely grows
> in deep compulsion, like water in the well,
> woven into the texture of the soil
> in a strong pattern. They have no rhymes
> to tailor the material of thought
> and snap the thread quickly on the tooth . . .

He describes how both the people and the place seem inimical to a developed art; and too stoic and harsh for an art of generous feeling.

> . . . They have no place for the fine graces
> of poetry. The great forgiving spirit of the word
> fanning its rainbow wing, like a shot bird
> falls from the windy sky. The sea heaves
> in visionless anger over the cramped graves
> and the early daffodil, purer than a soul,
> is gathered into the terrible mouth of the gale.

This theme is repeated, but with more acceptance on Smith's part, in a later poem, 'A Young Highland Girl Studying Poetry'. The furrowed brows of the girl puzzling over a subject she has no taste for will clear when she finds her natural place as wife and mother in a simple community.

> . . . And she – like them – should grow along these valleys
> bearing bright children, being kind to love.
> Simple affection needs no complex solace
> nor quieter minds abstractions of the grave.

Such a poem, one might say, is realistic; perhaps one should have no quarrel with it. Yet it is disappointing because of – to take the poet on his own terms – the absence of tension, the absence of disappointment on the poet's part that a life spent 'healing children, bringing lambs to birth' should have no access to the world of art.

Temporary acceptance of the physical environment, acceptance of its outward beauty, its colours and shapes, is of course natural, though in Smith's poetry there is very little indeed of the 'visitor's Highlands'. As he says himself in the BBC talk quoted above: 'I have never been interested in nature for its own sake. This may well be

because I was brought up in close hard contact with it.' There are
no raptures, no intimations of immortality. Instead, an ability to
focus a 'scene with figures' in which nature is as much the background of man's work as the object of a poet's contemplation. Such
is the attractively observed 'End of the Season on a Stormy Day –
Oban':

> . . . Boats lag on the waves untenanted.
> There's thinner patter of walking on the winded
> grey extended front. The soldier draws
> into his Great War stone from loose applause.
>
> A motor boat, stern-flagged, drives steadily through
> the seething waters. Braced to a splayed poise
> a yellow sailor digs his cockerel claws.
>
> And so! And so! His harvest in his hold
> he weathers another season, drives through cold
> towards his roped stone quay, his dead fish fold.

In other poems, nature may supply moments of an evocative,
rather Chekhovian symbolism, as in 'By Ferry to the Island', where
an afternoon picnic is remembered through three compared white-
nesses, the 'pure white' of a seagull, the 'lesser white' of the sand,
and the 'cool white' of a girl's dress.

> . . . And later, going home, a moon rising
> at the end of a cart-track, minimum of red,
> the wind being dark, imperfect cows staring
> out of their half-intelligence, and a plough
> lying on its side in the cold, raw
>
> naked twilight, there began to move
> slowly, like heavy water, in the heart
> the image of the gull and of that dress,
> both being white and out of the darkness rising
> the moon ahead of us with its rusty ring.

In the long, ambitious, but somewhat confused poem 'Deer on
the High Hills', which despite some fine passages is one of his less
successful works, Smith does his best either to work nature (both
animal mineral and vegetable) out of his system or to tell it to keep
its proper and decent place (it is not quite clear which). The elegant
ghost of Wallace Stevens, arch-tensionist as he was, glides rather too

openly through the strangely rough triplets of this meditation on man's place in the earth he has to inhabit. The poem seems loath to come to its conclusion that the deer, however 'noble' they may appear to the symbol-seeking eye as they flash their antlers or bound down the hills, are deer; that the 'starry metaphysical sky' they lie under is physical; and that although we may like to place the seemingly 'noble', 'proud', 'royal' manifestations of nature in a 'halfway kingdom' between earth and heaven –

> There is no metaphor. The stone is stony.
> The deer step out in isolated air.
> We move at random on an innocent journey.

But there is a tension in this poem which everyone must feel, and which at the end is movingly expressed. Man can neither shake off nature, nor communicate with it. There are moments in everyone's life when nature becomes more than a background, yet we have no way of measuring or explaining its suddenly active power – it may be no more than the moon rising over a stubble-field – or of acknowledging it to its face. If there are sermons in stones, they are sermons for other stones. Man can only overhear them, dimly, tantalized, fretting after a sharper deaf-aid than physics or metaphysics can so far provide.

> 'You called sir did you?' 'I who was so lonely
> would speak with you: would speak to this tall chair,
> would fill it chock-full of my melancholy.'
>
> So being lonely I would speak with any
> stone or tree or river. Bear my journey
> you endless water, dance with a human joy.
>
> This distance deadly! God or goddess throw me
> a rope to landscape, let that hill, so bare,
> blossom with grapes, the wine of Italy.
>
> The deer step out in isolated air.
> Forgive the distance, let the transient journey
> on delicate ice not tragical appear
>
> for stars are starry and the rain is rainy,
> the stone is stony, and the sun is sunny,
> the deer step out in isolated air.

Yet the poet Duncan Ban McIntyre, as Smith reminds us, did not hesitate to shoot deer, and 'the rocks did not weep with sentiment'. Nature means the fact of death, and a poet's attitude towards this fact becomes important. In two poems, 'In Luss Churchyard' and 'Sunday Morning Walk', he speaks of the necessary indifference of life to death. Both poems involve a walk on a hot summer day; in both, the grass and leaves are described as 'raging' in the brief desperate high growth of the season. In the first poem the poet broods over the gravestones and their inscriptions, and despite the raging of the grass and the 'savage' skull-and-bones carvings on some of the stones, his breast seems 'empty with indifference', and he moves out on to the road again and his steps quicken – though perhaps with a sense of escape. In the second poem, death is more immediate: a dead sheep buzzing with flies: and the poet, after vainly considering whether he should take his stick and beat off the dreadful indignity of the flies 'hissing ... out of the boiling eyes', leaves them to carry on the inevitable processes of organic nature and walks away, turning his back on 'a death of no weeping or mourning'.

But in a third poem where the telltale image of the 'raging grass' reappears (an image which haunts his poetry), Smith is brought more sharply up against the fact of human death, and here the protective indifference is broken open by pity and shame. In 'Old Woman', one of his best and most moving poems (though almost spoiled by the awkwardness of the last two lines), he wishes he could have the old epic indifference to anything so commonplace as death –

> . . . Greek or Roman men
> who pushed their bitter spears into a vein
> and would not spend an hour with such decay

– but although the pity he feels as he watches the dying, helpless old woman 'blindly searching the spoon' round her plate makes him feel equally helpless, imprisoned and impotent, this impotence being dissolved in poetry becomes active, and the reader has no sympathy with the 'Greek or Roman men'. The poet, though 'imprisoned' by his feelings and in no sense uttering a protest as such, makes of the poem itself a moral and social act. A tear, as Blake said, is an intellectual thing.

The broadening out of this theme to include the multiple suffering and death of war is a natural but difficult step. Smith has tried to deal with this in three poems of increasing ambitiousness: 'For the Unknown Seamen of the 1939–45 War Buried in Iona Churchyard', 'After the War' [on the drowning of two hundred servicemen near Stornoway in 1919], and *World War I*. The first two are not very successful; the absence of any defined attitude, the tone of uninvolved bafflement, gives the impression of something forced, and this shows equally in the flat phrases of the first ('These things happen and there's no explaining') and in the showy imagery of the second ('agile herring, drove on drove, go hissing/under their Hades of the blinded hound'). Only in *World War I*, a sequence of eight poems arranged in four sections, 'Haig', 'The Soldier's Wish', 'November, 1961', and 'Poppies', does the poet begin to dare to use his identificatory imagination, giving some hint of things as they were, and thereby taking those risks of involvement or commitment of which he is normally so sceptical. The risks add a fruitful tenseness to the poem, since this time the bafflement and the memorializing are countered by at least an elementary dialectic of protest. As the soldier himself is made to say:

> I want fat cigars to explode
> from God's lips. I want the dead
> to rise in their hideous truth,
> skulls, bones, smells, to writhe
> through blind speeches. I want
> the full dead to decant
> their blood into glasses, at feasts
> where the false praisers are guests.
> I want the girls who cried 'Heroes'
> to be raped by grunts on dead furrows.
> And all who spoke without thought
> of our 'young warriors' to rot . . .

Yet the poet still finds himself standing apart, saying that he 'can't cry for these men', that the weight of physical suffering is blunt and meaningless in comparison with the complexity and sharpness of what is enacted in the mind alone. The soldiers are

> like the stones of Stonehenge
> staggering about blind fields.

Survivors stand at attention and flaunt armistice poppies. Poppies are a false aesthetic, 'beyond good and evil'. But the poet ends on this wry note, having presented his own half-bitter poppy. The

soldier in his trench has almost disappeared. The poet hasn't sent
that box of exploding cigars to God after all.

> I write this down
> and bring them for a wreath
> not sympathy of pain
>
> but only a clear word
> in face of the absurd.

This very honest, very interesting, not wholly satisfying sequence
of poems shows Smith moving halfway towards a position he may
never in fact take up. The fascination the war theme has for him
indicates that he is not happy about a too complete reliance on local
and personal experience; at the same time, the severely unresolved
tensions in the poem – to a Lowland mind, indeed, the very 'honesty'
seems like a typically Highland evasiveness! – are the limits beyond
which his lack of optimism about human nature and its possibilities
for change will not take him.

I hope he will continue to investigate these bigger themes, because
I think he has laid too much stress on the value of narrow but deep
local experience. In his broadcast talk he said: 'I believe that one can
only write poetry about those experiences which are psychologically
important to oneself.' But to proceed to link this very reasonable
view with the belief that he can only write good poetry 'about High-
landers and about Highland places', as he went on to do, is surely a
false deduction. Place, nowadays, is not so all-important, important
though it must always be. The 'imaginary museum' of the arts is only
equalled by the 'imaginary cinema' of life itself. I may live in
Glasgow, but that means nothing to me when I read that a Buddhist
monk has set fire to himself in Saigon: for I am then in Saigon. When
Edith Piaf dies in Paris, or Joan Eardley in Catterline, I am moved
by these events just as much as by anything that I directly experience. Is there no wrinkle of the shrinking world felt at Oban? I am
sure there is, and the poet is the man who should acknowledge it.

At any rate, I would not be surprised if some of the wider themes
proved more profitable than that of the mind-body dualism which
Smith put first on his list of tensions. The poems which touch on this
subject – particularly the *Love Songs of a Puritan* – contain some
striking passages but seem curiously ingrown and static; the recurrent imagery of god and devil, theology and heresy, sermon and

saint makes little impact because the context fails to tell us how seriously it is to be taken; and for all the poet's expressed fondness for 'precision', these poems are sometimes vague and muffled in the too constant play of images and wit. A real 'Puritan', one feels, would never engage in such fiddle-faddle as

> . . . so there, before you, you enrich this earth
> or poor chaotic sea with the light you send
> like billowing skirts dear wind can make a froth
> of cloth like water not like shaping mind
> or like a shade predestinate that's meant
> to show the mercies of pure accident.

What seems wrong with these poems is that although they are ostensibly 'love songs', no actual human relationship very convincingly emerges from them. But Smith has claimed, 'I tend to be concerned with people', and it is quite true that when he succeeds in writing less subjectively the whole verse appears to open out and begin to speak, and some of his most attractive poems are character studies like 'School Teacher', 'The Widow', 'For Angus MacLeod', and 'For My Mother'. The tensions of mind and body are not lacking from these poems, but they have been properly distanced into an affectionate clarity. In 'School Teacher', for instance:

> . . . The classroom wavered. The four walls poured in.
> Her barren gown hung in the sea's spin.
> 'I want that apple. Bring it here at once'
> And smilingly he came to lay it flat
> on the clear desk. It hissed like a red cat:
> and standing quietly by her unlearnèd breast
> the boy's eyes shone with an oblique unrest.
> Sighing, she locked the lid. The apple lay
> placed in her loved desk, soon to decay.

These poems, like 'Old Woman', show one of the directions Smith's poetry seems to be taking: a poetry of sympathy and compassion, involving human beings, especially those of his own immediate experience. The other side of his art leads him towards something more abstract: his fascination with ideas of exactness, harmony, order, music, pattern, grace – ideas which tend to be expressed in non-human terms. What he calls 'a unity in spite of love and hate' makes an early appearance in 'Anchored Yachts on a Stormy Day':

> Nine yachts are rocking in the sullen water,
> one mast to each, one mast narrow and straight,
> almost (so one would think) about to break
> but never breaking quite. Indeed a kind of laughter
> a demon gaiety, lightens their dull weight
> so that the wave and wood, moving together,
> blend into one as if they yearned to make
> a unity in spite of love or hate
> and the dense rancour of the heaving weather.
> Though a tenth lies there capsized, the others dance
> their stormy demon dance as if awake
> they know the chances they must always take
> when seas are riding high: and that their tether
> is what will save them when the waters shake.

And a closer look is given to this conception of the united 'dance' or 'tether' in the later sequence called *Grace Notes*, where various kinds of 'grace' are presented: an acrobat's technique, a cormorant's diving prowess, the exactness of geometry, the strange percipience of the blind man's stick, the invisible grace that lies behind music and colour. These images of 'grace', beauty, precision, and propriety (which develop elsewhere in his poetry) seem a counterpart to the image of the 'raging grass'. Between the poles of rage and grace the human world has to move, and the picture of that world which the poet produces varies as his allegiance wavers. Under the pole of grace he is the poet who says in *Grace Notes*:

> . . . I speak of the central grace, that line which is
> the genesis of geometry and of all
> that tightly bars the pacing animal.
>
> Around it build this house, this poem, this
> eternal guesthouse where late strangers call,
> this waiting-room, this fresh hypothesis.

But at the other pole he sees things that are more important than grace, as in 'Money-Man Only':

> . . . . To slide your car along a riven road
> towards a house of the entire silver
> and a wife yapping from her glass kingdom –
> this I think is treachery to our kind.
> I excommunicate you from my undesigned

church of the crooked spire, the scrawled pane,
the minister wearing his clown's cloak,
the uncertain affirmations of my choir.
You own a grave I would not dare to share.
I know no crime graver than not to care.

I do not know how much of Smith goes with that fine last line, but I
hope it is a lot. A poet who is apt, through his very gifts, to be
seduced by a too salient imagery or music (e.g. 'from aloof azures let
its ariels go', or 'and from his Minch of sherries mumble laws') may
not find it easy to develop the human subject-matter in such a way
that the poem helps it to speak for itself, though this is done very
beautifully in 'Old Woman' and 'For My Mother'. But the root of
the 'caring' has been planted, in a sensitive intelligence, and we can
expect to see a broadening as well as a deepening of his already
marked and individual achievement.

Lines Review, 21 (Summer 1965).

James Bridie

THE only time I met James Bridie was a few years before he died, when I was in my final year at Glasgow University. My professor, Peter Alexander, had been lecturing to us on Shakespeare, and one day he announced that as a relief from the academic approach he had asked a living dramatist to come along and give us *his* views about Shakespeare. So we got a lecture from James Bridie. It wasn't a particularly well-delivered lecture, but I remember it very vividly. Bridie appeared as a rather shy and diffident speaker, but the views he was putting forward were far from diffident. He was talking about *King Lear*, but a large part of his lecture was devoted to a comparison between Shakespeare's *King Lear* and the old anonymous chronicle-play *King Leir* which was one of Shakespeare's sources, and his general argument was that the old *King Leir* was really a more satisfactory piece of work than Shakespeare's. It really was a better play – the king's motives were much clearer; there was none of that mad, lurid, extravagant poetry that cluttered up Shakespeare's dramatic action. You knew what the characters were saying, the whole thing developed lucidly and decently and was an object-lesson in simple dramatic construction. Shakespeare, in comparison, really didn't know what he was doing. – All this spoken quietly and without emphasis, as if it was the most natural thing in the world. And with one of the most distinguished Shakespeare scholars sitting a few yards away. Looking back now, I think this little incident says a lot about Bridie. It's quite clear that he was being impish and naughty in the extreme, and I think we all took the point – that here was in fact a little dramatic situation, an encounter between scholar, play-wright and students, and it was almost as if he was producing a little play, a little dance over the too rigidly deified body of Shakespeare. Well that's all right; one gets the amusement of what he's doing, and it was also stimulating, it made us think. But you're left with various questions, and these questions are unanswered. What did Bridie *really* think of Shakespeare's *King Lear*? Does he really admire a

direct well-made play more than a complex poetic one? Was he
being deliberately provocative, or only gently amusing? Was he
seriously trying to tell us something, or was he just the entertainer,
the licensed jester at the court of learning? No very satisfactory
answer to these questions is forthcoming – even when we read what
he has to say about *King Lear* in his collection of humorous essays,
Tedious and Brief (1945).

I mention this little episode because questions like these tend to
arise whenever you try to think hard about Bridie's work and its
meaning and value. Hs is still a very elusive figure, very hard to
estimate. My own feeling is that he is a good deal undervalued at the
moment. I want to discuss some of the reasons for this undervaluing
of Bridie, which can be traced to his conception of drama, a conception that is original and has to be understood. But first of all one
has to admit that Bridie was his own worst enemy in most of the
statements and remarks he made about drama outside the plays
themselves. From most, though fortunately not all, of these statements and remarks one would get the strong impression that here
was a man who was determined not to take his art seriously. There's
a persistent flippancy in nearly all his non-dramatic writings, whether
you read his autobiography *One Way of Living* or his essays and
squibs in *Tedious and Brief* or *Mr Bridie's Alphabet for Little Glasgow
Highbrows*. Some people are so put off by this flippancy that they
can never quite take Bridie seriously as a writer. But what exactly
does it amount to?

What does he say about drama and the theatre?

> A play is a method of passing an interval of time. A stage play is a
> method of passing an interval of time by putting an actor or actors on a
> platform and causing them to say or do certain things. If it is amusing,
> that is to say if it succeeds in making the spectators unconscious of the
> passage of time, it fulfils its functions and has merit . . . Other quali-
> ties of a play – its educative, its thought-provoking, its exciting, its
> poetic qualities – are not basic . . . Again I repeat that the Theatre is
> a Pass-Time; and, when we go on to consider the highly expert matter
> of some of the methods used to pass time, we must bear this in mind:
> that the eternal function of the Theatre is to entertain, to suspend, or
> at least to make tolerable the business of living . . . A work of art
> and particularly a play should be enjoyed and not judged.

> (*Tedious and Brief*)

This is a typical mixture of the jocular and the serious. It starts off on the jocular note, but by the end it is putting forward a perfectly possible view of the functions of a play – a limited view, but not necessarily a tongue-in-cheek view. Again, in *Mr Bridie's Alphabet* he says, 'The Play is not important to us today; not nearly so important as the films, for one thing. It would be fun if it was; it it still had the power to shock us, to make us weep, to make us rise in a howling mob and break the gallery benches.' You might say that it's almost incredible that a serious dramatist should write in this way. If the only result of the theatre becoming important again was that 'it would be fun' – *and* that this fun would consist in the audience going berserk and breaking up the gallery. And if you decide that Bridie is only being funny in a passage like that, you still want to know why he should think it worth his time, since he is playing into the hands of the philistine? I think he often writes in this way because he wants to dissociate himself from intellectuals and critics, wants to put himself forward as the practical man of the theatre whose first task is to keep the audience happy. (Cf. Byron. Byron was sometimes flippant or philistine in talking about poetry, and people often make the mistake of taking him at his word and then running down his poetry; they forget that the philistine joker is one of the many masks that Byron puts on, for his own purposes.) It has to be admitted that Bridie can at times irritate you intensely, but when you come across a sentence like this from his autobiography – 'If I appear to you a little smug and complacent, it is because I am smug and complacent' – certain warning signals should go off in your mind as you read this, and it should be clear that Mr Bridie is not a simple case, but has to be looked at with some care.

It's only fair to point out that on occasion Bridie does give us a more convincing account of his activity as a playwright. In his autobiography, in his last conversation with the Recording Angel who is still a bit dubious about the value of his plays, he writes:

'Just a minute,' I said. 'Listen to this. She came downstairs. She went to an office and sat there all day. She went back to her divan room at six-thirty and stayed there reading library novels. She had no friends and no money to spend.' . . . If I make her alive then I have told a story, a story out of which you can take your own meaning, a story you round off with your own moral. If I put in a murder in the next flat, a love affair with her employer or any such miserable incident I put it in because otherwise no one would buy this story. But they are not the story. The story is the girl herself, coming to life, reaching to you over the footlights and telling you that you are not alone in the world; that other human beings live, suffer, rejoice and play the fool within the same limitations that bind you.

In that more serious statement of Bridie's aims, there's one thing I'll like to pick on as a lead-in to a discussion of some of the plays themselves. He talks about the story in the play as being 'a story out of which you can take your own meaning, a story you can round off with your own moral'. Now this is a pretty fundamental idea in Bridie, and you can see it at work in most of his plays. I think it's an idea that comes essentially from the man himself and from his character and outlook on life, but of course it does also link Bridie back to Bernard Shaw whom he admired, and it links him forward to a playwright like John Arden. To all three, Bridie, Shaw, Arden, the same objection has at times been raised: that in the end you don't know where you stand as reader or spectator of the argument that's been presented – that either the author has not committed himself sufficiently to one point of view or he has not made his point of view sufficiently clear. E.g. in Arden's *Live Like Pigs* is he on the side of the gypsies or of the council house tenants? In *Armstrong's Last Goodnight* is he on the side of the outlaw or of the central government? In Shaw's *Major Barbara* is he on the side of the Salvation Army girl or of her father the armament manufacturer? In Bridie's *The Anatomist* is he on the side of Dr Knox or of Amelia or of Mary? One can't wriggle out of these questions by saying, Oh, Shakespeare didn't commit himself to expressing one particular philosophy of life, why should we get annoyed with Bridie and Shaw and Arden for sitting on the fence? But Shakespeare wasn't writing discussion plays as these dramatists are; these dramatists are deliberately taking up and tossing around some controversial point or idea and the idea is as central to the play as the characters are. It's interesting to notice that Bridie saw clearly what Bernard Shaw was doing and apparently approved of it. In an essay on Shaw in *Great Contemporaries* (1935) Bridie wrote:

> The most disturbing feature of *Widowers' Houses* was the judicial attitude of its author. He repeatedly stepped over from the prosecutor's desk to that of the Devil's advocate. We are still disturbed by this attitude. We like our author to take sides . . . How can a critic attack an author if he is for ever stating the converse to his own thesis in a much more brilliant fashion than the critic can achieve?

Well, Bridie never liked critics, and he obviously relishes any situation where the critic can be put at a disadvantage. As Winifred Bannister shows in her book on Bridie, the drama critics were often very much at odds, or very puzzled, by a new Bridie play. It was only rarely, in my opinion, that they really understood what Bridie was doing – they tended to put him in a category as a minor Scottish Shaw, a sort of pantomime Shaw with devil's horns on. In Scotland he tended not to be taken very seriously, though his plays were (by and large) enjoyed. In London the critics took him more seriously but seemed unwilling or unable to grasp the nettle of his Scottishness. In the end he emerged somewhat battered under that most particoloured and reprobated banner, an Anglo-Scots dramatist, with a strong right foot firmly planted in the West End and a much-tramped-on left foot weaving about between Glasgow and Edinburgh.

But perhaps this is all part of the plan, part of the man? Can we in any way define what he was trying to do?

To look for a moment at *The Anatomist*: Here is a strong play with a naturally dramatic, even lurid, subject, and within this lurid subject plenty of discussion of ideas. Bridie, with typical facetiousness, calls it in the subtitle 'A Lamentable Comedy of Knox, Burke and Hare and the West Port Murders', and also in his preface seems to disclaim any very serious intention. He says, for instance. 'The play does not pretend to be anything but a story with an historical background. If it illustrates anything, it is the shifts to which men of science are driven when they are ahead of their times.' There's a good deal of the smoke-screen about all this. The play may certainly be regarded as a comedy (a somewhat grim comedy perhaps), but it's doing more than Bridie says it is. It's a most vivid dramatization of an unresolved (and so far unresolvable) dilemma, and he manipulates our feelings by a series of alienation devices that draw him nearer Brecht than Shaw. I say Brecht rather than Shaw because it seems to me that the alienation is produced more strictly in terms of character, it isn't just an alienation of ideas or dialectic. Brecht wanted you to have strong feelings about what a character said or did, and then be able to stand back and judge your feeling, if necessary with a correction of it; Shaw, on the other hand, produces a continuous texture of wit in which the alienation devices are sometimes submerged. I think that if Brecht's work had been better known in this country while Bridie was alive, people might have had a closer sense of what Bridie was doing. In *The Anatomist*, Bridie is careful to involve us in a series of emotional reactions pro and con Dr Knox, and at a few points to remind us with a sudden cold shock that when we identify ourselves with Knox or feel alienated from him we're accepting or rejecting a whole philosophy of action. Knox is built up by opposites: he is rude, but he's vigorous and witty; he's arrogant and self-centred, but he's a man of genius who'll contribute something to medical studies; he's callous and brutal over the body of the murdered girl when she's brought in for dissection, but he's oddly sensitive and vulnerable when he's with Amelia Dishart; he's sinister, but also at times ludicrous. In the first Act we're swept up into a fascinated reluctant admiration for Knox; in the second Act against him, with the background of the horror and pathos of the Burke and Hare scenes; in the last Act we're not given a resolution or synthesis, we're left with all his contradictions still on our hands, and *we* have to decide. It's deliberately made difficult:

KNOX: And now, gentlemen, I should say ladies and gentlemen, I am humbly obliged to you. You are well aware that every sneaking scribbler in this intellectual Gomorrah who can smudge an ungrammatical sentence employs his miserable talent to scratch venom on the public news-sheets; that, for the benefit of those worthy citizens who are unable to read, gap-toothed mountebanks scream and splutter at every street corner. And I, gentlemen, I am the unworthy occasion of all this. I have argued with the great Cuvier, in the Academies of Paris. I shall not profane the sacred gift of human speech by replying to these people in any other language than that of the cudgel. With you I shall take the liberty of discussing a weightier matter . . . 'The Heart of the Rhinoceros'. This mighty organ, gentlemen, weighs full twenty-five pounds, a fitting fountainhead for the tumultuous stream that surges through the arteries of that prodigious monster. Clad in proof, gentlemen, and terribly armed as to his snout, the rhinoceros buffets his way through the tangled verdure engirdling his tropical habitat. Such dreadful vigour, gentlemen, such ineluctable energy requires to be sustained by no ordinary forces of nutrition . . .

[*While he is speaking the curtain slowly falls. The* STUDENTS *are listening with a passionate intentness which will, it is hoped, communicate itself to the audience.*]

This ambiguity chimes with both the intellectual core of the play – the argument about ends and means – and the popular reaction to Dr Knox. There can always be argument over ends and means. And at the popular level, we notice that although the mob is out howling for Knox's blood it is also already turning him into a folk hero, making up and chanting ballads about him:

> Up the close and doon the stair,
> Ben the hoose wi Burke and Hare,
> Burke's the butcher, Hare's the thief,
> Knox' the boy that buys the beef.

This awareness of how thoroughly mixed good and evil are in the world implies that Bridie was no social reformer; and in this, of course, he differs from both Shaw and Brecht. His peculiar quality is to suggest, though not to insist on, a certain trust in human adaptability and continuance. This trust is outwith systems of belief, whether religious or political, but it is aware of and subtly related to belief. Bridie is strongly attracted by the simple idea of belief in human genius; the risky, amoral side of this is seen in *The Anatomist* and *A Sleeping Clergyman*, and a more gentle side in the dreams and aspirations of *Mr Gillie*, still unsuccessful but still hopeful of launching genius among his pupils. But Bridie also wants to keep reminding us of the opposite of genius, that's to say, grace. He's never quite, even in his last plays, an existentialist. Man is not certainly or entirely on his own. Angels and devils appear; umbrellas walk off the stage; as Tobit says at the end of *Tobias and the Angel*, 'We have been visited'. The dilemma between genius and grace is, like all Bridie's antitheses, left as a dilemma.

It's natural that Bridie should have been attracted to William McGonagall, poet and tragedian, and written *Gog and Magog* on the basis of McGonagall's life. In Bridie's Magog, as in the real McGonagall, the interest lies in the ambiguity, the impossibility of deciding where the ludicrous ends and where dignity begins.

Similarly, in *Daphne Laureola* Bridie makes the question of ideals walk a tightrope. Is it better to have an unattainable Beatrice, even if you're not much of a Dante? Is it better for Ernest, the young man in the play, to lose Lady Pitts to her vulgar chauffeur and keeper Vincent? Is it better for Lady Pitts in the end to (as she says) 'settle down in a nice clean pig-sty'? Is a nice clean pig-sty better than loneliness, or worse? And linked with these dilemmas of personal life are larger questions pushing out into history and society: is innocence better than knowledge? should power be kind? can power be kind? Bridie never used the convention of drunkenness to greater effect than in the long tipsy monologues of Lady Pitts – the *in vino veritas* idea suits him perfectly because it keeps the ambiguity principle intact, i.e. you *may* be speaking the truth when you are in liquor but you are not really *responsible* for your statements. And these speeches are among the best things Bridie wrote.

> LADY PITTS: We had a laburnum tree at the vicarage. The pods were poisonous. We were told that we must not on any account eat the pods. It was like the tree of the knowledge of good and evil in the Garden of Eden. Only that was an apple tree. This was a laburnum tree. I ate some laburnum seeds and I was very ill, but I learned no more about good and no more about evil by that act. All that came later. But my father was very angry. He was terrible in his rage. I wore a white sailor suit when I ate the laburnum. My father thought I did it out of badness or to show off. There were several little boys there when I ate the laburnum. But he was wrong. Perhaps God was wrong about Adam and Eve. I only wanted to know about good and evil. That was reasonable enough. That was very, very reasonable. Even God is often unreasonable. (*She sings*]
>
> > Pull for the shore, sailor,
> > Pull for the shore,
> > Heed not the rolling breakers,
> > Stand to the oar.

In his last plays – *Daphne Laureola*, *Mr Gillie*, *The Queen's Comedy* and *The Baikie Charivari* – Bridie seems more and more to be setting his questioning against the actual background of the age. Lady Pitts is a sort of Archie Rice of 1949, and the broken-down Soho restaurant where she's drinking is a symbol of postwar Britain. This postwar feeling, and added to it the uneasy premonitions of a third and more terrible world war, are what lie behind *The Queen's Comedy*, which updates the Trojan War into our period. In this play unfortunately Bridie was tempted beyond his powers. Towards the end he decides to give, for the first time, answers as well as questions, and it doesn't work. After a splendid and most moving scene when the bloody maimed shades of dead soldiers appear in heaven and challenge the gods – as the medical orderly says, 'I'm dead and the dead can judge all gods and all men' – Bridie makes the mistake of bringing on Jupiter himself to explain what he has been doing, and his long speech, which ends the play, is merely embarrassing. But in *The Baikie Charivari* he returns to the theme of 'nobody knows'. At the end of this play the hero, Pounce-Pellott, who is also Punch and Pontius Pilate, has knocked out and rejected all those who would offer him advice and panaceas – the communist, the churchman, the scientist. Even the Deil, who comes to claim him on the last page but doesn't do it, is impressed. Punch is left to jest again. 'I must jest again and await my reply.'

Punch is a disconcerting figure, and Bridie enjoyed seeing himself as Punch. He was a bit of a Punch in the Scottish Theatre too. When he first joined the Scottish National Theatre Society in the 1920s he tells us how divided they were as to their programme for Scottish theatre. 'There were three main trends of opinion,' he wrote in his autobiography.

> John Brandane was for the pure milk of the Gospel. He considered that the Society should produce a Scottish drama by Scottish authors and, as there was no existing Scottish drama by Scottish authors, that the Society's sole function was to evoke one . . . Another trend of opinion was expressed mainly by the actors. They wanted to get their teeth into well-carpentered professional work, and were inclined to look down their noses at Scottish drama *per se*. A third trend was just beginning to make its appearance. A young professional producer had just been engaged . . . He was six feet four high and wore a jersey and sandals. Brandane did not entirely approve of him . . . The name of the producer was Tyrone Guthrie, and I need not tell any theatregoer that the Scottish National Players had got hold of a handful. His predilections at this time ran somewhat in the direction of song, mime, and stepladders; and Brandane, Gordon Bottomley, and Walter Buchanan of the St Andrews Society regarded these things as dangerous innovations, I think rightly.

(The situation doesn't seem to have changed all that much half a century further on – the Stage Company (Scotland) waves its banner for Scottish authors; the actors still looking for well-carpentered non-Scottish plays at Citizens'; and you've got the jersey and sandals and the mime and step-ladders at Traverse and Close.) Well, Bridie as Punch gives that rather mocking but sharp picture of the early days of the Scottish National Players, and then he goes on to describe how he took part it it himself, by writing his first play for them:

> My first step towards compromise was to write a play with almost everything in it but step-ladders. It was called *The Sunlight Sonata*, or *To Meet the Seven Deadly Sins*. Guthrie liked it. With magnificent courtesy and patience he helped me to iron out its amateur crudities. Brandane liked it, because, although it leaned over to the fantastic, it was as Scots as Freuchie. The Devil spoke from the top of Ben Lomond,

addressing the Seven Deadly Sins in braid Scots hexameters, and the eight of them interfered in the private lives of a bunch of quite justly observed Glasgow citizens picnicking on the Bonnie Banks. Three pantomine fairies called Faith, Hope and Charity intervened. It was the last and only extant survivor of my morality play period, and I thought it very amusing. I wrote it on a Sunday and had to ring up a clergyman of my acquaintance to find out exactly who the seven deadly sins were. He did not know.

All this banter is good fun as you read through it, and yet in the end you begin to sense underneath it the malaise of the Scottish theatre, its fits-and-starts development, its unagreed aims and policies. Bridie, officially an Anglo-Scots playwright but really an extremely Scottish one, is at the exact centre of any such malaise. He couldn't go along with those like Robert McLellan in later years who wanted a Scottish-language drama at all costs. He couldn't go along with those like the Unity Theatre group who wanted a committed 'people's theatre' in touch with Scottish radical traditions. But it would be quite wrong to suggest, as some who should know better have suggested, that Bridie sold out to the London West End and passed up his birthright. All dramatists are limited by something, and if Bridie has the obvious limitations imposed by his middle-class background and his lack of interest in political change, there are other, more committed dramatists who are limited by their incomprehension of the enigmatic, questioning needs and qualities in life which Bridie understood so well. His argumentativeness is Scottish, but the open-endedness of his arguments is twentieth-century, and I suspect that the impish elusiveness of his message will become more and not less interesting as time goes on. He wrote some very bad plays, but so do most dramatists. What we can say is that if we really did have a Scottish National Theatre, which I'm sure one day we will, Bridie's plays would be on eof the ornaments of such a company, and the best of them would be frequently performed in a variety of styles. There is more to Bridie than many people think, and it's time he was gently moved out of his little niche of neglect.

Scottish International, November 1971. (Text of a talk given to the English Association in November 1967.)

The Novels of Robin Jenkins

OVER the last twenty years Robin Jenkins has published almost as many novels and built up a considerable reputation. He is not the sort of author who has written one book of such unquestioned artistic success that all his other books have to be measured against it, and, in fact, reviewers have often been strikingly at variance in their estimates of his merits. But it would be fairly generally agreed that his most valuable and interesting work is in *Happy for the Child*, *The Thistle and the Grail*, *The Cone-Gatherers*, *The Changeling*, *Some Kind of Grace*, *Dust on the Paw* and *A Love of Innocence*. Most of his best books, though not all, are set in the West of Scotland (whether Lowland or Highland), where his naturally sharp observation combines with his sense of basic and recurring Scottish themes.

In an article in the *Saltire Review* in 1955, he argued that the novelist's job in Scotland was, above all, to be honest: to use the life he saw round about him, as a novelist in any other country would do, and be confident that it could be made interesting to readers outside Scotland. 'We have been a long time in acquiring our peculiarities: in spite of ourselves, they are profound, vigorous and important; and it is the duty of the Scottish novelist to portray them.' The wry awareness of that 'in spite of ourselves' is good, and typical of Jenkins, but perhaps the operative word is 'peculiarities', since there is no doubt that Jenkins's novels, for all their emphasis on honest reporting, do sometimes present an extremely peculiar world: a world that can only be regarded as in part symbolic and fabulous, however much local detail and dialect may be employed. It is there in the very vocabulary of his titles: 'grail', 'missionaries', 'changeling', 'grace', 'love', 'innocence', 'holy', 'Lord'. Even allowing for the irony with which some of these words are used, the religious preoccupation is constant, and it is the mingling of this preoccupation with two other things – the flavour of ordinariness, and the sudden very marked irruptions of violence and melodrama – which gives his books their characteristically odd and often enigmatic sort of reso-

nance. The religious preoccupation wavers between residual Northern Calvinism, observed both sympathetically and tartly, and intimations of a wider kind of grace. The ordinariness is children at school,
football matches, holidays at the coast. The melodrama is a hunchback shot in a tree by a neurotic gamekeeper, a schoolboy hanging
himself in a hut, a boy watching his mild father murder his faithless
mother with a hatchet, an orphan boy eaten by crows, a lay preacher
taking his hatchet to an American sailor who he thinks has seduced
his daughter and jumping to his death from a bridge. It is into this
grim wasteland of a gap between the placidity of everyday expecta-
tions of order and habit and the fearful potential of horror that
Jenkins drives his questions, which not surprisingly turn out to have
a metaphysical dimension. As the old roadman warns the hopeful
young hero of *So Gaily Sings the lark*: 'A man kens in his heart that
this is an unfinished sort of a place, not perfect like heaven; and
when he sees something that he thinks is complete he looks roond,
without meaning to, for the disappointment.' Yet this 'unfinished
sort of a place' is the novelist's domain, and he has either to glory in
it, or to find glory in it, somehow.

Jenkins concentrates, in the main, not on characters in the prime
of life but on children, the middle-aged and the old. This is unusual
in itself, but it helps him to present with greater immediacy and
sharpness contrasts between expectancy and knowledge, innocence
and guilt, obedience and freedom, as well as the tangle of frustrated or
late or twisted or consuming erotic experience in the over-thirties
which is another curious and at times grotesque feature of his work.
Some of the books offer a wary hope, some are tragic, some are
deeply ambiguous. In *The Changeling*, a Glasgow school-teacher
takes one of his East End kids with him and his family when they
go on holiday. The boy is a thief and a liar but intelligent, sensitive
but stoically inhibited, conditioned by poverty but capable of change,
yet dogged by an almost malicious bad luck so that the teacher begins
to feel 'inimical non-human forces' using the boy as their instrument:
he is a changeling. Although one can see that the changeling's anguish
has clear social roots – he can neither leave nor (by the end) rejoin
his own class, home and family – his suicide on the last page seems
rather forced, rather too didactic. The teacher (an unsuccessful one)
has been brutally rewarded for his do-gooding.

Children are again at the centre of *A Love of Innocence*. Two
brothers from an orphanage in Glasgow are boarded out in the

Western Highlands, into a God-fearing community. Must the sin of their father, who murdered their mother, be visited on them? Even to those who are sympathetic and who like the boys, 'they seemed to lie under some kind of guilt.' But those who would send them away as contaminators of Highland purity are defeated, and the novel ends in some optimism. Its title, however, is not unambiguous, since if it offers a positive on the one hand, this seems to be turned inside out on the other, considering the fact that the main adult character, a philanderer, bigamist, fraud and blarneyman, and very far from 'innocence', is presented as a likeable rogue and by no means devoid of good qualities.

Extreme vulnerability is shown as, in the end, defenceless in *The Cone-Gatherers*, the most atmospheric and mysteriously suggestive of his books, marred only by novelettish touches (great ladies and their gamekeepers are not Jenkin's forte). Here, guilt and cruelty and suffering are shown, not as social or personal, but as written into the world of nature of which man can only be a part. During a world war, two brothers are working in a Highland forest, gathering cones for seed. Both are strange, Hardyesque earth-creatures. Against malice and rumour they have poor defences. The grimness of the ending, when the hunchback brother is killed by the gamekeeper, is only relieved by the implausible catharsis of Lady Runcie-Campbell, weeping in pity on her knees among the pine-cones.

For some years Jenkins taught in Afghanistan and Borneo, and he uses these countries as background in some of his novels. It is generally thought that he works best with Scottish material, but the attempt to break out from this was certainly justified in *Dust on the Paw* and *Some Kind of Grace*, if not in *The Tiger of Gold* or *The Holy Tree*. *Dust on the Paw* is a long and ambitious novel. The main theme of mixed marriage is probed with insight and humour, within the broader political context of a recently independent state trying to find its identity among the new dollar and rouble imperialists. Although a certain whiff of *tour de force* hangs over this book, its reiterated preoccupation – whether it is better to be humble dust on the paw of the lion or to be the lion – strikes the Jenkinsian note of weighing compassion and assertion.

In his novels since *A Love of Innocence* (1963) Jenkins has shown some uncertainty of aim, and his last book *A Toast to the Lord* was an exceedingly odd production. There are improbabilities in many of his stories, but here they are as bold as brass and as hard to swallow.

It is as if James Hogg should be talking about justified sinners, go out half-way, come back disguised as Muriel Spark and start talking about miracles. The setting (despite the author's canny disclaimer) is the environs of Dunoon and the Holy Loch, with US nuclear submarines and their personnel, and a variety of local attitudes towards them, as background to the extraordinary central character. Agnes, daughter of a narrowly bigoted sectarian preacher, has been assured of God's favour since childhood, and her antinomian imperturbability survives not only sordid and calculating episodes with two American sailors but equally her ensuing pregnancy, her mother's death from cancer, her father's murder of the pious sailor she had seduced and his subsequent suicide, and the horrible death of a lonely orphan boy on the moors. Without benefit of irony, such a character will really not wash. Yet on the last page we are asked to believe that the indomitably happy Agnes is not only a first-rate schoolteacher but has completely won over her normally sensible headmistress to an equivalent flush of God's-in-his-heaven rejoicing.

There is much greater satisfaction to be had from his new book, *A Far Cry from Bowmore*, which is a collection of six short stories. Here, the Malaysian setting in a post-colonial era, where a large part of the inhabitants are Indian or Chinese, though many an angular expatriate Scot is also to be seen, provides a jungle of ironies which he picks his way through humorously and well. He is good at illustrating his recurring theme of the clash of moralities, not only Western v. Oriental but intra-Oriental as well, until terms like 'bribery', 'flattery' and 'veracity' are turned inside out, and nothing solid seems to remain except the ability to hold on to threads of tolerance or hope or the mere persistence of life. The title-story shows the loveless and prejudiced Presbyterian rectitude of a Scottish engineer being broken into at last by pagan funeral gongs and the dignity of a Malaysian woman at the death-bed of her Scottish husband, whom he had once met in Islay. But in this story the narrative is rather contrived. In the freer, more comic, novella-length 'Bonny Chung', which is the strongest story in the collection, didacticism is kept at bay: this spectacle of a young expatriate Chinese on the make, with the unfolding of his educational and sexual adventures in a mixed-race society, is excellently done, and ends the volume on its best note of irony.

Listener, 12 July 1973.

Part Four

Part Four

The Bicentenary

Now that the bicentenary celebrations are over, their glory no doubt slightly dimmed by the unexpected launching of the Chinese probe to Alpha Centauri, it might be an interesting moment in history to ask ourselves, from the vantage-point of 2070, what the celebrators of 1970 would make of the university as we know it today.

Although in respect of numbers we are not among the giants, having approximately 53,000 students on our three campuses at Gilmorehill, Gartocharn, and Lochwinnoch, our ancestors would probably be struck by what would seem to them to be an inordinate amount of activity going on in all three places. This impression would be inevitable, since of course like all substantial institutions we are now a continuously self-renewing organism which is at work 24 hours a day and 365 days a year. The old concepts of 'term', 'session', 'semester', and 'vacation' have long been given up. Naturally, full utilization programmes could not be developed until plant and machines on the one hand, and human teaching staff on the other, became much more resistant to any deterioration, stress, or fatigue brought on by continuous functioning. A great deal has now been achieved in both these directions, and the fact that we have to sleep only one night in seven has been described as the 'liberation of the century'. The teaching arrangements are in any case so extremely flexible that no member of staff who wishes some restoration period is likely to be denied it. Temporary staleness is readily relieved by simply plugging oneself in at one of the scores of Vibrators scattered throughout the university. For more extended mental refreshment, involving change of environment, anyone requiring leave of absence may spend it either where he wishes or at one of our 'external campuses' on Rum, Ibiza, or Madagascar. Rum is extremely popular: the whole island is covered by an almost invisible geodesic dome, erected many years ago by the Buckminster MacBrayne Combine, and in the delightful controlled climate under the dome, visitors enjoy every sort of lush vegetation, semi-tropical sport, and semi-feral adjunct that could be devised. On Madagascar, the Electronic Hammocks are a strong attraction (amounting at time to an addiction) which it would be tedious to describe in detail.

But this is by the way. In the day-to-day working of the university, our ancestors would find that some subjects have disappeared, and some others that might be strange to them have come on the scene. They would look in vain for Moral Philosophy, Latin, Greek, or English, or for a faculty of Divinity. Part of what they would know as Philosophy they could discover, a shade transformed, in the quaintly named but highly important department of Sociosophy; for Logic they would have to enrol in the huge separate faculty of Computer Studies; as for Metaphysics and Divinity, they would find the remnants of these being taken care of in Thinkout, an interdisciplinary body devoted to – in the Chinese phrase – the 'turning over of stones'. The classical languages went entirely, and the modern European languages suffered an almost catastrophic decline, after the Sino-American Concordat of 2044, when it was ruled that English and Chinese would be the only two recognized world languages. Our friends of 1970 must realize, of course, that the Chinese Confederacy now reaches from Tokyo to Paris, and that the decline of the USSR which had begun before 1970 continued into the twenty-first century until Russia had become virtually indistinguishable from other large but inefficient semi-capitalist states. Chinese is therefore, of hard necessity, our second language, and Glasgow University is fortunate in having fostered an outstanding department of Chinese Studies, whose seven professors and vast staff can attract research students even from Peking itself. The disappearance of English from the curriculum may cause some surprise, but it must be remembered that the best of its functions have been taken over by the brilliant Word Institute at Rowardennan, while the worst have just been allowed to lapse. The idea that a study of literature, involving mainly an analysis and interpretation of historical texts, was in some way to be regarded as 'central' to an educated and civilized person's experience because of the moral energies it clarified and transferred, began to seem less and less true even towards the end of the twentieth century, and was of course greatly (though no doubt unfairly) discredited when a group of Cambridge English graduates were found to be the perpetrators of the peculiarly horrible series of Stonehenge murders in 2010 and 2011. The petulant suicide of the literary critic F. R. Leavis at the

age of 102, on hearing that a record company had endowed a second
chair of Pop Music at Corpus Christi, had done nothing to halt the
decline of academic literary studies, and despite some warning and
some girning voices, there was general relief when these studies
were discontinued, concurrently with the establishment of a number
of activist, non-historical, non-researching Word Institutes devoted
to the verbal transformation of life. The Rowardennan Institute has
already become internationally famous, as its former students include
such well-known Scottish wordsmen as Gully McDaid, Cornelius
Coia, and Fung Mei-fan. Indeed, the curious phenomenon known as
Scottish Word dominated the great Word Rally held at Crewe last
year by the four members of the Federated British States.

There are two twenty-first-century innovations at Glasgow University which would prove of considerable interest to our forefathers. These are the large, flourishing departments of Zoics and
Nude Studies. Although such old categories as 'science' and 'art'
have little relevance today, these two studies in their origins at least
belong to science and art respectively. Zoics is a not very good word
for the experimental study of the 'creation' of life. A wide range of
life-forms can now of course be synthesized, and many non-fertile
variants and mutations are produced in the laboratory for educational
(including aesthetic-educational) purposes. All biggish universities
are encouraged to build up a Zoics department and to concentrate
on varying some particular species, genus, or family at the lower end
of the zoological scale. Very strict, internationally agreed limits of
biological complexity must not be exceeded; ferocious penalties are
attached. Specialists in teratology keep constant watch on all labora-
tories. Glasgow has created a notable range of new jellyfish, some
of them of extraordinary limpidity and grace. These are exhibited,
and constantly replaced by fresh mutations as they die off, in the
spectacular Tank Gallery in the basement of the Zoics complex.
The intense debate which began about ten years ago between
Zoics and Sociosophy, the latter trying to insist that higher forms
of life, including the mammalia, must be created if the study is not
to stagnate (to quote one of their proponents) 'at the pretty level of
an outmoded kinetic art', and the former insisting that proper con-
trols have still not been established (to quote one of *their* proponents)
'for three-eyed hawks or men with mandrills' bottoms', will no doubt
rage a long time yet.

Nude Studies is, as I believe our ancestors would say, a different kettle of fish. As its name implies, it is the study of every way in which the human body can be used simply as a human body. There would never have been such a study proposed if it had not been for the remarkable growth of the Nude Theatre, and yet, looking back now on those early days of the century, it is hard to realize how very vehement and vocal the opposition to these studies once was. Many axes have been studiously ground over the obscure history of the Nude Theatre, but it would appear to have arisen in the first place as a mainly commercial gimmick to revive the theatre's sagging fortunes, and then to have surprised its shady promoters by rapidly settling down to become a generally accepted, non-titillating artform which in fact succeeded in giving the theatre a genuine new lease of life. It did this because, once complete nudity had been established as the norm for all the actors in a production, a new convention with great dramatic potential had been invented, and it was not long before an entire new school of dramatists, choreographers, and media-men pushed into view, with the result that the Nude Theatre accounts now for about 40 per cent of all theatre in the Federated British States. In Nude Theatre, which has developed a set of conventions of almost Japanese strictness, a few temporary props, and some make-up and partial masking, are allowed, to help indicate character or action, but no clothing may be worn by any actor or actress without the express permission of the Living Arts Council sitting in Crewe, and this is rarely given. At Glasgow University, Nude Studies is a well-established discipline shared between the several chairs of Drama, Art, Dance, Television, Cinema, Sociosophy, and Physiology.

Some people would connect the rise of Nude Studies with the Marydomes, but I myself consider this case to be not proven. Of course our forefathers of 1970 will not know about the Marydomes. Glasgow University has seventeen of these structures, some of them capacious enough to hold three thousand persons, others of varying degrees of snugness and intimacy. The city of Glasgow itself must now have, I imagine, around six or seven hundred, and new ones go up every month. Following on the general social acceptance of soft drugs, and their consequent legalization early this century, there was an obvious need for some sort of congenial place where a man might take his wife or family for an evening's smoking and listening to music or watching electro-flicks. With the rapid decline of alcohol as a social solvent (nowadays it is only very old or eccentric people who are seen 'drinking' – the very word has an odd archaic ring to it), many derelict public-houses began to be taken over as shebeens for smoke-ins, but the sleazy barbarities of such meeting-houses caused such widespread criticism that clearly an entirely new type of building was called for. The fabulously enterprising Buckminster Lawrence Buildcorp started designing a special series of geodesic domes, cheap, light, strong, well-appointed inside with all audio-visual-tactile appurtenances and air-conditioned to any required degree of 'atmosphere'. No doubt the popularity of marijuana gave them the name Marydomes, shortened in popular usage in Glasgow to 'the Merries'. The universities obviously had to have their own 'Merries', and the very large ones at Glasgow, Strathclyde, and East Kilbride Universities have admittedly earned some notoriety. At Glasgow University's biggest Marydome, not long ago, the Nude studies and Drama departments combined to stage a show in which at least half the actors were clothed, and this was certainly scandalous, but the University President refused to close the dome, and the situation remains tense, with rough gangs of non-smoking youths trying to infiltrate the Merry and handle the clothed actresses.

I have no doubt that the old graduates of this university would like to hear, finally, about the fate of one of the city's noble treasures, the Burrell Collection, especially as the university is concerned with that fate to some extent. After the disastrous fire which destroyed the newly built Burrell Museum at Pollok in 1988, a few days before it was due to be opened by Sir Robin Philipson, and because of the inexplicable failure of the builders to insure their new property, the whole project was thrown back, both financially and architecturally, into a very deep melting-pot, and not until 2017 was anything like the required sum of money raised again. A new competition for architects was just being organized in the early 2020s when un-fortunately the protracted National Emergency period, declared when Chinese kites were discovered floating across the English Channel, put a stop to all large-scale and prestige building. When this ban was lifted in 2031, it was found that the master-plan of the huge number of dispersal-points where the collection had been sent for safe keeping during the emergency was lost, and it took ten years' hard searching to unearth at least a majority of the main items. Then, of course, with the development of the Nude Theatre, the Marydomes, and the electro-flicks, there was a general apathy about 'mothy tapestries and stained-glass Tang horses' (as an anti-Chinese wit dangerously put it), and it is only within recent years that the subject of housing the collection has been mooted once more. By this time, so many of the putative exhibits have been lost, damaged, faked, stolen, or destroyed that it will need only a small building to show them in, and Glasgow University, with commendable local patriotism, has now proposed that it might rent one of its older Marydomes on the Rum campus to the Burrell Trustees to house what is left of the great collection. I understand that the Trustees have indicated their willingness to engage in talks with the University President in this matter.

These are some of the things, then, that our ancestors can look forward to. As for ourselves, we are very conscious of being one of the four universities selected by the Sino-American Academy to set up the first extraterrestrial campuses on the moon. Our tercentenary report may be dated therefore from the Sea of Tranquillity.

College Courant, Martinmas 1970, (celebrating the centenary of Glasgow University's move from the High Street to Gilmorehill).

A Hantle of Howlers

THESE wild and various aberrations have been collected from University Entrance papers in English Literature, marked in Scotland by the compiler during the last eight years. They are offered mainly as a comedy of errors; but an attempt has also been made to classify and comment on the mistakes, in the notes which accompany each section. Some of the results suggested by this analysis may be of interest, and throw a little light on the rather obscure subject of 'examination psychology', as well as on wider issues in education.

To all my anonymous contributors I owe my thanks. Their words have been reproduced with all faithfulness, both in spelling and in punctuation. Square brackets indicate additions made by me for clarity's sake. The masculine pronouns have been used throughout in my comments, though about half the examples are, in fact, from girls' papers.

I. RARE WORKS AND QUEER FACTS

1. Jane Eyre's 'Pride and Prejudice'.
2. Scott's 'Atlantis'.
3. Scott's 'Treasure Island'.
4. 'Henry Esmond' by Burke.
5. 'Waverley' by R. L. Stevenson.
6. Milton's Defensio pro Publicano Anglicano.
7. Wordsworth's Ode to the Imortations of Imortality.
8. The Bigendians and the Weeendians [in *Gulliver's Travels*].
9. Milton in his sonnets was a pupil of Plutarch.
10. The first man to bring the sonnet to England was Wycliff.
11. One of the best young sonnet-writers today is Rossetti.
12. The conquerors spared Athens when they heard the Electra singing.
13. Pluck and Buttons are comic in A Midsummer Night's Dream.
14. Hythrosney is the daughter of Zephur and Aroura.

15. Mincius, the goddess of wind.
16. Scott's portrayal of human character has earned him the name of 'Cock of the North'.
17. The form of these two sonets are ABBA of Quatra tetra in the first two verses.
18. Milton did much to influence Wordsworth, and he in return made Milton think of nature.
19. Strangely the only artist of note was Sir Christopher Wren who built St Giles in Edinburgh.
20. Then one night Laburnam Woods [Birnam Wood] begin to move towards the castle. The Labarnum wood is a army carrying a branch of the laburnam tree each person carrying one.
21. The famous ending, Beauty is truth, and truth beauty, But the better of these is truth.

A candidate sitting an examination has his head temporarily crammed with an uncomfortable number of facts: names, dates, technical remarks, important quotations, causes and results – in addition to normal general knowledge. It is only natural that some of the apparently unconnected facts will reveal their subconscious connections under the stress of answering the paper. 'Examination fever', like any other heightening emotion which involves the whole person organically, has the effect of increasing the mind's susceptibility to association. Unsuspected links are brought abruptly to the surface, and are expressed in written words which have to be set down too rapidly for a conscious rational or corrective control to operate. These links can usually be traced when we begin looking for them in the mistakes that are revealed, though sometimes they are purely personal to the candidate. The examples given above are almost all in the former category.

It is quite clear that Birnam Wood (20), if you forgot the actual name itself, would naturally convert its sounds to the nearest arboreal name you knew – laburnum. The varying spellings of 'laburnum', none of them correct, indicate neatly the candidate's lack of certainty about the term which his mind has thrown forward. Similarly, the interesting conflation of Keats and Corinthians (21), which perhaps shows a Calvinist conscience at work, is explained on the verbal level by an overlapping of patterns of rhythm and rhyme involving abstract nouns. The nouns are all different (faith, hope, and charity as against truth and beauty); but this only underlines the magnetic power of these subconscious patterns, more musical than semantic, within the candidate's memory. The charming and ironical novel of (1) owes its existence to the writer having thought, 'Who was the author of *Pride and Prejudice*? I'm sure it was a woman. What woman's name have I seen on a book of that period? Jane Eyre of course!' The work adumbrated in (6) would make interesting reading; presumably Milton, defending various liberties, turned from divorce to drinking; 'Licence they mean when they cry Liberty'.

Not all the mistakes, of course, involve a subconscious associational element. The writer of (12) obviously had no idea what 'the *Electra* of Euripides' was, though he had heard his teacher use this strange phrase with its unexplained definite article when Milton's sonnets were being discussed, and he was making the best of a bad job by attaching what meaning he could to it. He seems to have visualized the Electra, perhaps as a chorus (of electors?), or an exotic bird, or an early kind of gramophone.

11. A PUNNETFU'
22. Bassanio was in need of money to go and press his suit.
23. Gray's Elegy is full of picturesque illusions.
24. The immotal sole.
25. The Americans are a people of English dissent.
26. Keats wished to 'load every rift with awe' [ore].
27. It was only after Flora's repeated objections that Waverley withdrew his suite.
28. At this time the weighing of air caused much ignorant levity.
29. Was Milton militant?
30. Milton had acetic taste.
31. The friar was constantly in the taverns amongst the knight hawkes.
32. Two men gambol over Belinda whilst she amuses herself [in *The Rape of the Lock*].
33. When the Senior Decon of the church is ill, his friends each attend his bedside with a will to help him.

A first-grade or classic pun, as in (25) or (33), arises when a candidate believes he is making a clear and unexceptionable statement but has chosen one of those situations where an ironical or contradictory co-statement is lurking very near the surface and is betrayed into actuality by a helpful verbal link. Many Americans are, admittedly, of English descent, but merely to say so is to invite qualification, because everyone knows that an American is not like an Englishman. The statement as it stands implies that he is. It is therefore an unstable statement, and the slightest disturbing factor, such as the emotional pressure of an examination, will bring out whatever verbal possibilities of apparent distortion but actual revelation it contains. The use of 'dissent' is particularly nice because it is both historically true (in relation to the religious dissent of the early settlers) and an up-to-date commentary (on the natural differences, today, between American and English opinion). It is a double pun, and almost deserves an extra mark.

The rather macabre and Volpone-like situation of (33) has a parallel and fairly obvious explanation in terms of human experience. And in (22) it would be quite the expected thing for Bassanio as a young lover to want to press his suit sartorially before doing so in a different manner at the winching. These are all proper puns, and the fact that they are all involuntary (and are such as are constantly recurring) argues in favour of what Freud suggested (and what James Joyce illustrated) about the subconscious origins of our wit and humour. But this leads me to my next section.

III. CARROLL, LEAR, JOYCE, ETC.
34. Prince Hal behaves magnaminiously.
35. The curfew tells the knoll of parting day.
36. The ship [in 'Lycidas'] was shaped like an eclipse which was a bad omen.
37. Percy Blythe Shelley.
38. In Lycidas he talks of the clergy as a shepherd and the people as his folk.
39. His sister-and-law.
40. The blastphemers.
41. Then Jenny's sweetheart arrives [in *The Cotter's Saturday Night*] and after being seized up by the mother is invited to stay.
42. The Franklin's house was well stalked with food.
43. The Squire led an active life and was sinuous.

44. The franklin, an epiquerien.
45. It would be shear butchery.
46. 'Last did come and last did go
    The Pilate of the Gallilean Lake' ['Lycidas']. . . . .
47. Antony is a frivalrous character [in *Julius Caesar*].
48. Antimony is something of an enigma [in *Julius Caesar*].
49. 'Fame is no plant that grows on moral soil' ['Lycidas'].
50. Richard II was a weak irresolute man pandied by his favorites.
51. George Elliot betrays village life very well.
52. Bolingbroke then proceeds to dismantle the king.
53. It was a great condensation on their part when they spoke to any-
    one beneath their rank.
54. Lady Macbeth rambling out her horrible memoirs.
55. Michael is a pastoral poem in blank worse.
56. But Miss Bingley's schemes go nowwire.
57. Brutus has just finished agrueing with his friend Cassius.
58. Caesar is proud and pompeous.
59. Elizabeth Bennet is, to some, one of the greatest characteratures
    in English literature.
60. More's Uptopia.
61. Swift's misagony.
62. After Gulliver has been shipwretched . . .
63. Only a demigogue.
64. In the West Wind Shelley has a whish to bring joy to the world.
65. We feel Keats's volumptuousness.
66. Burns's songs are all based on Highland girls he had seen or even
    loved. He likened many of his subjects unto flowers, who blomb
    and are forgotten. He also describes girls who have existed and
    nobody has noticed them accept him.

Some of the errors here, especially in the portmanteau words, are
most interesting. Indeed, they are hardly 'errors' except to a niggardly
imagination. How beautifully do the two views of Prince Hal's
character dovetail in (34): Hal the magnanimous, Hal the ignomi-
nious! Or in (57), how neatly is the quarrel scene patched up, with
Brutus and Cassius changing insensibly from argument to agreement!
And the bold distortion of (60) has an easy (if unintentional)
priority in time over our fashionable 'Subtopia'. In (66) the flowers
that 'blomb' are admirably transient, whether we think of 'bomb'

or 'tomb'; though the real kick of this extract is withheld till its penultimate word.

This is something different from a pun. Words like 'magnaminiously' and 'blomb' and 'shipwretched' and 'nowwire' (nowhere + haywire) have a creative or poetic element added to their punning base, so that a slight shot of fantasy gives the joke a lift and it gets above itself, and this inventive high-spiritedness gives more pleasure to the reader. It may seem extraordinary that such brilliant compressions of relevant meaning as the examples show should all start up unbidden out of mere confusion and hastiness of mind. Yet that is a fact that must be explained. How far, for instance, is (63) no more than the error of someone who can't spell 'demagogue'? Or may we surmise that at the back of that candidate's mind is the notion that many a demagogue thinks of himself as a demigod, and that this notion silently intrudes into his spelling, though the thought has not become conscious enough for him to sort it out in so many separate words? This a question we can hardly answer; but when 'error' becomes creative in this way, I feel reasonably sure that the requisite elements of the mosaic must have been present in the examinee's mind, and must have been scanned, however delicately and quickly, just under the threshold of conscious thought. The examiner, at any rate, may well give him the benefit of the doubt. These are the vorpal burblings that refresh his spirit.

So many 'meaningful mistakes' of this kind occur that one wonders how far the influence of James Joyce is in fact at work. It is a type of error that has probably always been made, just as it is a type of verbal humour that is found long before Joyce or Lewis Carroll (in the sixteenth-century Marprelate Tracts, for example); but its frequency in exam-papers today seems to owe something to modern writers such as Joyce. The influence of a Joycean word-play, though indirect, is more pervasive than the ordinary person suspects. In advertising and journalism, particularly, he is subjected to a continual barrage of Joyceanisms, from the 'Schweppervescence' fantasies of Stephen Potter and the glorious mishandlings of Messrs Accles and Pollock to the zestful headlines of the sports pages of his daily newspaper. No conscious awareness of the linguistic or aesthetic techniques employed in these inventions is needed for their impact to be recorded on the mind; indeed, it is probably true that the less consciously they are imbibed the more lasting is their effect. We live in a world of *double entendre*, and I doubt whether we realize it. Children growing up in this world take its ambience for granted, and if they were ever encouraged to write quite freely, I expect we would find their style, like the franklin's house described above, 'well stalked' with the fowl and flesh of Joyce's cupboard.

IV. REALITY BREAKING IN

67. The Lilliputians – those skelfs of humanity.
68. Falstaff is a study in utter shambles.
69. Long John Silver was a man greedy for gold and fond of bloody deeds, he thought nothing of killing a man, in fact he was a real bad one.
70. The Rape of the Lock starts by Belinda waking and putting on her battle dress.
71. In late 17th century a means of air travel was adopted. A flying helicopter was invented.
72. Milton's mythological taste is noticed when he refers to the 'Hours' who were some sisters who led a charabanc.
73. But Cassius is only taking a lone of him.
74. A nun could not show her forehead, or keep a dog but this lady ignored the rules for she done both.
75. The Poor Parson [in *The Canterbury Tales*] was very like our modern Billy Graham, except that in those days he was not so well known as communications were very poor.
76. Balnibarbi [in *Gulliver's Travels*] – the land beneath the flying saucer.
77. The 3rd voyage includes Gulliver's visit to the Mormons.
78. With Hamlet are sent to England Frankienstien and Guilderstern.

The 'reality' referred to in the title of this section is irrelevant 'out-of-period' information more familiar to the candidate than the historical facts he is dealing with, and also it is the use of local everyday words or phrases which slip out with no thought of their applicability in a literary context. In both cases the humour comes from incongruity. It is curious to note that even what appear to be merely absurd errors of fact turn out in most cases to have a *verbal* confusion which has derailed the relevant material and allowed some bold and specious substitute to push into its place. In (71), for example, it is not the dating that is wrong. The reference is to the seventeenth century, but the candidate has been reading about a new and speedier long-distance coach of that period called the 'Flying Coach', and it is the word 'flying' that has given wings to his pen. Even so, it is a remarkable mistake to make, and it shows the obsessive power a word can have. The candidate knew that the term 'flying' came in somewhere, and how could anything on land be flying? He probably forgot the word 'coach', but association would easily slide 'copter' into its place, and what could be more relevant? Satisfaction at having solved the 'flying something' problem would then block any further mental effort, and so the now anachronistic date would pass into his text. Much the same sort of thing accounts for (76), where 'flying saucer' represents 'Flying Island'; and what is Part 3 of *Gulliver's Travels* if not science fiction? In (70), this not untruthful statement is firmly based on the poem which tells us that 'now awful beauty puts on all its arms'. Incongruity without any verbal confusion is seen at its best in (75); this is just honest simple-mindedness, but its somewhat startling understatement about communication reveals the writer's sudden faint suspicion that this comparison might be less than likely – and his determination to cling to it for all that.

In general, I find that modern or local instances and analogies are rather sparingly used in these answers, and they are seldom very illuminating. The ability to use them easily, casually, and yet accurately only comes to people after a good deal of practice, and it is the trial and error stage that we most often see here, especially under these circumstances of tension and haste. It appears that most candidates think it safer for the world inside the examination room to remain an insulated world, far from the charabancs and the Mormons. (The writing of an essay on a general subject is of course another matter; but I am not concerned with that sort of paper.) Each question answered is itself a little period world, insulated by natural diffidence or by lack of time from most of the wider issues which, if glanced at, might make a pass mark soar to a considerably higher figure – though as things are found at present it more commonly opens the floodgates of misapplied ingenuity, or stimulates the polychronic montage of (78) or (72). Sometimes the unspoken comment from 'reality' on the literary past makes its presence felt as unmistakably as if it had been formulated as a comparison. 'Milton's social life', one examinee confessed, 'was not much; if it was wet he would go to friends but otherwise he was writing'. With these words a boy in 1949 looked back three hundred years, and compared not only himself and Milton, but two societies.

Further remarks on these points in a broader educational context will be found under Section VIII.

v. Not What I Meant – Or Did I?

79. Chaucer never fails to lose our interest.
80. Milton speaks of 'sweetest Shakespeare's fancy child' [in 'L'Allegro'].
81. Chaucer loves to emblemish a tale with matter not strictly relevant.
82. The Wife of Bath was a real woman's man.
83. Gray's Elegy was made famous by the remark of General Wolfe on his death bed. He said that he would have rather taken Quebec than write the elegy.
84. The King's horse is terrified, and the King, being an excellent horseman, is unseated.
85. The late King Edward, a friend of Milton's [Edward King].
86. His passion new know bounds.
87. Darcy asks Elizabeth for his hand which she refuses.

If Freud was right in arguing that slips of the kind shown in this section – reversals of the expected statement – often betray by their confusion the speaker's or writer's disbelief in what he is stating, then this is a common enough form of self-revelation. Examples like (79) could be multiplied. The writer here starts off with one construction ('Chaucer never fails to keep our interest') and shifts halfway to an alternative ('Chaucer never loses our interest'), and his hesitation – like the famous mis-spelt 'hesitency' of Earwicker in *Finnegans Wake* – indicates his personal lack of conviction. He feels that the first form is not positive enough to convince the examiner, and strikes out into the second, where the feeble 'fails to' is avoided; but in the process he creates the third form, where his murky thought willy-nilly comes clean. Not that what he says is absolutely unacceptable, even if it is unspeakable. Chaucer was a writer of long poems, and no writer of a long poem fails somewhere to lose our interest. It is our realization of this unhappy truth that gives us the necessary sympathy to see the mistake as a good joke and not merely as a grotesque blunder. A parallel element of truth gives body to (81), where the two possibilities (the approved but improvable 'embellish' and the taboo but tempting 'blemish') have become fused in a single Joycean term. (80) is a beautiful hypallage by someone who was probably quite ignorant of Sir William Davenant. (82) is an interesting comment on the limitations of English idiom: we speak of a 'man's man' and a 'lady's man', but what do we say if we are talking about a woman? The pull of the two existing phrases was too strong; the answer could only be, by analogy, a 'woman's man'! Again, there was probably enough truth in the result to smuggle it past the candidate's inner censor – the Wife of Bath does have certain clearly masculine traits of character. (87) with the delightfully absurd visual image it calls up, is entertaining because it also draws attention to the absurdity of the phrase it mocks. We aren't usually aware of this, because 'asking a lady for her hand' is only figurative (even with a manual accompaniment) and non-visualized. The seriousness of the request, were it real, is shown by Darcy's predicament. What lady would give her hand, if she thought she might never retrieve it?

VI. A Fine Figure of a Speech

88. He might have niped the bud on the head and removed Antony at the same time as Caesar.
89. In the night full of Portents the graves opened up and the dead rouse. It was raining blood. These are Shakespeare's make-up.
90. Falstaff, the ball of craft.
91. Falstaff is the most decorated spoke of the wheel in which the hub is Prince Hal.
92. The lights were hushed.
93. Bolingbroke made Richard taste the pills of deposition.
94. 'Richard II' might be described as a centifruge with its vortex being Bolingbroke.
95. Brutus is being pricked with the horns of Delima.
96. Rome and Greece fell through.

Mixed or ridiculous metaphors are not so frequent as one might expect. I can only speak for recent years (1949–56), but certainly there are few candidates in my experience who will now risk purple passages or even attempt any sort of imitative stylishness or personal eccentricity in their writing. In some ways this is a good thing, because I think it is true to say that a particular kind of hollow rhetoric and pomposity, which did exist, has gone out; and this reflects changes among those who teach as well as among those who learn. We are more suspicious of uplift than our fathers and grandfathers were. Too many crimes can be committed in *that* name. And so rhetoric is put in a drawer, and grows rusty. It is significant that Shakespeare is the only author who appears in my examples; his rhetoric is a continuous challenge, and it is catching, as the answers to Shakespeare questions show. But even this is no more than a sprinkling. The fault of present-day answers tends to be drabness, not pretentiousness, and those who suddenly display an eagerness for distinction are apt, through lack of practice in rhetorical tricks, to find themselves like Brutus in (95), pricked with the horns of Delima. Shakespeare and Lamb, one sometimes feels, are the two writers who should *never* be taught at school, because they cannot do any good to people who are painfully learning the art of writing, and they can do a great deal of harm – especially Lamb. It is a fact that many pupils leave school thinking that 'poetry' is 'what Shakespeare writes' (mixed metaphors, archaisms, anachronisms and all), and that 'good prose' is 'well, Lamb's for instance'. It is only the absence of imitative and rhetorical training that prevents this from becoming a fairly disastrous situation for the future of the way people write. We face our pupils, in fact, with a great gap between masterpieces which they are told to admire and any style which they themselves are required to develop. This might not matter so much if the rhetorical basis of style was explained; but is it? The few flights into style that one sees would argue that it is not, for they are shaky and inconsistent. That is why one is apt to put up with the existing drabness, even while being disappointed by it, since any alternative visible at the moment holds out no prospect of giving pleasure.

The state of our prose writing in general is not good. There are hardly any writers today who are capable of uniting the two important qualities of vigour and refinement in one prose style. Our Elizabeth Bowens have little vigour; our John Wains disclaim refinement. There is no common twentieth-century style which could easily take a stress in whichever direction the author and his subject required. To better this situation is no easy task, but it is something that can be helped by people other than 'writers'. It can be helped by everyone, and especially it can be helped in schools and universities.

I believe we still put too much emphasis on correctness, on mere adherence to rules of grammar which for the most part are in need of extensive revision. The concept of correctness is important, but it must have an intimate relation to the contemporary state of the language, including the spoken language, and it should never become absolutely rigid. Pupils' and students' mistakes must be corrected, but not automatically or without comment, for there are two kinds of error: the one that has no virtue from any point of view, and the one that can be used to show its perpetrator which way vigour of style is to be found, since vigour (like refinement) springs up at the edge of error. For an example of the second type, see (67) or (92). In both of these, the only 'error' is a disturbance of the *tone* of the context. 'Skelfs' is a perfectly applicable spoken term in Scotland for describing the Lilliputians, but it will not stand being written at that point in its 'Southern English' surroundings; its effect is too startling and too funny. What we ought to point out to the candidate would be that 'skelf' must not therefore be laid on the shelf; that with a little care it might well be manipulated even into an English literary context; and that in any case its presence showed a refreshing refusal to disconnect writing from speech. In the same way, 'the lights were hushed' might have been used by Virginia Woolf or Ronald Firbank; it is its prosaic context which condemns it, not its seeming illogicality. We want to encourage people to be vigorous without being slipshod, and delicate without being whimsical, and the difficulty of doing this usually issues in the safe advice to pray to God and keep your powder dry – with the result that the force of prose is kept in a complacent suspense, and nothing is ever fired.

A bolder approach seems indicated. It is no doubt true, for instance, that there should be a difference between written and spoken English, if only because speech is both evasive and repetitive. The question is whether it is wise to set so much store by this difference. Could both speech and writing not be improved by some reconnaissance and raiding on the part of each? Would everyone not admit that there is a wershness about educated speech today? Only a fraction of the vocabulary the speaker actually possesses comes into utterance. Social timidities and taboos repress half the colloquial element – racy phrases, vogue words, popular allusions – while half the intellectual element of uncommon but apt or brilliant words is kept back by fears of pedantry or eccentricity that would have astonished Shakespeare's or Dr Johnson's contemporaries. The educated English voice tries to slide past language, disturbing it as little as possible. What is not disturbed may be preserved, but will it increase and multiply, will it grow and change?

And if educated speech is unsatisfactory, and if one can see why it is, then ill-educated writing appears in much the same position. To take one instance: the person who leaves school at fifteen has very often no idea how to write a letter. Business letters can be learned – if he goes into business; but personal letters he never masters, for he carries into them a mistaken idea that certain stilted phrases and inexpressive clichés are 'correct'. He would write a more natural letter if he had been better educated – or if no one had educated him in letter-writing at all. As it is, his correspondents have to become accustomed to adding the right overtones to a series of practically dead counters variously arranged. They do this, of course, and such letters can be more subtle than one would think; but what an amount of natural talent is straitjacketed when the private letter – of all forms – becomes a vehicle for half-remembered rules of literary procedure and not for the quick free turns of thought of one person speaking to another!

We must work hard if we want to bring into existence, in these and other directions, a more supple, buoyant, generous, and forceful English.

[And let schoolmasters, when they are penning a careful diatribe for the national Press as they sometimes do, remember that their well-articulated sentences, their plethora (a favourite term) of abstract nouns, and their ironical pseudo-negatives may not save them from one besetting fault – unreadability. One can see such a communication (it is hardly to be called a letter) a long way off. It stands forbiddingly foursquare like a great black thicket of -ence and -ing and -ation and -imum. The ordinary man may be forgiven if he thinks there must be something wrong with a letter of this kind, and with the mental outlook which could believe it was putting things in the best possible way. O, reform it altogether!]

VII. SPELING BE

97. 'O what can ale the night at arm' [Keats, 'La Belle Dame'].
98. In Milton's sonnet to his dead wife she appeared like Alastic [Alcestis].
99. Gaunt laks tack [in *Richard II*].

100. Travel in the 17th century was abominal.
101. Richard II has a feminent temperment.
102. Hamlet suffered from a slit personality.
103. The two tercets of the testet.
104. Licencenitiousness.
105. The Gohst.
106. London, the huge micropolis.
107. A lifetime of rescherch.
108. The Decacelaric Couplet.
109. The stopped heroic couple.
110. The Episcable Church.
111. Cycology.
112. Tinety Abbey.
113. Mr Collins is a hauty overbeary man.
114. 'Wakedst Duncan with thy knocking! – I wouldst thou couldst!'
115. Swift is a suturist.
116. The Wife of Baths history is rathered mottled.
117. We feel, though mingled with remorse, a ping of satisfaction at Macbeth's death.
118. It was out of the point to paint Caesar as 'the all Saints' or the 'Holy of Hollies'.
119. Poirot is a famious french dective.
120. A climax of antithesises.
121. George Elliot is only her pseudom name.
122. In writting the 'Silas Marner', Mary Ann Evans came to the end of her creative carrier.
123. The king's coffers are empty, so he farms out the revues.
124. His secret unsavoury marriage with a slaterny woman from Bathery.
125. He develops an affection for his golden sovereigns . . . for their trinsic value.
126. Richard II's introvercy.
127. The Wife of Bath could enjoy all the ribbled tales of the men.
128. Lady Mac Beth has to take spirits to keep her from going into a delema.
129. 'Hamlet' poses severable almost unanswerable problems.
130. Remorse at having killed altrobus. ['The Ancient Mariner'].
131. The state is compared with the micro of the garden [microcosm].
132. Swift has some small inaccuracies in his grammer.

133. Beware the fiftheenth of March!
134. It brought me a sense of my great inadadaquicy.
135. The King of Brobdingnag thought Gulliver couldn't be a darwf. His professors thought he might be a emybro, but they really didn't know.
136. Keats creats a fine effect of delicasy by useing these single sylable wordes.
137. His boat was of the yatch type.
138. A humourous toutch.
139. The first glimspe.
140. Natural phoenoemia.
141. Greatly exadurated.
142. Flirtations, cochetery and the like.
143. The Strugglebruggs is a satyr on the belief that perpetual life is to be sort after [Gulliver's Travels].
144. Miusic.
145. Shakespierre.
146. For all Falstaff's jocual outward appearances, we love this old dear cartricure of the English-man of the period.
147. Falstaff the roystering old profligacer.
148. A Leffow of the Royal Society.
149. Peremptorarily.
150. Pope's machinery includes slyphs, nmyphs, and knombs.

In this section I have gathered together a murrain of mis-spellings which are amusing for reasons too various to be reducible to principle. They are rather too quaint, fanciful, and accidental for Section III. There are errors of haplography (109, 123, 125, 131); of dittography by obvious collateral contamination (113, 114, 116, 129); of metathesis (130, 135, 137, 139, 148, 150); of (apparently) mishearing (108, 110, 127, perhaps 102); of wild stabs at the unfamiliar (98, 121, 126, 140); and of the too logical mind (120). The most Joycean are the caterwauling 'miusic' of (144), the revolutionary 'Shakespierre' of (145), and the startled 'Gohst' of (105).

I have listed, of course, only the more spectacular and entertaining mis-spellings. A full list of the commoner mistakes would make interesting reading too – of a different kind. Books on spelling, or books that deal with spelling difficulties, seem to bear little relation to the errors that people actually make. Certainly it is a good thing to have columns of -ABLE and -IBLE, or rules about -IE- and -EI-; but why do so many people write ASKES, ORIGONAL, POLOTICS, DISCRIPTION, RELIGOUS, SPEACH, WRITTING, REFERING, BE-GINING, DEFINATE, PAYED, LAYED, LEAD (for LED), OFFICIER, SIMILIAR, CHARACHTER, VALUBLE, and INCIDENTLY? These spellings turn up repeatedly. Some of them are of course covered by the existing rules, but others are not, and perhaps these particular examples are ones that should be held out as warnings. Although there is a difference between ignorance (140) and carelessness (129), it would help matters if we payed more attension to the latter than we do, and tried to understand what the *psychology* of error is like, since its *mechanics* is not enough.

The other solution is to return to the old toleration of variant spellings. It could be argued, in the instances I have given, that no harm is done because the meaning remains clear; and that spelling should be as personal as hand-writing, so long as it obeys the minimal demands for conformity and intelligibility that we make of our penmanship. One may preferre to wryte with a certein Flurrich; anuthir wil hav sum pashn for fonetiks; a third will be normally law-abiding but on occasion will exhubberate into enthusiasmus. A price has to be paid for the grand march of grammar and education: in this case, quite simply, the disappearance of spelling as a source of pleasure or 'character'. My examples show, however, that this pleasure is dormant rather than dead. Those who would like to see its reawakening may study the letters of Ezra Pound, the essays of Robert Bridges, and the novels of James Joyce.

VIII. DEPARTMENT OF STATEMENTS AND DESCRIPTIONS

151. Warren Hastings ruled like a true Englishman, taking all and giving nothing.
152. Ophelia being young has not lived so long.
153. Ophelia – Hamlet's child lover.
154. Hamlet says he will play off his head.
155. Lady MacBeth asks the evil spirits to come and unsex her. Having been unsexed, she then takes control of Macbeth.
156. When all hope of a son had vanished, Mr Bennet secluded himself in his libreray.
157. In Brobdingnag Gulliver becomes the favourite plaything of the Queen, and it was the King's custom to question him.

158. Mr Collins' parish was situated just within the Rosings park, the residence of Lady Catherine, wall.

159. Being so self-centred Richard little worried about others, but he worried about his queen and told her to go to France.

160. Macaulay, discussing the degradation of morals, went on to say how the latest fashion was for all men and women to know something of physical science, and all men of fashion had a laboratory where they played around and made some very important discoveries.

161. Burke's morbid philanthropy.

162. Milton was saturated with his fellow-beings.

163. The Monk even had a gold waggle, in the shape of a love-knot.

164. Scott did not frequent any places where he could meet women during his life.

165. Henry Morton, portrayed by Scott as the hero is well nigh a failure as a character for he is sex-less.

166. Edith [Bellenden] faints at the very times when her prolonged consciousness would be of the greatest help to her lover.

167. He goes on to that lycidas has died before his prime and asks who would not sing for him. I did not know lycidas and I don't feel like mourning his death. (He does)

168. When Milton felt the need for a new stanza he simply took one.

169. Hamlet calls himself a muddy mettled minded rascal and aptly so.

170. Bessie McClure [in *Old Mortality*], an old death who shelters friend and foe alike.

171. L'Allegro begins with the song of the lark and the bellowing of the cock.

172. L'Allegrow is happilly pleasant without being indecent.

173. The innocent and skulking Macduff.

174. Pepys, our ablest sailor.

175. Claudius had plenty of courage, and his favourite way of murdering was poison.

176. Falstaff is mysterious, kind, and odious.

177. As the play progresses Hamlet's madness declines in quality.

178. But Macbeth has a powerful weakness.

179. In Hamlet the ghost appears to Hamlet (the ghost app) and asks him to revenge his death.

180. And the Victorian period had straightened up the women of the cities and courts.

181. Mr Collins [in *Pride and Prejudice*] is in all, but structure, a woman.
182. Mr Collins is verbose toady.
183. And whether Shakespeare was a naturalist or a super-naturalist could be agreeably debated on.

This section (and also the next one) will show the examinee struggling with the expression of ideas and truths, losing his way somewhere, and often setting down inconsistencies, or paradoxes, or conclusions that are very remote from what he intended. These statements break down less because of lack of knowledge than because candidates who are mostly of school-leaving age lack the necessary experience or sophistication of mind to be deft in sorting out the complex strands involved in literary criticism. Most of the statements, though ridiculous or amusing, are true. The fault is a fault partly of expression, partly of confusion of mind. The confusion comes from having to make rapid selections among the clutter of facts that are stored in the mental attic, bundle them up in the right packages, and bring them down into the open at the exact moment when they are required. The writer of (160), for instance, has really been unable to decide in his mind whether he is talking about the degradation of morals or the development of science, and so his account hovers ambiguously between the two, with entertaining effect. Macduff as described in (173), Claudius as in (175), and Falstaff as in (176) could all be found in Shakespeare; these adjectives could be defended; the absurdity of each total picture derives from lack of practice in describing human character – from the fever of haste in which all available knowledge is brought to bear on the subject without pause for a critical glance – from an inability to reduce what is complex to a manageable sample, where discordant elements are still kept separated by tiny buffers of explanation.

In an English paper, literary criticism has to be attempted, since it is always asked for in some of the questions. The results show again and again just how hard – how impossible, I have heard it said – this is, for most candidates. Many of them take refuge in technical description ('The sestet was composed of an octave plus a couplet'), listing rhyme-schemes and figures of speech and leaving it at that. Some will hazard a concluding 'I like this sonnet because it is clearly expressed and the language is flowing'. The majority of those who do try to say what is good and why, or even to give a detailed description of the meaning of the work, come up against a paucity of vocabulary – a vocabulary, too, which one feels in any case they disbelieve or are at least indifferent to. They have, in the main, only two ways of praising a poem: (*a*) 'It is clearly expressed and easy to understand', and (*b*) 'It shows how sincere the poet was in describing his feelings'. Now I doubt very much whether this represents their real reaction to poetry. It may represent what they are told to say about poetry. If so, there is something wrong. When I was at school I enjoyed Tennyson's 'Lotos-Eaters' and Coleridge's 'Christabel', and so did many other boys in the class, but neither I nor they thought for one moment that we liked these poems because they were 'clear and easy to understand', and the idea of 'sincerity of expression' never entered our heads. I think we might, if pushed to it, have described how and by what stages we were carried away by that poetry; but no one in an examination admits to being carried away by poetry, or suggests that one should be carried away by poetry. It is surely curious, and wrong, that one of the special distinguishing marks of poetry – its electric charge, its shock, which comes from its placings of words that are at once unexpected and yet ravishingly right – should be the one thing that examinees either don't know or are inhibited from mentioning? A very clear poem may be very good, but is it good because it is clear? It may be a hideously fraught question for the schoolmaster, but should that 'because' not in many cases be 'although'? The author of 'Marmion' would seem to have all the virtues demanded by these candidates, but is 'Marmion' a great poem, or its writer a great poet? From the evidence I have collected, it is clear that both passionateness and intellectuality are very faintly seen in the vision of poetry that is current. Those who may be tempted to add, 'And a good thing too!' should pause to consider whether in that case poetry ought to be taught at all. Poetry is not wishy-washy by nature, and a wishy-washy view of poetry is a perversion.

I freely admit that to those who have no interest in poetry (and that must include a large percentage of those who sit these examinations) it is very difficult to know what to say about it. What I am querying is the quality or relevance of the aids that are at present being supplied to fill this void. There does seem to be a tacit agreement to leave the real difficulties undiscussed (the difficulties, for example, inherent in the catchword 'sincerity'), and to give the subject a specious air of 'higher knowledge' by going into purely schematic technical details at some length. God forbid that the already overburdened teacher should have to institute Empsonian analysis of Donne and Hopkins! - but what he tells his pupils about poetry should at least not be inconsistent with the fact that writers like Donne and Hopkins - or Dunbar and Dryden - did write poetry. Was Dunbar 'sincere'? The word is meaningless, but Dunbar was a poet. Is Hopkins 'clear'? Again, the word is meaningless as it stands, yet Hopkins was a poet.

There is no easy solution to the problem of teaching literary appreciation, and any attempt will be limited according to the age and experience of the pupils. I do feel, however, that in comparison with some subjects (science subjects most obviously) English is falling behind in its sharpness, in its awareness of what is going on; it seems too often to be taking the easy way out, assuming (over-pessimistically in my opinion) that pupils who have to know something of the most recent developments in physics or chemistry 'would never understand' modern poetry, drama, or novels - or, dare I add, modern criticism.

There is indeed a disturbing unreality about these examinations. Sometimes candidates will boldly criticize what they call 'ivory tower' writing. What they fail to realize is that it is they who are in the ivory tower - locked up with the voltas of Milton's sonnets and Macaulay's portrait of Warren Hastings. It is hardly their fault. They have been taught - and rightly - something of the literature of the past, but they have not had it related to the present. What I miss most of all in the papers I have marked is a convincing sense of the growth and continuity of literature, of traditions being recognized as traditions and original things being recognized in their specific originality. The clever schoolboy of seventeen who has studied science would not be entirely at a loss if he was asked where the discovery of the transuranic elements, or of new particles like the anti-neutron, 'fits in'. Yet if you were to ask the best English pupils where the novels of William Golding and the poetry of Thom Gunn 'fit in' - well, the answer would be a lemon, or thereabouts. There are those, I know, whom this lemon would not upset. 'Literature, unlike science, does not progress.' But the retreat into history is unhealthy; and it is the present that suffers. To dismiss the relevance of the present is to meet halfway the fairly common belief that 'things would not be any different if Shakespeare had never lived'. Surely it is immensely disappointing if boys and girls who have studied Shakespeare at school come away themselves with this belief; and yet that is the impression that only too many answers continue to give. Is it so difficult to tell our children why our great writers are great, and what they mean today?

IX. CONFUSION UNBOUNDED

184. Milton did not write about love because he had to look after his insane sister who killed their father.

185. Milton wrote this sonnet ['When the Assault was Intended to the City'] on the temple of Athene against Lord Elgin, who was at the time removing the Elgin Marbles.

186. Macbeth meets Macduff who was plucked from his mother's woman before her time was up. This finishes Macbeth.

187. Hamlet's mother remarries her dead husband's uncle.

188. Lady Macbeth goes mad and one day her body was found floating becide the lillies. Shortely after that Macbeth dies a nartural death. Mostely of wory.

189. Eppie, the childless baby girl [in *Silas Marner*].

190. Shakespeare forms his characters from the heart outwards whereas Scott forms his characters from the heart inwards, never quite reaching the heart.

191. This passage comes from Macaulay's essay on Warren Hastings. Warren meets and falls in love with the author's wife. This shows with what class Milton associated with.

192. The height of Scott's achievements in portraying character are the limitations to which he can rise.

193. It was in Greece that Caesar crossed Egypt and became en-armoured of Cleopatra.

194. Burns was very good to small flowers . . . The poem goes on to adress the mountain daisy and then cuts it down.

195. 'Pride and Prejudice' means the thoughts of those which might be hurt and the dislike of the people whose thoughts have been hurt of the people who hurt them.

196. The Style of Wordsworth sonnet starts of with an Apostrophe which gives it the impression of a wale. But ends in a soft note.

197. Sonnet was a poem which was set to music. Their first writers included Petrach and Boccachio. This form is of 15 lines of iambic pentametre. The poem is divided into an octave, and

the terset in the last 6 lines. The terset is divided into 2 sestets. The sonnet is a poem which expresses a thought with great exactitude and within the framework of the little air.

198. The Same [Wordsworth's sonnet to Milton in the *Golden Treasury*] is different it tell of England being 'a stinging fen' and calls on milton to come to life

'O milton! thou should'st live at this hour' –

anthysis. So that he may revive life in England as in his own day that everthing was death at this time the time of the industrial revolution.

199. Scottish life is very simply and more natural, unlike English which is more artifical. They are more christen, friendly, generous and more hospitalble. 'A man for a Man and that for a man.'

The preceding thoughts may be left to speak for themselves. Here, the absurd reaches heroic proportions, and illiteracy (like absolute zero) begins in some of the examples to be approached. The total impression left by this group is striking: one can sense the whole examination-room ferment of disorganized recollections, and the painful attempt to organize them which issues in broken logic and bad grammar. The heads of the writers lie open, and we can gaze deep into them at the jumble of knowledge they contain. The scene may perhaps shock and surprise, as well as amuse.

200. 'And thus ends my cathecism.'

Twentieth Century, Dec. 1956–Jan. 1957.

The Compleat Writer's Guide, USA–USSR

Scriptistics: An Introduction
by Virgil Wigwam

SOME time ago it was my good fortune to read the interesting article by Mr Alvarez on 'The Poet in the University' (in *The Twentieth Century*, June 1955). I could not help feeling that the writer took a somewhat negative view of his subject, and as I myself am in charge of a creative writing centre at the University of Laredo in Texas, I judged that a communication about our ideals and practices might not be wholly out of order.

I am well aware that the idea of Scriptistics, or the practical study of creative writing, is something which arouses deep suspicion in these islands. You have in Great Britain, as you yourselves seem happy to reiterate from time to time in your literary journals, an ancient tradition of inspired amateurism in the critical sphere and of the wild untutored genius in the creative sphere. You take pride in having escaped the fate of France in hoisting on to its shoulders, like a more foolish Sindbad, the incubus of a National Academy. You rejoice that Shakespeare is so unlike Racine; you make a cult of *Tristram Shandy* because it causes the canons of the art of the novel to explode; you carefully count up your rather large number of mad poets – Hoccleve, Cowper, Collins, Smart, Blake, Moore, Clare, Beddoes; and in criticism you cling lovingly to your Charles Lambs and your Maurice Morganns. The point is, however, can you continue in this direction, in our very professional twentieth century? Your amateur poet is like a man toiling uphill on a home-made bicycle, while our trained professional poet flashes past him in a Cadillac. You yourselves have expressed dissatisfaction with the present state of poetry; why do you persist in blocking progress by believing and asserting that nothing can be done about it? Because the wind of genius bloweth where it listeth? What the wind of genius needs is a trap, a tunnel, a wind-machine, an Anemoelectric Scheme. To lure and tame the wind of genius we need a little know-how. That know-how is not so inaccessible, not so impossible as you in your country assume. Just as a poet can be taught a great deal about using the tools of his trade with maximum efficiency, so also can he be helped towards attaining that receptivity of mind which begins like radar and ends like magnetism: he can be helped towards making himself the sort of person genius will find it easy to inhabit.

Is this so strange? Is literature so different from the other arts? Your best painters, sculptors, and composers do not hesitate to submit themselves to the discipline of Colleges of Art and Colleges of Music. Are Benjamin Britten and Vaughan Williams any less spontaneous, any more pedantic, for having gone through the Royal College of Music and passed examinations in the subject they hoped to create in? The young composer studies harmony and counterpoint and must produce exercises showing that he understands their principles both historically and theoretically. Why should the young poet be exempt from studying metric and rhythm and producing exercises to show that he has understood the principles of technique in his own art? Poetry is not less but more complex than music, since it has a counterpoint of sound and sense each of which is a so-called 'incalculable' effect; why therefore should the poet spend less and not more time as an apprentice in his art? Because he already speaks and knows his own language? But surely the language of poetry is (if we take everything into account) as different from the language of everyday conversation as music is different from an aimless humming or whistling? To believe otherwise is disastrous, as the more extreme poems of Wordsworth will show. Genius without art is like love without the senses: 'a great prince in prison lies'. Blake would be a greater painter if he was a better draughtsman. Shelley would be a greater poet if he was a better versifier. Every virtuoso is not a great artist, but every great artist is a virtuoso. For these reasons it seems to me to be unnecessarily self-spiting if we refuse to teach what *may* produce works of genius merely because we know that it *will* produce some that lack genius. A course in Scriptistics should make the mediocre writer interesting, the good writer brilliant; and it should extend the range and deepen the power of the writer of genius.

What we aim at is something quite different from the normal university class – something that is nearer the studio, the *atelier*, of the Renascence artist. The instructor must himself be a poet, dramatist, or novelist, not perhaps one of major importance but someone who has already proved himself, already been found acceptable, publicly, who has mastered his own medium and is capable of sympathizing with beginners in the same activity. The contact must be personal, the atmosphere informal. Apart from teaching, such classes should offer something less easily defined, a series of 'availabilities' – availability of books, of kindred minds, of non-dogmatic comment, of constantly practical help. (I should perhaps add that in the Scriptistics Centre at Laredo we also make available whatever scientific and mechanical aids to composition have been devised. We have, for example, not only the most recent models of translation machines, but also our famous Electronic Thesaurus, which is in some ways a modern development of the machine Gulliver saw at the Lagado Academy of Projectors; on 'feeding' the thesaurus with the words or ideas he desires to develop, the student depresses a few simple keys and the instrument within a matter of seconds will begin to utter in a clear ringing tone and at dictation speed a continuous stream of all possible figures of speech and other rhetorical devices which could give force to the original word or idea, until its associations are exhausted.) To enter a Scriptistics course, intending students must produce some evidence of ability to write in either prose or verse. By 'evidence' I mean this: that if the writing is careful or learned or smooth or correct after the style of the prize poem of former days it must also show enough vigour or enough strangeness to counterpoise these negative virtues, and conversely if the writing is uncouth or ungrammatical or ill-organized it must also show enough sensitiveness or enough force to make the regulating of those positive faults seem worthwhile. If Scriptistics had always been available, what would it not have accomplished! Hopkins would have been prevented from becoming eccentric, mannered, and grotesque; Coleridge would have learned how to finish a poem; Scott would have learned how to begin a novel; Mrs Browning would have written *Aurora Leigh* in prose; Emily Dickinson would know a rhyme from a rowing-boat; and Blake would learn the difference between pouring steel from a measured ladle and just opening the furnace door . . .

But at the present time, what would be the results? I argue along three lines, that Scriptistics would be good for (i) the individual, (ii) the State, and (iii) literature.

(i) It would benefit the individual pupil, even if he never became anything like a 'great writer'. As things stand at the moment, nothing is more noticeable or deplorable than the sudden drop in spontaneity, in fire, in freshness of writing in the transition from school to university. At school, imaginative writing is still being permitted and encouraged, and the results are often admirable; many people are writing far more vividly before they are sixteen than they will ever write after it. If they come to the university, they are forced to write critically, abstractly, to develop an argument, to present facts which are often new to them and are retailed without much understanding, interest, or feeling. The power of the individual word or phrase seems now of no importance; *it* will not get them an A or an Alpha. They lose, through mere atrophy, that verbal creativeness which almost every child possesses and enjoys, and their prose becomes stereotyped and pithless. I would affirm therefore that even if a complete course in Scriptistics is thought to be too revolutionary, it could not but be helpful as a subsidiary subject to any Arts student. I have already mentioned that I think the course would benefit each grade of serious writer, from the mediocre to the first-rate. From the point of view of the individual instructor, the course would be one of the most humane and rewarding in the university. I may perhaps remind you that in the First Book of Rabelais, in that most humane of all colleges, the Abbey of Thelema, whose motto was 'Do What You Will', we are told that 'so nobly were they taught, that there was neither he nor she amongst them but could read, write, sing, play upon several musical instruments, speak five or six several languages *and compose in them all very quaintly in both verse and prose.*' Nor was the more orthodox education recommended by Castiglione in his *Courtier* any different in this respect, for the young gentleman was there advised to

> exercise himself in poets, and no less in orators and historiographers, and also in *writing both rhyme and prose, and especially in this our vulgar tongue* . . . And if he shall not attain unto that perfection that his writings may be worthy much commendation, let him be circumspect in keeping them close, lest he make other men to laugh at him. Only he may show them to a friend whom he may trust.

Well, we hope that Scriptistics will supply 'a friend whom he may trust'.

(ii) One argument which as an American I must not neglect to put forward is that by encouraging writers to learn their trade in a recognized and responsible institution the State will gradually be able to exert that gentle but not inutile control over literature which is so desirable in an age of subversive ideologies. As Plato wisely remarked in his *Republic*,

> Our first duty is to set a watch over the makers of stories . . . We shall have to throw away most of the stories they tell now . . . when they say that many unjust men are happy, many just men miserable, that injustice is profitable when undetected, and justice the good of another, but a man's own loss . . . We shall forbid them to make statements like that, and shall order them to make songs and stories to the contrary effect.

Here the universities may do good work by setting subjects and encouraging approaches and attitudes, in Scriptistics courses, which will both integrate the writer into his community and imbue his writing with a further integrating effect once it is read by the people. Naturally there is no pattern of coercion in this, but set exercises may occasionally include, as for example they have done at Laredo, odes on presidential elections, marching-songs for United Nations forces, and lyrical evocations of specific nodes or nubs of the American way of life such as the supermarket, the motel, the drive-in, and tollvision.

(iii) For the effect of Scriptistics on literature, I would ask you to compare the following two extracts, each from a long poem:

> (*a*) But almost as soon as it was made,
>   death wanted to destroy
>   timelessness
>   by what he called
>   time, and he persuaded me
>   against my better
>   judgement, that the timelessness
>   which it had made, and I
>   consented to, would have
>   no meaning if there were
>   no time.

> (*b*) Sailors, who pitch this portent at the sea
>   Where dreadnoughts shall confess
>   Its heel-bent deity,

> When you are powerless
> To sand-bag this Atlantic bulwark, faced
> By the earth-shaker, green, unwearied, chaste
> In its steel scales: ask for no Orphean lute
> To pluck life back. The guns of the steeled fleet
> Recoil and then repeat
> The hoarse salute.

I think you may agree with me that although these passages have superficially the same look of irregularity on the printed page, the second has discipline, character, and strength where the first has not. Now the first passage is from 'The Creation' by one of your younger poets, James Kirkup; and the other passage is from 'The Quaker Graveyard in Nantucket' by one of our younger poets, Robert Lowell. And Robert Lowell is a product of Scriptistics. He has studied how to write poetry at American universities; he has studied under American poets like Allen Tate who teach creative writing. Talent of his own he certainly had, but he has been shown what to do with this talent and how to develop it. 'The Quaker Graveyard' advances literature; 'The Creation' spins in a void. It seems to me (though as one from outside I say it with some hesitation and diffidence) that much of your poetry has become slipshod and uncraftsmanlike, and that the only recognition of this fact among poets themselves has been a retreat by some into the palisade of the syllable-and-rhyme-bound stanza with no very great sharpening of the weapons of diction. In this, as you will appreciate, I may be wrong. I am a little confirmed, however, in my doubts about your professionalism when I look at your prose fiction. Your novels show neither the good writing of the nineteenth century nor the intense expressiveness of the twenties and thirties of this century. Also, your 'revival' of poetic drama can scarcely be called a success. Given these circumstances, would you find it impossible to be persuaded that Scriptistics is worth a try?

Now I should like to say something concerning our practical organization. What would be most useful in your country would be a three-year 'non-graduating' Diploma course (Dip. Script.), and also a four-year graduating M.A. Honours course in conjunction with a second recommended subject (preferably a science). The extra year in the Honours course would be devoted to deeper theoretical considerations – what we call in Laredo 'creativational dynamics' – and also to more original work. Any student who failed in his final Honours year would have sat his Diploma examination at the end of the third year, and would therefore still have the Dip. Script. qualification. This qualification should be a hallmark indicating a reasonable level of competence in writing and a reasonable amount of imaginative power. Here is a rough outline of the work:

1st Year: Vocabulary – extending its range, making it a precision tool. Observation – training of eye and memory, seizing of sense-impressions, association of descriptive phrases with things and events; use of that famous object 'the poet's notebook' (as Hamlet says, *My tables* . . . '). Elementary stylistic imitation to induce verbal suppleness and also to 'keep the eye on the object'; exercises in onomatopoeia, in re-creation of realistic conversation, in use of dialect. Some imaginative writing, mainly descriptive, for criticism by instructor and class.

2nd Year: Some specializing in either the novel or drama or poetry. Experiments in group-writing, both prose and verse. Imitation of more complex events and situations and styles, but with some study of parody and irony as well (e.g. James Joyce's recapitulation of English prose styles in *Ulysses*). Students to attempt to produce a short story, a one-act play, a group of lyrics or a narrative poem.

3rd Year: Study of selected works where something is known of inception and growth (e.g. 'The Ancient Mariner', *The Prelude*, 'The Lady of Shalott', *The City in the Sea*, *The Portrait of the Artist as a Young Man*; the Prefaces of Henry James). Some study of the doctrine of 'inspiration', not neglecting its practical and methodical aspects (e.g. Houseman's beer, Hart Crane's cider and records, De Quincey's opium, Milton's books, Pope's spleen). Study of new forms and mediums: film, radio, television. Practical study of markets and trends, publics, fashions; proof-reading; copyright. Diploma examination at end of year will have written questions, and will include creative work submitted, i.e. a novel or a collection of short stories or a play or a long poem or a collection of short poems; this to be 'judged worthy of publication' by the examiners, though not necessarily published previously.

4th Year: Honours students must make a more special study of one subject according to the branch they have chosen to be most interested in, i.e. in the novel they must do either 'World Social History from the Eighteenth Century' or 'World Psychologies of Personal Relations'; in drama they must do 'the non-verbal aspects'; in poetry they must do either 'metric' or 'prose' (study of prose as a discipline from which the poet has much to learn). Also, study of lessons to be gleaned from famous unfinished works (e.g. *The Faerie Queene*, *The*

Recluse, Edwin Drood, Weir of Hermiston, The Last Tycoon, Sweeney Agonistes, Hyperion, The Triumph of Life). Literature and character; literature and life. Honours students must produce work that has either been published commercially or accepted for publication.

In our examinations we endeavour to keep questions fresh and imaginative, as we are after fresh and imaginative answers. Here are a few examples from recent years:

Describe as carefully as you can the prose style of (*a*) Defoe; (*b*) Norman Mailer; (*c*) *The National Geographic Magazine*.

If Milton is to Spenser as Tennyson is to Keats minus what Keats took from Dryden, and if Spenser is to Tennyson as Milton is to Keats, what is the relation between Dryden and Milton?

Outline a possible poetic development, assuming an ode-like, stanzaic form, of ONE of the following subjects: (*a*) The Launching of the First Atomic-Propulsion Submarine; (*b*) The Death of Chatterton; (*c*) The Secret History of Tartan.

What steps would you take if you were asked to make a dramatic version, for the live theatre, of one of the novels of Ivy Compton-Burnett?

Discuss, with examples, the smallest grammatical, verbal, or phonetic unit in which poetry can inhere (e.g. paragraph, sentence, clause, phrase, word, syllable, sound).

'A man writes much better than he lives.' (Johnson.) 'Judge no man by his books; a man is better, higher than his books.' (Coleridge.) – Discuss.

What can be learned about filmscript-writing from the dialogue of the following films: (*a*) *Scott of the Antarctic*; (*b*) *All about Eve*; (*c*) *Murder in the Cathedral*; (*d*) *The Thief*.

Does a poet think he has something to communicate to others? If so, does he have it before, or after, or all the time? If not, does he think he has something to express to himself? If so, does he have it before, or after, or all the time? If not, does he have any *other* conscious reason for writing? If so, what is it, and does he have it to begin with, or find it at the end, or discover it gradually all the time? If not, do *you* think he still has any reason for writing even if *he* does not think he has? If so, what is it? If not, can we still ask the question, Why does he write?

That will perhaps give you some idea of how we do things at Laredo. From the academic point of view, the Laredo thesis is also that held by the University of North Carolina, that literary study should be 'a fourfold discipline: language, literary history, literary criticism, and imaginative writing'. Without the last of these, the first three become inbred, haemophilic, and desiccated. From the creative point of view, we believe that the time is past when the writer could rely on his own efforts. The rabbit will not come out of the hat nowadays; you must learn how to run a rabbit farm. Today the writer has so much to learn that we think he must put himself (however unwillingly) to school, and we think that if he does so he will be surprised to find that much of what he imagined must descend to him from heaven can in fact be prospected for on the ground, provided only that he has patience, quick senses – and a geiger counter. And while as a man he may have the first two, only a college course in Scriptistics will give him the third.

Scriptistics: A Second Glance
by Laika Droshky

I am an instructress at the Gorky Scriptistics Institute in Moscow. I wish to say, in answer to Dr Virgil Wigwam, that we in the Soviet Union have been both studying and practising the organization of creative writing for many years, and have gained considerable proficiency in teaching this subject. The Institute to which I belong trains young writers, partly by the lecture and seminar system and partly through practical exercises in individual and group creative activity, and sends them out well-prepared to report on the cultivation of virgin lands, the rigours of the northern taiga, or the sands of the Kara Kum, in verse or in prose. We also, I should add (and I recommend the idea to you in Britain), run courses for older and established writers who wish to renew their creative strength at the sharply bracing fount of friendly criticism and co-operative emulation.

I wish to draw your attention to a little anthology of poems which was published in Moscow in 1956. This was called *The First Word*, and it was a collection of work by students of the Gorky Scriptistics Institute. The authors were mostly in their early twenties or late teens. I thought it might promote the enlargement of international cultural understanding, which we on our part so much desire, if I acquainted readers in Britain with the tenor and contents of this anthology. At the same time, I wished to attempt to correct some dangerous impressions which might emerge from a few of the remarks of Dr Wigwam.

Our young poets are encouraged to write on subjects drawn from everyday experience – the peaceful labours of Socialist construction, the conquering and moulding of man's environment, the ardent thoughts and feelings of those who are engaged in building up a new life. We should agree with Dr Wigwam that Scriptistics can prove its usefulness to the State as well as (or rather than) to the individual; but I suspect that his reference to 'an age of subversive ideologies' is an ill-concealed attack on the inevitable spread of those ideals of man's brotherhood which he might find indelibly inscribed on the pages of his own countryman Walt Whitman. I find it hard to accept the necessity of an exercise on such a palpably aggressive subject as 'The Launching of the First Atomic-Propulsion Submarine', or such a frivolous one as 'The Secret History of Tartan'. And why should students be required to investigate *Sweeney Agonistes*, which is (I believe, though I have not read it) a work of decidedly ambiguous moral tone? In our anthology you will find a healthy and well-balanced choice of themes, and as far as attitudes of mind are concerned, the well-known poet Evgeny Dolmatovsky points out in his Introduction to this volume that it has 'no place for whiners, aesthetes, and empty vessels'. In the young post-war generation of poets, Comrade Dolmatovsky goes on, we see the 'springlike optimism of youth', and there is now 'no division between the personal and the public'. I expect that in British Scriptistics Centres, once they are established, you will have lessons on the finding of the Objective Correlative. In our society this is no longer required. The doctrine of the Objective Correlative assumes a normal split (which can sometimes and by great effort be bridged) between inner emotional life and external artistic theme, just as it tacitly assumes the same in life itself – e.g. that a man is not normally happy at his work, and that his 'real' or 'emotional' life begins only when work leaves off. This is what makes Western Man (if you will forgive a liberty of terminology uttered in a comradely didactic spirit) such a deeply divided Centaur, with his aspiring torso doing its best to ignore the plodding undercarriage, and the perspiring undercarriage unaware of the music of its hoofs.

I have been interested to notice how differently from ourselves you advertise or announce new books of verse. It is instructive, I think, that you recommend in the first place (and often exclusively) pleasures of style or tone or manner, whereas we recommend content, subject, theme, and purpose. This habit of yours comes clearly from a lack of confidence that your new poet has unearthed a series of subjects objectively correlative to his experience. The experience, for you, lies open in the style, and your critical weapons are sharpened for that; but towards subject-matter you are lenient to the point of indifference. Here, for instance, is what your blurb-writer has to say about a recent volume (Anthony Thwaite's *Home Truths*, 1957). After a reference to Comrade Thwaite as a 'reflective' and 'lyrical' poet, we read:

> In this first collection, readers will find something more than mere *grace* and good *organization*, though these may still be counted among Mr Thwaite's qualities. He shares the feeling for *clarity* and *structure* and what has been called 'the hard *thrust of intelligence*' with those poets who have recently been grouped together as 'The Movement', but he has managed to avoid any close identification with this group, perhaps because he is younger and belongs to a later poetic generation.

My italics will serve to beg you to notice that the emphasis throughout is on style, and the reader is given *no* indication of what the poems are about. The assumption is that he is not interested. Would you now compare this with a recent Russian volume (Veronica Tushnova's *Heart's Remembrance*, 1957), announced as follows:

> Veronica Tushnova is a lyrical poet. Her new book of verse is devoted to the rich and varied world of the feelings and experiences of Soviet man and Soviet woman, of a friend, a wife, a mother; filled with a burning love for her native land, its people, and her own kith and kin. The poet fights for purity of feeling, she wants the people who are dear to her to be unremittingly and endlessly exacting to themselves and to others . . . and not to become reconciled to worthless emotions and worthless relationships.

Our emphasis speaks for itself, and I would only ask you, in judging us, to judge yourselves against the views of your own Northern English critical realist William Wordsworth, whose admirable Preface to the *Lyrical Ballads* we are (in your defection) now endeavouring to realize in the USSR.

I proceed, after these preliminary comments, to illustrate my general argument with examples from *The First Word*.

One of our youngest contributors is a seventeen-year-old hunter from the Siberian taiga called I. Kharabarov. He writes a poem, 'Let there be no sorrow', which may seem to you to be immature and slight, but which I quote as the type of poem regarded by us as

promising (for its freshness and sincerity) and central (in its attitude
to the dignity of man's labour).

Let There be No Sorrow

Let there be no sorrow,
                let there be no grief.
Better to go out
              into meadow and field
Raking in the hay
              for heart's relief,
For the heart's relief
              stacking the July hay.
It dries and dries
              in the swaths of the scythe,
Clover-red
              and speargrass-green.
Scarcely is it scorched
              underneath by the sun
When it quietly crackles
              in the rake's teeth.
Your hand is busy –
              your soul sings.
Injuries are forgotten,
              the mind is true
To its clearest springs,
              to live and to breathe
And to sleep by the hay
              so fragrant and so new.

The next poem, by Herman Florov, deals with the exploring and
adventurous spirits of those who are opening up new communities in
harsh and remote territories of the Soviet Union. It describes the
first moment of realization of the immediate and awesome nature of
their task, as new settlers plunge in their train deep into the frozen
Siberian landscape.

The Woman

She brought into the compartment with her
The spicy scent of Siberian pines.
The blizzard, as if tired of drifting,
Sleeps in a downy shawl. Snow shines
Briefly where a flake is melting

On her lashes; she blinks, her eyes screwed up . . .
The Major smoothed his cigarette: his
Match remained in air, unstruck.
The architect took off his glasses
With care from laughing hazel eyes.
Again as we listened we saw the fabulous
New Siberian township rise.
The train sped on.
                    The woman was gazing
At the slumberous volcanic hills.
She was silent: it was nothing she was singing or saying
That caught and fused their separate wills
To read her profile, her clear forehead;
They saw the far had come near, they could pass
Into the unfabulous life of the forest.
Their tea reached them sweet in the glass.

Although we like to underline the importance of social themes, and of the individual's place in society, I must make it clear to you that the expression of personal feeling is by no means discouraged. On the contrary, much effort is directed in our Institute towards ensuring that young writers with strong emotional reactions shall find the means both of embracing a deserving object and of writing about it in such a way as to make others love it too. Of the following poem, by Bella Akhmadulina (one of our very promising young poetesses), Comrade Dolmatovsky says in his Introduction: '"At Night" will be copied out, I'm sure, into the notebooks of more than one young student and working girl, who will find in this poem a reflection of their purest feelings.' I imagine the natural chastity and restraint of the English mind will appreciate the charm of this verse.

At Night

How should I call, how should I cry out?
Brittle as glass is the house in its quiet.
The telephone yonder is sleeping sound,
Its head at rest on the hook all night.
As for me, I want to walk through
This shining town, I want to reach you
By snow-filled lanes, to reach your window
So softly, so quietly, never to wake you.
The palm of my hand will cover the tinkle
As icicles drop from eaves to the street.

I'll have all the lamps extinguished
To keep your eyelids closed in sleep.
I'll issue orders to the springtime
To still its dark and stirring feet.
For now I can see you, dreamer, at last . . .
Your arms relaxed, the day's work past . . .
Deep in the tiny lines at your eyes
A weariness lies half concealed.
Tomorrow I shall kiss these lines
And each tired track will soon be sealed.
Till morning comes I'll guard you so,
In the white dawn I'll disappear,
My footsteps buried in the snow
With the dry leaves of a dead year.

Many of the students who pass through our hands have come to Moscow from far-off corners of the Soviet emp— – of the Soviet brotherhood of nations. The open gaze and eager malleable spirit of these distant visitors make them very often the apple of our eye, and we treasure their verses as we would treasure the first hardy flowers springing from a new and unknown soil. Don't laugh (though you may smile) at the 'first word' of Khodzhamurat Turumbetov which I now quote. This poem was written first in his native Karakalpak, a Turkic language spoken near the Aral Sea. Perhaps to your young people Comrade Turumbetov would appear what I believe is called a square. But out of this square, and the book which holds him to his appointed task of self-betterment, we raise the Sputnik. On second thoughts, the Institute does not mind whether you laugh or not.

A Good Book

The lights will soon be lit beyond my window –
There in the park, winking among the trees . . .
Nothing holds me from going into the city
Except this book that's resting on my knees.

Over the park a yellow moon is floating,
Hanging above the plane-trees are the stars,
And hurrying with headlamps brightly glowing,
On go the gay and bounding trucks and cars.

The girls are singing now outside my window,
A song that is part gladness and part pain;
A mouth-organ calls me, calls me over and over;
But here, in spite of the spell, is where I remain.

You too, my friend, will not find this unheard-of.
Although the soul demands its idleness
We'll not stir out of doors for any pleasure
Less than the pleasure that good books possess.

I should like to give you another example of poetry from our
national minorities: written this time by a young woman who is
using (and using with some skill) her own native (Daghestan) poetic
traditions. Here is a pastoral ballad by Fazu Aliyeva, composed
originally in the Avar language of the North Caucasian group. (I and
my colleagues, I might intimate at this point, should be glad to hear
sometime from Dr Wigwam about the literature of the American
national minorities; we have always found it most difficult to obtain
any information at all concerning the modern trends of prose and
verse in the numerous American Indian languages.)

The Milkmaid and the Shepherd

One day I came back to my farm from the hills.
A rain-storm relentlessly scurries and spills,
It runs from the rocks in a boisterous flood . . .
And who should I meet but a young shepherd lad.

– O listen, dear shepherd, say I, drawing near him,
Let your cloak be my roof till we see the rain clearing.
So frozen, so soaked have I got on the road –
O wrap me and warm me, your breast is so broad.

– My lovely! I see that your stars are against you.
An emptier cloak would soon have encased you,
But look, my poor heart will need all its warm flames
To thaw in my cloak these cold little lambs.

The following day began burning from dawn
Till valley and hillside were scorched with the sun.
At evening I went where a craggy path led
Right into the path of the young shepherd lad.

– My lovely! you don't really know me, I know,
But cool me in your kerchief as white as the snow.
I have walked with my flock in the heat all day,
Let me rest in the shadow of your hair, I pray.

> – I'm sorry, bright falcon, an emptier kerchief
> Would soon have encased you; but look how my heifer
> Would pant in its absence. If your soul is on fire
> Then girls that you *do* know will quench your desire.

Poetry for children has always been regarded as an extremely important category of writing in the Soviet Union, and for this I see no real provision made in the Scriptistics programme of Dr Wigwam. As a woman and a mother, I cannot but feel that this is a serious omission. The Child, if I may revert to your excellent Northern English revolutionary thinker and practising aesthetic pediatrician William Wordsworth – the Child is father of the Masses. We must foster those writers who will some day foster the mind of the young. In the following poem Y. Korinyets gives an admirably light introduction to the deceptive possibilities latent in imaginative fiction, and the importance of having the truth finally revealed when it serves as basis for an entertaining fantasy of the riddle type.

The Hare

A hare came over
The garden wall.
It wasn't big, and it wasn't small.
It climbed by a plank to the garden shed
And ran about on the roof overhead.

O this hare was clever, clever –
Now like a mouse in a trap it would quiver
In the dark window-pane,
Then hop along
The wall again . . .

Tell me I'm wrong,
Say you don't believe me,
I never saw the beastie!
Only in a dream at all at all
Can grey hares run along the wall!

No, and no, my children, my dears.
These verses I have written here
Are not about the hare in the wood
With dew for his drink, birch-bark for his food,
And a grey fur-coat slung over his back
And a fear in his eyes for the huntsman's track.

> It was simply this –
> I took a mirror in the palm of my hand,
> I sat down here on the window-sill,
> And I trapped the sun in the mirror, and
> Sent him dancing to do my will.

There I end my examples. Why did I give them? I will answer this question. I had a vehement desire to present the evidence which would show that the development of Scriptistics need not (and should not) preclude the one quality we ourselves prize most: *prostota*, simplicity, *prostoserdechnost*, the plainness of the heart. I do not suggest that Comrade Wigwam is unaware of the statement made by one of his compatriots, Louise Bogan, when she wrote in 1951:

> Modern poetry has now reached the stage where whatever can be taught about its methods and material has been assembled into a well organized set of rules. Any intelligent young student, having absorbed the essentials of this poetic code, can turn out a plausible poetry directly derived from literature, without so much as a side glance at life.

I would urge on him, however, a reconsideration of his scriptistic principles, and assure him that the hand of friendship continues outstretched from the Gorky Institute, should he ever feel inclined to draw upon the experience we have amassed. Failing any such immediate contact, a study of the half-dozen poems here translated may help to accustom him to the directness and concreteness which the form of the future has already assumed.

The future is shy, but in our Institute we have a kind of Life Class where students are invited to delineate such of her features as may present themselves, and she has this property, that the more she is searched for, the more she is revealed. The student poet, like every pioneer, lives on images perhaps naive or clumsy, but burning with what your remarkable Northern English prophetic peasant poet William Wordsworth called 'something evermore about to be'. What is time, what is history? I will answer this question. A past that shows many laws of change and development; a present that is complex but can be understood; a future that can be seen as distinct tracks leading to a noble life or to disaster. And just as a piece of music like Dmitri Shostakovich's *Song of the Forests* can sensuously evoke the heroic struggles of the days of Stalingrad, the busy joys of liberated post-war constructive effort, and the far-off tranquil exalted happiness of 'A Walk in the Forests of the Future' – so surely, and in terms even more unmistakable, should literature be made capable of holding up its own great and stimulating images of real time and real history, until man himself *makes* the time and history he today in so many parts of the world still suffers to wash over him like idle and insolent waves.

Such is our programme. I have outlined it only in general terms, but details will be supplied on request. I have every confidence that the value of Soviet Scriptistics will emerge even from the strictest international scriptistical statistics.

Twentieth Century, March 1958.

Index

Albers, Josef, 21ff.
Aldan, Daisy, 33
Alexander, Peter, 232
Apollinaire, Guillaume, 29, 39, 69, 195
Arden, John, 235
Arnold, Matthew, 81f., 137, 142, 167
Arp, Hans, 21
Asimov, Isaac, 36

Bacon, Francis, 184, 215
Baildon, H. B., 136
Bannister, Winifred, 236
Barnes, William, 139
Barrie, J. M., 137, 169
Baudelaire, Charles, 133
Beaumont, George, Sir, 118
Beckett, Samuel, 184
Beckford, William, 36
Beethoven, Ludwig von, 133
Bell, J. J., 169
Bill, Max, 21, 27
Black, D. M., 183
Blaine, Julien, 25
Blake, George, 169, 170, 226
Blake, Patricia, 58
Blake, William, 32, 55, 100, 194
Blok, Alexander, 189
Bold, Alan, 184
Bory, Jean-François, 27
Bosch, Hieronymus, 78
Brecht, Bertolt, 174, 195, 199, 236, 238
Bridges, Robert, 81
Bridie, James, 232–41
Brogan, Colm, 161
Brontë, Emily, 35
Brown, George Mackay, 164, 182f.

Brown, Pete, 7
Browning, Robert, 12, 133, 215
Bryden, Bill, 163
Buber, Martin, 197, 219
Buchan, Tom, 160, 183
Buchanan, George, 17
Buñuel, Luis, 54
Bunyan, John, 36
Burke, Kenneth, 11
Burns, Robert, 66, 97, 140, 166, 168, 169, 172, 178, 194, 196, 197, 220
Burroughs, E., 216
Butter, P. H., 187
Byron, George Gordon, Lord, 130, 194, 198, 234

Camões, Luis de, 197
Campbell, Donald, 163
Campbell, Roy, 196, 197, 198
Campion, Thomas, 111
Campos, Augusto de, 20, 25
Campos, Haroldo de, 20
Camus, Albert, 178
Carpenter, Edward, 215
Chagall, Marc, 76
Chaplin, Charlie, 196
Chapman, George, 104
Chaucer, Geoffrey, 82f., 85, 86, 89, 94, 194
Chekhov, Anton, 40, 169
Chesterton, G. K., 215
Chomsky, Naum, 27
Chopin, Henri, 25
Claudel, Paul, 197
Coleridge, Samuel Taylor, 3, 209, 221
Columbus, Christopher, 47
Colvin, Sidney, 147

Conn, Stewart, 163
Conquest, Robert, 195
Coolidge, Calvin, 53
Conrad, Joseph, 215
Corrie, Joe, 169
Cowell, Edward, 3
Cowley, Abraham, 112
Cowper, William, 100
Crabbe, George, 104
Crane, Hart, 43–47, 48, 53, 54, 55, 57
Crashaw, Richard, 111
Crockett, S. R., 169
Cruickshank, Helen, 164

Dalí, Salvador, 54
Dante Alighieri, 18, 105, 202, 238
Darwin, Charles, 148
Davidson, John, 8, 136, 137, 146, 169, 172
Davie, Donald, 194
Defoe, Daniel, 194
Dickens, Charles, 133, 169
Donn, Rob, 167
Donne, John, 101, 102, 104, 131, 215
Dostoevsky, Fyodor, 161, 181
Doughty, Charles, 10, 139, 206, 219, 220
Douglas, Gavin, 83, 84, 86ff., 167
Dryden, John, 100–17, 197
Dunbar, William, 66, 81–99, 167, 178

Eardley, Joan, 228
Einstein, Albert, 196
Eliot, T. S., 5, 7, 8, 14, 123, 133, 167, 187
Enright, D. J., 194, 195

Fergusson, Robert, 18
Fergusson, Samuel, Sir, 140, 166
Finlay, Ian Hamilton, 21ff., 24, 145, 159, 173, 175, 184f.

FitzGerald, Edward, 3ff.
Fitzsimon, Shaun, 173
Franco, Francisco, 197
Freud, Sigmund, 196
Fry, Christopher, 36
Fulton, Robin, 183

Gagarin, Yuri, 14, 76
Galsworthy, John, 215
Galt, John, 166, 169, 170
Garioch, Robert, 17–19, 164, 178f.
Gascoyne, David, 14
Gatherer, W. A., 196
Geddes, James Y., 172
Genet, Jean, 118
Gibbon, Lewis Grassic, 138, 170
Gide, André, 122, 196
Ginsberg, Allen, 7, 15, 54, 178, 210
Glen, Duncan, 163
van Gogh, Vincent, 68
Gogol, N. V., 169
Golding, William, 40
Gomringer, Eugaen, 20–27, 32
Gosse, Edmund, 136
Graham, Cunninghame, 168, 170
Graham, Dougal, 168
Graham, W. S., 173
Graves, Robert, 69, 186
Gray, Alasdair, 163
Gray, Thomas, 112

Hamilton, Janet, 172
Hanley, Cliff, 164
Hardy, Thomas, 139, 244
Havergal, Giles, 163
Harvey, William, 168
Hay, George Campbell, 161
Haynes, Dorothy K., 171, 175
Henley, W. E., 141, 146
Henryson, Robert, 83, 85, 89
Herbert, Zbigniew, 67–70
Hind, Archie, 156, 164
Hogg, James, 244
Hollo, Anselm, 15

Holloway, John, 193
Hopkins, Gerard Manley, 82, 139, 149, 215
Horace, 114, 115
Houédard, Dom Silvester, 32
Housman, A. E., 146, 149, 221
Hughes, Ted, 24
Hume, David, 166
Humphreys, Emyr, 40n.
Huxley, Aldous, 196, 210

Ibsen, Henrik, 133

Jackson, Alan, 159, 178, 183
James IV, 91
James VI, 85
James, Henry, 194, 215
James, William, 215
Jenkins, Robin, 175, 242-5
Johnson, Samuel, Dr., 94, 101, 102, 103, 105
Joule, J. P., 210
Joyce, James, 84, 120, 217
Jung, Carl, 178, 196
Juvenal, 113, 114, 115, 116

Kafka, Franz, 36, 40, 75, 161, 181, 187
Kahn, Otto H., 45
Kamensky, Vasily, 29, 62, 63f.
Kandinsky, Vassily, 21
Keats, John, 3, 130, 132, 133
Kennedy, Andrew, 90ff.
Kerouac, Jack, 7
Khlebnikov, Velemir, 29, 62
Kipling, Rudyard, 146
Kirkup, James, 13
Kneller, Godfrey, Sir, 101
Kokoschka, Oscar, 185
Kruchonykh, Alexei, 62, 63

Langer, Susanne, 194
Langland, William, 89, 92
Larkin, Philip, 159

Lauder, Harry, 169
Lawrence, D. H., 7, 14, 204
Leavis, F. R., 7, 14, 250
Lenin, V. I., 60, 197
Leonard, Tom, 179
Lewis, Wyndham, 64, 197, 198
Linklater, Eric, 170
Lissitzky, El, 28, 62
Logue, Christopher, 7, 194, 195
Lorca, Federico García, 53-57
Lowell, Robert, 24, 74, 161
Lucretius, 105, 124
Lunacharsky, Anatoly, 60
Lyndsay, David, Sir, 83, 178, 196

McGonagall, William, 171, 238
McGrath, Tom, 160, 177, 178
McLellan, Robert, 241
McLuhan, Marshall, 216
MacAulay, Donald, 161
MacBeth, George, 135, 136, 138, 142, 144, 146, 147
MacCaig, Norman, 164, 173, 181f.
MacColla, Fionn, 164
MacDiarmid, Hugh, 9ff., 15, 66, 139, 144, 162, 168, 169, 172f., 173, 174, 176, 178, 184, 194-221
MacDonald, Alexander, 167
MacIntyre, Duncan Ban, 167, 226
MacLeod, Sheila, 164
Macfarlan, James, 172
Machiavelli, Niccolò, 60
Mackenzie, Compton, 170
Maclean, Sorley, 154, 156f., 161, 164, 182
Macpherson, James, 167
Malevich, Kasimir, 22ff.
Mallarmé, Stefan, 29, 33
Malraux, Andre, 77
Marinetti, Filippo, 27, 60
Marlowe, Christopher, 104
Marshall, Herbert, 6
Martinson, Harry, 10
Marvell, Andrew, 111

Marx, Karl, 196

Mayakovsky, Vladimir, 6f., 29, 47–53, 54, 55, 57, 58–66, 100

Mayer, Hansjörg, 32

Mayo, Bernard, 16

Melville, Herman, 40

Miller, Henry, 44, 174

Miller, Hugh, 170

Millet, Jean François, 133

Miłosz, Czesław, 68n.

Milton, John, 100, 102, 103, 111, 119, 126, 194, 197, 202, 210

Moir, D. M., 169

Mondrian, Piet, 21, 185

Monet, Claude, 133

Montale, Eugenio, 71

Moore, Henry, 73

Morgan, Pete, 184

Muir, Edwin, 139, 173, 176, 186–93, 219

Munro, Neil, 170

Neizvestny, Ernst, 73

Neruda, Pablo, 24

Newton, Isaac, 16

Nichol, B. P., 27

Niikuni, Seiichi, 28

Olson, Charles, 159, 178

Orwell, George, 36, 40

Osborne, John, 175

Pasternak, Boris, 60, 64, 78

Pauwels, Louis, 3

Peake, Mervyn, 35–42

Persius, 113, 115, 116

Philips, Katherine, 104

Piaf, Edith, 228

Pignatari, Décio, 20, 25

Pitter, Ruth, 206

Poe, Edgar Allan, 36, 146

Pope, Alexander, 100, 101, 103, 105, 167

Pound, Ezra, 5, 8, 14, 32, 48, 64, 159, 187, 198f.

Proust, Marcel, 122, 161

Quasimodo, Salvatore, 174

Rabelais, François, 36, 84, 97

Raine, Kathleen, 13

Ramsay, Allan, 139, 166, 167

Read, Herbert, 196

Robbe-Grillet, Alain, 219

Robinson, Henry Crabb, 132

Rodchenko, Alexander, 62

Rowll, John, Sir, 90

Ruskin, John, 4

Sartre, Jean Paul, 77

Schrödinger, Erwin, 16

Scott, Alexander, 164, 166, 177, 185

Scott, Peter Dale, 68n.

Scott, Tom, 159, 173, 174, 176

Scott, Walter, Sir, 168, 170

Sempill, Robert, 197

Shakespeare, William, 81, 82, 89, 101, 102, 103, 105, 107, 108, 128, 210, 216, 232

Shaw, George Bernard, 174, 235, 236, 238

Shelley, Percy Byshe, 114, 132

Sholokhov, Mikhail, 158

Shostakovich, Dmitri, 194

Simpson, Louis, 74

Singer, Burns, 196

Skelton, John, 84

Smith, Adam, 166

Smith, Alexander, 172

Smith, Iain Crichton, 154, 161, 175, 180, 181, 182, 222–31

Smith, Janet Adam, 135

Smith, Sydney Goodsir, 164, 173, 174

Snow, C. P., 17, 35

Soloviëv, Vladimir, 200

Solt, Mary Ellen, 24
Solzhenitsyn, Alexander, 158
Soutar, William, 169
Spark, Muriel, 244
Spence, Alan, 163
Spencer, Herbert, 142
Stella, Joseph, 44
Stevens, Wallace, 14, 69, 194, 202, 210, 224
Stevenson, Robert Louis, 135–49, 170
Stone, Irving, 53
Stopes, Marie, 196
Swan, Annie S., 169
Swift, Jonathan, 78, 116, 198
Swinburne, Algernon Charles, 215

Taylor, C. P., 163
Telford, Thomas, 166
Tennyson, Alfred, Lord, 4
Thomas, Dylan, 7
Thomson, Derick, 161
Thomson, James, 57, 103, 136, 137, 172
Tolstoy, Leo, 133, 134
Traherne, Thomas, 131
Tse-tung, Mao, 201
Turner, W. Price, 173

Ure, Joan, 163
Urquhart, Thomas, Sir, 84, 92

Vantongerloo, Georges, 21

Virgil, 86, 210
Voznesensky, Andrei, 7, 29–32, 47, 71–78

Wagner, Richard, 133
Waller, Edmund, 101
Watson, Roderick, 184
Watt, James, 166
Ważyk, Adam, 196
Weaver, Mike, 24
Webb, Mary, 211, 212
Wells, H. G., 8, 36, 37, 61
Whitman, Walt, 4ff., 9, 11, 45, 54, 81, 137, 142, 194
Williams, Gordon M., 154, 155
Williams, Tennessee, 174
Williams, William Carlos, 9, 11, 12f., 167
Wittgenstein, Ludwig, 181
Wolfe, Thomas, 43f.
Wood, Peter, 36
Wordsworth, William, 100, 115n., 118–34, 147, 148, 187, 194, 195, 199, 203, 204, 205, 207, 215

Yeats, William Butler, 5, 7, 8, 14, 141, 167, 187, 194, 204
Yevtushenko, Yevgeny, 7, 47, 71
Young, Douglas, 135, 172
Young, Edward, 103

Zdanevich, Ilya, 28